Praise for *Courage or Complicity*

"In a nation much devoted to hero worship of veterans, too little attention is paid to actual life in the military and its aftermath. Steve Early and Suzanne Gordon offer the most comprehensive and honest accounting of what my fellow veterans have experienced post-9/11 and the challenges we face today. Their new book is sweeping, authoritative, and bold. As more Americans stand up against the politicians and corporations falsely claiming to be on our side, the authors show how military veterans can join the charge against them."

—Matthew Hoh, former marine captain and State Department officer, Iraq War combat veteran

"As this timely book reports, the unlawful use of National Guard units in a nationwide assault on immigrants and DOGE-driven attacks on federal jobs and services has led to a new wave of labor, community, and political activism by former service members and military families. In their dispatches from the frontlines, the authors chronicle the role of veterans and their organizations in this critical defense of democracy against authoritarianism."

—Joanna Sweatt, Marine Corps veteran and national organizing director, Common Defense

"Early and Gordon provide us with an urgent guide to understanding how and why the ruling class has turned and always will turn its back on veterans. Veterans looking to harness their sense of betrayal to the struggle for a more just world should read this essential book—and then spread the word about it."

—Rory Fanning, Afghanistan war veteran, former army ranger, and author of *Worth Fighting For*

"This book chronicles the struggles of veterans whose disillusionment with traditional advocacy organizations led them to form new networks, more labor-focused, grassroots oriented, and engaged with social justice issues. The result is a new generation of incredible warriors whose presence in unions and progressive movements is needed more than ever before."

—RoseAnn DeMoro, former executive director, California Nurses Association/National Nurses United

"*Courage or Complicity* describes the use of past military service by politicians from both major parties. As the authors show, most who are elected to Congress champion bloated defense budgets that are now bigger than the total expenditures of the next nine largest military spenders in the world. The authors provide a useful scorecard for assessing candidates whose brand of patriotism includes little solidarity with fellow veterans in need of jobs, healthcare, and workplace rights."

—Larry Cohen, founding chair of Our Revolution and former national president of Communications Workers of America

"The authors are longtime advocacy journalists who reveal how corporate profiteering is cannibalizing both Medicare and the VA, thus undermining the possibility of real healthcare reform in the US. Reading this book will make you want to march, organize, and lobby to defend the single-payer financing and public delivery of veterans' healthcare, which provides such a good working model for broader systemic change."

—Ana M. Malinow, National Single Payer Steering Committee

"In recent years, few nonveterans have done more reading, writing, critical thinking, and public speaking about veterans' issues than the authors of this collection, which highlights the past and present role of former soldiers on the left, in labor unions, electoral politics, and antiwar campaigning."

—Jon Melrod, attorney, labor activist, and author of *Fighting Times*

"Combining deep research and first-rate journalism, this book deftly exposes the machinations and terrible results of corporate militarism. Early and Gordon expertly cut through the fog of class war, showing how the profit-driven system of the US warfare state routinely shafts veterans, workers, and society as a whole."

—Norman Solomon, author of *War Made Invisible: How America Hides the Human Toll of Its Military Machine*

"Gordon and Early expose the great injustice of VA privatization and union busting, which has an adverse impact on veterans as federal workers and patients. Their reporting and commentary tells our story and uplifts our voices, as we carry on the fight!"

—Aimee Potter, VA clinical social workers and AFGE Local 789 Steward in Chicago

"The Trump administration's billionaire-backed push to hollow out and privatize large swaths of the federal government is an attack not just on critical public services but also on the many veterans who deliver them. At the VA, former service members who signed up to continue serving their country have faced unlawful firings, mass reductions in force, ongoing understaffing, and the gutting of their workplace rights and protections. This book shows how federal workers are fighting back—by building power through rank-and-file organizing on the job and in cross-union formations like the Federal Unionists Network."

—Mark Smith, president of NFFE-IAM Local 1 at VA in San Francisco

"Once again, Steve Early and Suzanne Gordon are providing a rare worker-centric perspective on veterans' problems, which the Trump administration claims to care about but actually doesn't. I look forward to sharing their well-researched new book with veterans in my community, union coworkers, and other labor activists trying to save the VA from further privatization and eventual dismantling."

—Betsy Zucker, retired VA nurse practitioner, member of AFGE 2157 and FUN supporter in Portland

"Anyone who has worked on difficult strikes and organizing fights knows the kind of rank-and-file leadership that military veterans can provide. This book tells the story of former soldiers, like the late Tony Mazzocchi, who campaigned for job safety and health, union democracy, and a labor party. We meet younger veterans who are now frontline resisters to Republican union busting and defunding of essential public services."

—Rand Wilson, union activist and organizer, CHIPS Communities United

"*Courage or Complicity* exposes how bipartisan support for outsourcing VA care has undermined, rather than improved it. Let's hope this book will spur collective action among my fellow caregivers in our rank-and-file fight to restore workplace protections and contract rights that benefit us and our patients."

—Latisha D. Thompson, organizer with Federal Unionists Network and rank-and-file member of AFGE at the VA in Philadelphia

"The book is an excellent introduction to the politics surrounding military labor and veterans' affairs. It provides a timely reminder of the long history of left organizing and dissent from within the US armed forces and among military veterans. For a socialist left looking to rebuild links with the US working class—and vying with right-wing populist appeals to labor—it's a vital read."

—Derek Seidman, contributing writer, Truthout

"In this wide-ranging and important collection, Steve Early and Suzanne Gordon document how VA care is the canary in the coal mine of a broader corporate drive to undermine and privatize all public goods and services. They argue that veterans can become a bulwark against the divisive and corrosive politics of the MAGA right and a force for progressive social change. Anyone looking for hope in these difficult times should read this book."

—Mark Dudzic, Labor Campaign for Single Payer

"*Courage or Complicity* asks how a country always ready to spend billions more on war can't find money to meet the basic social needs of millions of poor and working-class Americans, including those who served in the military? As the authors document, veterans who challenge 'forever wars' and fight social injustice are helping to build a more broad-based progressive movement today."

—Gene Bruskin, poet, playwright, and labor solidarity campaigner

"If you're a student thinking about joining JR ROTC or talking to a military recruiter about what to do after high school, you need to read this book, *before* signing up!"

—Kim Scipes, Marine Corps veteran and emeritus professor of sociology at Purdue University Northwest

Courage or Complicity?

How Veterans Are Responding to the Assault on Democracy

Steve Early and Suzanne Gordon

Courage or Complicity? How Veterans Are Responding to the Assault on Democracy

ISBN: 979–8–88744–020–0 (paperback)
ISBN: 979–8–88744–199–3 (ebook)
Library of Congress Control Number: 2026931289

Cover by John Yates / www.stealworks.com
Interior design by briandesign

10 9 8 7 6 5 4 3 2 1

PM Press
PO Box 23912
Oakland, CA 94623
www.pmpress.org

Printed in the USA.

To the memory of RN Alex Pretti, an AFGE member at the US Department of Veterans Affairs (VA) whose heroic activism and tragic death helped turn the tide in Minneapolis (and America?)

Contents

Authors' Note and Acknowledgments

Neither of the coauthors of this book ever served in the military, but participation in the movement against the Vietnam War was a formative experience for both of us. Steve's single semester in the Reserve Officer Training Corps—a program discussed later in this book—made him a strong supporter of removing ROTC from campuses, abolishing conscription, and ending the Vietnam War, in whatever order any of those goals could be achieved, locally or nationally.

Steve's first job after graduation was as Vermont field secretary for the American Friends Service Committee; in that capacity, he worked with Vietnam Veterans Against the War and other peace campaigners. After becoming a journalist, Suzanne covered the GI coffeehouse movement and related expressions of antiwar sentiment by active-duty military personnel in the early 1970s.

A decade later, she helped trade unionists in the United States and Europe—some of whom were veterans—promote "economic conversion." Working with them, she organized an international conference on this subject and coedited *Economic Conversion: Revitalizing America's Economy*. This book critiqued the cost and wastefulness of global military spending. Its cross-border contributors showed how factories engaged in arms manufacturing could be converted to the production of socially useful goods and services.

Over the past forty years, Suzanne has been a vocal advocate for a publicly funded national healthcare system in the United States. As a longtime coeditor of a Cornell University Press series on the culture and politics of healthcare work, she published her own books (and work by other authors) on patient safety, hospital funding and administration, home care and long-term care, nursing and medical education, and how national health systems function more effectively in other industrialized countries.

Suzanne's first contact with the Department of Veterans Affairs (VA) was via a series of "team building" workshops that she conducted for caregivers at the VA Medical Center in Palo Alto, California. Since then, she has written or coauthored three books about the VA—*The Battle for Veterans' Healthcare: Dispatches from the Frontlines of Policy Making and Patient Care* (Cornell University Press, 2017); *Wounds of War: How the VA Delivers Health, Healing, and Hope to the Nation's Veterans* (Cornell University Press, 2018); and *Our Veterans: Winners, Losers, Friends, and Enemies of the New Terrain of Veterans Affairs* (Duke University Press, 2022), coauthored with Steve and journalist Jasper Craven.

Suzanne also coauthored (with Phil Longman) a report for the American Legion titled *VA Healthcare: A System Worth Saving* and received an award from the Disabled American Veterans for her VA-related reporting. She has also received an award from the American Public Health Association for her work on healthcare and the VA.

In 2019, she wrote a nationally distributed guide for Rotary Clubs about how they can better partner with the VA on local programs to support veterans. More recently, she collaborated with the American Federation of Government Employees on a staffing study called *Disadvantaging the VA*, based on a survey of the agency' front-line workers. In 2024, she worked with the *American Prospect* to produce "Veterans Healthcare Choice: Myth or Reality," an investigative report on the "false promise of VA privatization."

Suzanne helped found the Bay Area–based Veterans Healthcare Policy Institute to provide ongoing analyses of VA-related developments and has been a frequent speaker before audiences of veterans, VA staff members, union members, healthcare reformers, and Rotarians across the country.

In addition to coauthoring *Our Veterans*, Steve has written four other books about labor or politics. While attending law school in the 1970s, he worked with union members—some of them recently returned Vietnam veterans—in a high-risk industry (coal mining). In that and other labor organization roles until 2007, he assisted campaigns for workers' rights, safer and healthier workplaces, and affordable medical care. While serving as national union representative for the Communications Workers of America, Steve was involved in many difficult contract negotiations and strikes over job-based benefits. That experience has made him a strong supporter of Medicare for All.

Steve was drawn to the subject matter of this book (and our previous one) because of the overlap between labor and veterans' issues in three areas. They include military service as a form of work (albeit nonunion), the occupational health and safety hazards faced by military personnel, and how their later need for medical care and disability benefits is addressed through a national system of "workers' compensation" (the VA) that is much better than any state program for injured workers.

Steve has also been struck by the parallel erosion of veteran organization influence and infrastructure, nationally and locally, and labor union decline in the United States. As chronicled in *Our Veterans* and this collection, both trends have had adverse consequences for an overlapping working-class constituency. One upside has been the emergence of newer groups advocating for younger veterans of post-9/11 wars—and organized labor's rediscovery of the million or more workers in unions who previously served in the military.

We have collaborated for a second time on a veterans-related book because of our continuing interest in the work experience of seventeen million veterans during and after their military service, their use of VA programs and services, and their role as voters, labor and veterans' organization members, and in some cases as political candidates and public policymakers. Advocacy journalism dealing with this subject matter or any other is only as effective as the work of the advocacy organizations that one chooses to work with. We've been privileged to partner with scores of dedicated activists in labor, veterans, and healthcare reform groups, some of which overlap with the progressive media outlets thanked below.

Suzanne is now and always very grateful for the invaluable insights of Dr. Ken Kizer, a transformative leader of the VA in the 1990s who has had a long and varied career in public health. At the Veterans Healthcare Policy Institute (VHPI), Russell Lemle and Jasper Craven have been invaluable collaborators. Many thanks also for all the information and advice provided by past or present VHPI steering committee members, including Bruce Carruthers, Paul Sullivan, Paul Cox, and Lou Kern. VHPI's work is supported by many generous donors and the advisory board, which has included Oscar Arbulu, Hugh Foy, Charlene Harrington, Bridget Lattanzi, Phil Longman, Larry Cohen, Marilyn

Park, Essam Attia, and Joan Zweben. Andrew Pomerantz, Joe Ruzek, Dorothy Salmon, Jay Youngdahl, H. Westley Clark, Joseph Riotta, and Eddy Machtinger and Craig Newmark. Special thanks also to Steve Holt and Peter Dickinson.

To keep up with VHPI's work, consider subscribing to its e-newsletter at veteranspolicy.org/contact and signing up for Suzanne's Substack posts, VA Champion and The Team Intelligencer.

Suzanne has also worked very closely for nearly a decade with the "Save Our VA Campaign" of Veterans for Peace. Its stalwarts include Bruce Carruthers, Jeff Roy, Arlys Herem, Mark Foreman, and many others who have devoted countless hours to this cause. Many thanks also to Susan Schnall, Buzz Davis, Denny Riley, Dan Shea, Mike Ferner, Mike Wong, John Ketwig, Michael McPhearson, national executive director of VFP and its Labor Working Group (Greg Miller, John Braxton, Kym Valadez, Patrick McCann, and Steve Morse).

We also want to thank all our past or present allies and helpers at Common Defense, including Jose Vasquez, JoJo Sweatt, Perry O'Brien, Naveed Shah, Eric Goepel, Jessica James, Lakiesha Lloyd, Zach Shrewsbury, Alexander McCoy, and Kyle Bibby as well as John Kamin and Alex Rich. As noted in the first part of this book, Kyle is cofounder and now co-leader of the Black Veterans Project.

Fellow CWA members involved in joint work with Common Defense, the union's Veterans for Social Change program, or both now include David Marshall, Britni Cuington, and Keturah Johnson whose work is hailed in part 4 of this book.

We also want to salute the always amazing work of Swords to Plowshares, the product of a San Francisco–based team that includes Michael Blecker, Colleen Corliss, Amy Fairweather, Tramecia Garner, and many others. Many thanks to Kyleanne Hunter for her leadership at Iraq and Afghanistan Veterans of America. And Brittany Ramos DeBarros, the always formidable and effective organizing director of About Face: Veterans Against the War.

At the American Federation of Government Employees, National Nurses United, National Federation of Federal Employees, and Service Employees International Union, we have had scores of well-informed sources and fact checkers, along with VA caregivers and patients themselves. These valued helpers, past and present, include Lisa Swirsky, Daniel Horowitz, Tim Kauffman, Brittany Holder, Ian Hoffman, Jessica

Early, Jon Rose, Mark Smith, Matt Stevenson, Ali Parand, Naveen Reddy, Timir Mehta, Essam Attia, Ryan Mimms, Kimberly and Dave Bump, Betsy Zucker, Dan Shea, Linda Ward-Smith, James Driscoll, David Rosenblatt, Tabitha Niemann, Brittany Holder, Latisha Thompson, Buzz Davis, Andrea Johnson, Aimee Potter, Patty Hoyt, Irma Westmoreland, Rachel Berger, Kevin Pietrick, Joe Henry, Randa Ruge, Tiffany Nguyen, Matt McLaughlin, Jessica Fee, Jeanine Packham, Missy Miklos, Jason Freeman, Adam Pelletier, and Kayla Williams.

Suzanne also wants to thank the many VA staff members around the country, who shall remain nameless due to their understandable concern about job security threats during the second Trump administration, which has made their day-to-day work harder than ever before. Among healthcare reformers, Suzanne would like to recognize the tireless work of Ana Malinow, Kay Tillow and their colleagues at National Single Payer; Rose Roach and Mark Dudzic at the Labor Campaign for Single Paye; Gillian Mason at Healthcare-Now; and Gordy Schiff, Mardge Cohen, and many other longtime friends at Physicians for a National Health Program. We have more recently met and learned much from navy veteran Theresa Aldrich, a tireless researcher, writer, and critic of the VA "entitlement reformers" profiled later in this book.

Labor Notes deserves much credit and thanks for publishing our work on the subject of veterans in the labor movement. At the last three Labor Notes national conferences, VA union activists, patients, and labor defenders have been able to strategize together. The Vets-in-Labor / Save the VA session at Labor Notes in Chicago in June 2026 should be the largest such gathering ever, in part because of the growth of the Federal Unionists Network (FUN). As reported later in this book, FUN's development as a critical cross-union network has been nurtured and supported by Labor Notes. At FUN, many thanks to Mark Smith (again), Griffin Mahon, Jerry Jones, Chris Dols, Colin Smalley, Anna Bakalis, Shaye Skiff, and other key activists, along with valued FUN advisors and volunteers like Dave Snapp, Joe McCartin, Eric Blanc, Ellen David Friedman, Jon Melrod, Joe Fahey, Ken Paff, and Benjamin Zucker. Jamie Partridge has long been a promoter of similar cross-union solidarity among postal workers in different labor organizations; his information and insights on the job threats facing veterans in that public workforce are reflected in this book and our previous one.

Writers don't reach readers in any audience, large or small, without receptive editors. For their encouragement, support, and role in the original publication of material reshaped for this collection, we'd like to thank the following:

David Dayen, and his great coworkers at *American Prospect*, Gabrielle Gurley, Ryan Cooper, Bob Kuttner, and Hal Meyerson; , Micah Uetricht, Nick French, Sean Gude, and Bhaskar Sunkara at *Jacobin* (plus Derek Seidman and Megan Day for their much appreciated *Jacobin* interviews); Matt Cooper ,Paul Glastris, and Phil Longman, at *Washington Monthly*; Katrina van den Heuvel at *The Nation*; Jeffrey St. Clair and Joshua Frank at *CounterPunch*; Randy Shaw at *Beyond Chron*; Dick Price and Sharon Kyle at *LA Progressive*; Michael Albert, Alexandria Shaner, Bridget Meehan, Arash Kolahi, and Fintan Bradshaw at Znet; Margaret Flowers at *Popular Resistance*; Wade Rathke at *Social Policy*; Peter Olney and Bob Gumpert at *Stansbury Forum*; Miles Kampf-Lessin and Alex Han at *In These Times*; Marci Rein and Max Elbaum at *Convergence*; John Russo and Sherry Linkon, at *Working Class Perspectives*; Russell Mokhiber and Ralph Nader at *Capitol Hill Citizen* (and Ralph for several *Nader Radio Hour* invites) Jeff Machota at the *Veteran*; Norm Stockwell and Bill Lueders at the *Progressive*; Alexandra Bradbury, Jenny Brown, Dan DiMaggio, and their coworkers at *Labor Notes*; Dianne Feeley and David Finkel at *Against the Current*; Dan LaBotz, Nancy Holmstrom, and Saulo Colon at *New Politics*; Craig Brown at *Common Dreams*; Alana Price at *Truthout*; Chris Lombardi and Maxine Philips at *Democratic Left*; Hugh Jackson at the *Nevada Current*; and multiple moderators at the always invaluable Portside—David Cohen, Marti Garza, Jay Schaffner, Stephanie Luce, Kurt Stand, Leanna Noble, Judy Atkins, Meredith Schafer, and their growing number of colleagues.

Last but not least, we'd like to thank our comrades at PM Press—Ramsey Kanaan, Joey Paxman, Gregory Nipper, Chris Dodge, Stephanie Pasvankias, Steven Stothard, Courtney Davis, and all their associates. We could not have reached the finish line without the essential help of K.M. Slade, copy editor, fact-checker, and formatter extraordinaire. She did double duty—first, by getting part 5 material in shape for original publication in the *American Prospect* and then helping us get the entire manuscript together.

Introduction

"People Are Waking Up"

"No one has done more for veterans than me." Like any utterance from the mouth of Donald Trump, that statement needs fact-checking, which we gladly provide in this book. For the record, no recent resident of the White House has directed more unfriendly fire at former service members, their families, friends, and neighbors than Trump.

The president is right about one thing: in three successive national elections, more military veterans voted for him, by varying margins, than for Hillary Clinton, Joe Biden, and Kamala Harris. And therein lies the political challenge—and organizing opportunities—highlighted in the pages that follow.

How can opponents of an increasingly authoritarian regime reach more of the seventeen million Americans who served in the military, may have leaned conservative in the past, but are now, for different reasons and to varying degrees, experiencing Trump voter remorse?

Without a doubt, Trump has done much for the high-profile veterans you will meet in this book. JD Vance, Doug Collins, and Pete Hegseth all landed leading roles in Trump's second administration as a big thank-you for their service—as Make America Great Again (MAGA) loyalists in the Senate, House, or Fox News.

Arrayed behind this "Gang of Three" are other former officers, also leaning far right, who returned to the federal payroll in 2025, as Trump appointees. In some cases, they are still deeply involved in implementing the antilabor agenda of the Heritage Foundation's Project 2025. This includes eliminating the jobs of three hundred thousand federal workers, many of whom served in the military, and turning National Guard members into what one federal judge called an unlawful "national police force" (in a nation with too many police already).[1]

Of course, getting sacked as a federal worker or being forced to leave your day job to join an unlawful Guard deployment to a "crime-ridden, Democrat-run city" is not as bad as being personally detained by Immigration and Customs Enforcement (ICE). Or losing a family member to the Trump-Vance attack on millions of undocumented workers.

Or worse yet, losing your life as RN Alex Pretti did in late January 2026, when his fatal encounter with ICE "burst a dam," as the *New York Times* put it, and helped trigger a massive and inspiring community-labor protest against the brutal occupation of Minnesota by thousands of federal agents. (For more on that, see the epilogue).

Amid the ongoing life-and death struggle against a violent and lawless roundup of immigrants, even being part of a "military family" provided scant protection, as several high-profile cases confirmed in California, Oregon, and Missouri. In each instance, military veterans found themselves either personally detained or struggling to get a loved one out of jail, until either legal action or political pressure won a temporary reprieve from deportation.

Three Boys in the Marines

In Santa Ana, California, a patriotic noncitizen named Narciso Barranco encouraged all three of his sons to enlist in the Marines. Alejandro, age twenty-five, served as a combat engineer in Afghanistan. Jose Luis, twenty-three, completed his service in August 2025 and planned to attend nursing school on the GI Bill. Emanuel, twenty-one, remained on active duty. All three had hoped to use their enlistment to sponsor their father's application for a green card. But, according to Alejandro, "everyone was so busy in the military," and a lawyer they consulted "wanted $5,000 just to start the process."[2]

In June 2025, after working in the United States for thirty years without papers and no brushes with the law, Narciso was doing landscaping work outside an IHOP. It was, unfortunately, located right next to a Home Depot parking lot targeted by ICE. When the slight forty-eight-year old Mexican American was accosted by masked federal agents, he raised his weed whacker—more in surprise than self-defense.

Their response was to pepper-spray Narciso, pummel him to the ground, shackle his hands behind his back, and shove him into an unmarked vehicle, along with a day laborer nabbed in the same raid. To no avail, he told them, in English, "I have three boys in the Marines." Narciso's thank-you for their service was two months spent in a crowded, privately run federal detention center. An immigration court judge rejected a government request to keep him behind bars indefinitely without bond, so he was then released.

Narciso was required to wear an ankle monitor and check in with ICE three times a week, until an immigration judge terminated the deportation case against him, paving the way for his belated bid for "parole in place." Much touted by military recruiters, this process allows the undocumented parents of service members to remain in the United States while becoming a legal permanent resident.[3] "There are many people in the military with immigrant parents like my dad," Juan Luis told the *New York Times*. "I never thought this could happen to him."

A Vet for Peace and a Veteran's Wife Detained

Like the Barranco brothers, Muhammad Zahid Chaudhry served in the military, lived legally in the United States for twenty-five years, and earned a green card, while doing much skirmishing with the government about his immigration status.[4] In 2000, he enlisted in the Army National Guard, then served for five years until he was honorably discharged due to a back injury suffered while training for a deployment to Iraq. Requiring a wheelchair for mobility due to his service-related condition, the Pakistani native became president of the Veterans for Peace chapter in Olympia, Washington, and served on the Washington State Governor's Committee on Disability Issues and Employment.

On August 21, 2025, Chaudhry showed up for an immigration hearing in Tukwila and ended the day in solitary confinement at a Homeland Security Detention Center. Despite an active campaign to secure his release, Chaudhry remained in custody, separated from his wife and two young children, for 124 days. Fortunately, Melissa Chaudhry is a two-time Democratic congressional candidate in Washington State who had the organizing experience and political contacts necessary to make Muhammed's case a local cause célèbre. As a result, the mayor of Seattle and many others in the community called for his release.[5] In her new book, *Service and Sacrifice*, Chaudhry describes their ordeal—and continuing uncertainty about Muhammed's legal status—as "a case study in what happens when constitutional guardrails fail," even for veterans who are foreign born.

Like Melissa Chaudhry, James Brown is a US citizen married to an immigrant. Brown is a Gulf War vet who lives on a farm in Missouri. His wife, Donna Hughes-Brown, is an Irish citizen who was a lawful US resident for thirty-seven years, regularly renewing her green card so she could do healthcare work. In 2015, she wrote a bad check for a small amount, quickly repaid the money, and received probation for her minor offense.

Nine months after James Brown, who served in the US Navy for twenty years, voted for Trump in 2024, Donna was coming home from a trip to Ireland. She was detained at O'Hare Airport and transferred to ICE custody in Kentucky, separated from her husband, four children, and five grandchildren. While imprisoned under what she described as "deplorable conditions," Hughes-Brown faced possible deportation for a "crime of moral turpitude." Mike Kehoe, the right-wing Republican governor of Missouri, declined to get involved in her case claiming it was a "federal issue" only. After 143 days, Hughes-Brown was finally released when a judge found she posed no threat to the community and her (still unresolved immigration) case was highlighted at a congressional hearing.

"I want somebody to have the guts and the fortitude to stand up and say, 'You know what? This is wrong,'" James Brown told a British newspaper. "It's crazy that this is happening. It's just crazy that this is even allowed in this country."[6]

Two, Three, Many Openings

The multiplying injustice of situations like these (and so many others) has impacted millions of people who did not participate in the 2024 presidential election. And some who did—like James Brown—now regret their vote for the Republican candidate "100 percent." To build a broader, more diverse movement against the craziness of Trump, new allies and activists are needed, many of whom have been showing up by the tens of thousands at a succession of nationwide "No Kings" rallies, and other anti-Trump protests.

Among them, notes journalist Micah Sifry, is one big group of "people who are already on fire: federal workers." As Sifry describes this newly aroused and now highly motivated segment of the population: "America's 2.4 million civilian federal workers are, by their nature, generally patriotic and politically moderate. Nearly 30 percent of them are veterans. They all take an oath to defend the Constitution. Also, unlike many politicians from both parties who went to elite schools and are worth millions ... most federal workers are just like the people they serve: working-class."[7]

As Sifry argues—and we hope to demonstrate in this book—one result of the Trump-Vance assault on the civil service is its "radicalizing of the very people who can best explain how the government does so much good for so many."

Some of the best explainers of that sort were already "well developed" in their labor, left-wing, or antiwar politics before becoming frontline defenders of government jobs and services, the rights of immigrants, and federally funded healthcare for the poor. Their past organizing experience helped them figure out how to best engage their coworkers and fellow veterans, who were sometimes one and the same. And, when existing unions or veterans' groups failed to mobilize their members in response to multiple threats, these rank-and-file activists helped create new formations that could better address those challenges.

The left in the United States has always embraced the small band of veterans who became antiwar activists or conscientious objectors. By the early 1970s, the GI movement in favor of military withdrawal from Southeast Asia had become so broad-based and disruptive that it helped shorten the Vietnam War and end mass conscription. To this day, the aging cohort responsible for those achievements—still active in groups like Vietnam Veterans Against the War and Veterans for Peace—garner well-deserved applause at progressive events everywhere.

Organizations formed by men and women who served in post-9/11 wars in the Middle East—like Iraq Veterans Against the War (which morphed into About Face) and Common Defense, the largest grassroots network of progressive vets today—follow in Vietnam veterans' footsteps but do so in very modern, media-savvy ways.

Outside that progressive vet milieu lies the much larger ex-military population of popular imagination. Thanks to much media stereotyping, the former soldier that comes to mind in that cohort is pale, stale, and male but definitely not sporting the graying ponytail of a sixties radical. A red-state Republican, he wears a US flag pin and a Legion cap, marches in patriotic parades, and cheers every new war coming down the pike. Worse yet, his successor in the post-9/11 generation is an eager recruit for right-wing militias. This is the kind of angry, conspiracy-minded vet who donned camo again and stormed the US Capitol on January 6, 2021, to protest an election that was not stolen.

A More Diverse Vet Population

In reality, as described in our previous book, *Our Veterans*, the military has developed far greater gender, racial, and ethnic diversity than many people realize, while continuing to attract a workforce that is predominantly young, working-class, and poor. After much struggle, the Pentagon was forced to accept more women as well as openly gay and transgender recruits. (As noted in part 6 of this book, the latter have been disgracefully targeted for expulsion by Secretary of War Pete Hegseth). According to Pentagon statistics, about a third of the 1.3 million men and women on active duty identify themselves as a "racial minority (Black or African American, Asian, American Indian, or Alaska Native, Native Hawaiian, or other Pacific Islander, Multiracial, or Other/Unknown)."

Unofficial estimates put the percentage of people of color in uniform even higher—at 43 percent. Nearly three hundred thousand women were deployed to Iraq and Afghanistan; thousands served in combat roles after a ban on that was lifted in 2013. About 16 percent of all enlisted personnel and 18 percent of all officers are female. Reflecting the overall demographic shift in the enlisted ranks, a quarter of all veterans are now people of color. One little-noted dual identity in the veteran population derives from the "union density" of the latter. More than a million former service members belong to private or public sector labor organizations.

In the struggles that unfolded in the year after Trump's return to the White House, some of the earliest whistleblowers on the depredations of Elon Musk's Department of Government Efficiency (DOGE) were unionized caregivers at the largest public healthcare system in the country, run by the Department of Veterans Affairs. And a few, like Mildred Manning-Joy, an African American vet and VA nurse in Durham, North Carolina, had already been skirmishing with would-be privatizers of the VA for eight years, under Biden and Trump before him.

Manning-Joy was among the National Nurses United (NNU) members and other VA union activists who picketed and rallied in 2022 to block a Biden administration plan to close veterans' hospitals and clinics in many states.[8] At stake for Manning-Joy in that fight was not just her job and healthcare access; after multiple tours of duty in Afghanistan and Iraq, her own son had returned home with "the invisible scars of his time in combat" and was much dependent on VA care too.

In May 2025, Manning-Joy headed to Washington, DC, as part of a delegation speaking for fifteen thousand VA nurses represented by NNU. Their mission was to sound the alarm about the "staffing cuts impacting patients' ability to receive proper care for wounds and chemical burns, patients waiting an outrageously long time for medication, nurses left without support staff and experiencing moral distress while trying to perform tasks such as turning over beds in addition to their patient care duties." On Capitol Hill, they criticized the Republicans for "trying to silence VA nurses' protected union voice ... and eliminate health care for more than 8.6 million lower-income patients."[9]

On the other side of the country, NNU caregivers at the VA Medical Center in San Diego delivered the same message, surrounded by patients, their families, labor, and community supporters. "No matter who you cut from the VA, veterans are going to be affected," warned RN Safiah Dhada. "If you cut housekeeping, nurses will be bagging trash, taking time away from patient care. If you cut supply techs, nurses will need to chase down supplies, delaying our veterans' care. Our veterans deserve timely care, not delays that negatively impact health outcomes."[10]

The Anti-privatization Fight

Helping to coordinate such protest activity around the country is NNU national vice president Irma Westmoreland, a VA nurse for twenty-six years and, like Manning-Joy, a veteran of struggles against Trump during his first presidential term, after which "we came out stronger," she believes. "[Nothing that Trump does now] will keep us from doing the things we need to do to represent VA nurses," Westmoreland told us. "[But] taken together, all of his actions are aimed at crippling and then privatizing the VA.... And only the unions are standing in the way of that."

Latisha Thompson is a VA social worker in Philadelphia who belongs to an American Federation of Government Employees (AFGE) local that was slow to respond with similar membership mobilization and outreach to the public. So, at the risk of her own job, she landed an appearance on *Democracy Now*, with hosts Amy Goodman and Juan Gonzalez, one month after Trump's inauguration. On that show, she pulled no punches about the new president's "ultimate goal of gutting public services and paving the way for his disgustingly wealthy allies, like Elon Musk, to gain more profit."

A member of the Federal Unionists Network (profiled later in this book), Thompson reminded her listeners that this assault threatens more than a century of progress made by civil rights campaigners who marched, organized, and lobbied so that "everyone in the federal government had more fair working practices, safer conditions, and stronger collective bargaining rights." She added, "Today, 20% of ... all Black workers ... work within in the public sector, earning a living wage, living with more stability, and, importantly, receiving lifesaving, life-changing benefits.... Black families cannot afford to lose these jobs. As a predominantly working-class population, we have to fight, resist DOGE, and these austerity measures, [as part of] the larger struggle for racial justice and ... to save our democracy."[11]

In Chicago, Aimee Potter, a fellow VA social worker who serves as an AFGE shop steward and local treasurer, was similarly outspoken in multiple media outlets, locally and nationally, about the cascading threats to her fellow workers and patients. She comes from a distinguished union family, which includes two members involved with the Chicago Teachers Union and another, her late stepdad, who was a founding member of Teamsters for a Democratic Union.

At the VA, Potter specializes in opioid overdose prevention. Federal funding of harm reduction programs that focus on addiction treatment is a major budget-cutting target of the White House.[12] Among veterans, substance abuse tends to overlap with the problem of thirty thousand also being homeless. Yet, as Potter told the press, the new administration "fired a slew of employees, who were veterans themselves, working with homeless vets, as well as outreach teams working in the community. Part of the VA's mission has been to increase community connections and build collaborative relationships among the VA and outside resources."[13]

"There's less support for those of us doing this work daily, so some of us are going to be looking elsewhere for other jobs, which then impacts the availability of in-house services for veterans," she points out. "We have lost seasoned clinicians who have not been replaced, and that leads to longer wait times for appointments."[14] But that's OK with VA Secretary Doug Collins because he can then justify even more outsourcing of mental healthcare to the private sector.

To be fair and balanced, it should be noted that VA press secretary Peter Kasperowicz, an alumnus of Fox News (like Pete Hegseth), frequently assures the national media that any such concerns about privatization—raised by "union bosses" like Westmoreland, Thompson, and Potter—are just "a far-left canard."[15] When his boss, Collins, eagerly implemented Trump's illegal cancellation of collective bargaining agreements, Kasperowicz called that "a huge win for veterans"—even though one hundred thousand vets working at the VA were covered by them.[16]

Far Left Turnout?

In red-state America, Micah Sifry's thesis had an early field test in the few town meetings that Republicans held in their home districts in the spring of 2025 (against the advice of their House and Senate caucus leaders). Such meetings with predominantly white, often rural constituents—who were definitely not leftists—became increasingly risky as popular anger grew over DOGE-driven service disruption. And audiences became particularly agitated about pending threats to Medicaid in the "One Big, Beautiful Bill" that the Republican majority passed for Trump, a few months later, in July.

One initial confrontation occurred when Rebecca Reinhold, vice president of AFGE Local 85 at the Dwight D. Eisenhower Medical Center in Leavenworth, Kansas, unloaded on Rep. Mark Alford in a widely viewed YouTube exchange. She reminded Alford that her twelve hundred members provide critical services. "We make sure veterans are cared for from the moment they become a veteran," she said. "But you want to cut my job?" In response, Alford insisted there would be "appropriate funds for veterans" and that any VA cuts "would not affect services" because "we're going to make sure veterans are supported."[17]

In Oakley, Kansas, Sen. Roger Marshall abruptly ended an already contentious town hall meeting when local resident Chuck Nunn similarly questioned the wisdom of VA service cuts. His concern was shared by another member of the crowd who declared "I'm not a Democrat, but I'm worried about the veterans." Marshall did not respond to either comment and left the room hurriedly, amid jeers and boos.[18]

In other House member encounters with constituents in the Southwest around the same time, it was the same story. Veteran Louis Smith drew approving applause from an East Texas audience when he warned Congressman Pete Sessions that "the guy from South Africa [Elon Musk] is not doing you any good—he's hurting you more than he's helping."[19]

During a more easily controlled "telephone town hall," Rep. Stephanie Bice from Oklahoma got an earful from a self-identified former army officer and Republican voter who demanded to know how "some college whiz kids with a computer terminal in Washington, DC ... have determined that it's OK to cut veterans benefits."[20]

In Illinois, Jacob Bushno, a veteran of the Iraq War who had become a Forest Service worker, was one of an estimated six thousand vets impacted by Trump's February 2025 dismissal of twenty thousand federal workers still in "probationary status" (some of whom were not "new hires" at all but had just recently changed jobs at an agency, like the VA, that had employed them for years). Bushno was let go seven days before his one-year probationary period ended, a decision he tried to appeal. He also reached out to his Republican congressman for help—figuring that fellow veteran Mike Bost, chair of the House Committee on Veterans' Affairs, would be sympathetic to his plight. He got no response from Bost.

What was happening then, in early 2025, only got worse by the fall of that year. Democrats in Congress tried to spare twenty million Americans, including many Trump voters, from insurance coverage price increases resulting from Republican cuts in Affordable Care Act subsidies.[21] This led to another government shutdown, like the five-week one during Trump's first term. After that major payroll disruption, Congress passed a law mandating that federal workers furloughed or forced to work without salaries during any future shutdown receive their back pay afterward.

Nevertheless, Trump mused publicly about not paying some workers this time, even though he signed the 2019 legislation requiring him to do so.[22] This left House Speaker Mike Johnson to deal with worried callers on C-SPAN, like a military wife and self-identified Republican voter from Fort Belvoir, Virginia, who told Johnson that her family "lived paycheck to paycheck" and had two sick kids in need of medication that they could not afford if the shutdown continued.[23]

By the second week of the October 2025 shutdown, the president was boasting on social media: "Meeting today with Russ Vought, he of Project 2025 fame, to determine which of the many Democratic agencies, most of which are a political scam, he recommends be cut, and whether or not those cuts should be permanent."

Tackling Trump, with Courage and Care

In North Carolina, one fifty-five-year-old former Trump voter, now an archenemy, was quick to recall how, during his presidential campaign, "Trump had waddled from rally to rally yapping that he had no ties to Project 2025 ... because he knew voters hated that wrecking ball blueprint."[24] This White House critic is Richard Ojeda, a fiery former paratrooper, two-time Bronze Star winner, and veteran of the wars in Iraq and Afghanistan, who knows a thing or two about "political scams."

Ojeda began his twenty-five-year army career as an enlisted man and then went through officer training after completing college; he retired with the rank of major. In 2016, Ojeda—soon to become a Democratic state senator—voted for Bernie Sanders in West Virginia's Democratic presidential primary. But in the general election that year he thought mistakenly that Trump—as a political outsider, like Sanders—was more likely to "drain the swamp" in DC than Hillary Clinton.

Two years later, Ojeda became the West Virginia politician most supportive of the pay and benefit demands of the twenty-five thousand public school teachers who staged an illegal statewide walkout. He spoke on the strikers' behalf at rallies throughout the state and, inspired by their "red state revolt," decided to take his own populist working-class politics to Congress, via an uphill fight against right-wing Republican Carol Miller. During Ojeda's 2018 campaign against her, he expressed public regret for his Trump vote two years before. In his view, after winning the White House as a self-proclaimed adversary of corporate interests and their lobbyists, Trump only "took care of the people he's supposed to be getting rid of."[25]

Ojeda's own congressional race became so unexpectedly close that Trump had to personally intervene. During a campaign rally for Miller, the president made a point of pronouncing Ojeda's last name with an affected Hispanic accent, as a way of mocking him. Miller ended up winning, but Ojeda's 44 percent of the vote—garnered with little national Democratic Party support—was a thirty-two-point improvement over the performance of the Democrat running in the same district two years before. According to *FiveThirtyEight*, Ojeda outperformed his district's partisan lean by 25 percent, the strongest showing for a non-incumbent anywhere in the country that November.[26]

In 2025, Ojeda launched another bid for Congress in his adopted state of North Carolina.

During his successful Democratic primary campaign, Ojeda found encouraging signs that other former Trump supporters are having second thoughts as "they're looking around at the wreckage so far, the ICE kidnappings, the censorship, and the economic pain." More people, he believes, "are realizing that they were pawns in the oldest con in the book—blame immigrants, blame workers, blame anyone who doesn't look or pray or live the day you do."[27]

"People are waking up. They're fed up that they've been lied to. They're angry, and they damn well should be. Our job now is to meet that anger with something stronger than shame, because mocking people who got conned won't win anything. The only way to defeat a movement based on fear and division is to build one rooted in courage and care."

"We have to talk to people who were misled by Trump and give them something to believe in other than a cult of personality," Ojeda says. "If you give people something worth fighting for, they will fight for each other."

PART I

THE MILITARY EXPERIENCE

Military service, stripped of its patriotic trappings, is just another blue-collar or white-collar job. It involves work in a highly unregulated industry, with no collective bargaining or protective labor legislation and no anti-discrimination statutes. Today, half the active-duty military workforce of 1.3 million is between the ages of eighteen and twenty-five. So that's a young population without much prior full-time job experience.

Many teenagers enlist because their moms and aunts or uncles and fathers or grandparents served. The result is many multigenerational "military families," even if they don't include career military people. New recruits largely hail from nine or ten states that also have a disproportionate number of military bases. Men and women lacking civilian job options are understandably drawn to the promise of stable employment, steady pay, health insurance coverage, subsidized housing, food, and clothing.

When recruiters woo young people with immigrant parents, spouses, or children at risk of deportation, they play up "Parole in Place," a program to protect military family members from deportation. In 2023, about 11,500 relatives of military recruits benefited from the program, a 35 percent increase over the previous year; a flood of new applicants is expected, in response to Trump's roundup and detention of so many undocumented workers. Family members lose their protective status if their relative, who is a citizen or permanent resident, drops out of the National Guard or is dishonorably discharged from the active-duty military.

Opportunities for job training are another part of the enticing package rolled out by recruiters, along with signing bonuses worth up to $50,000. Where else, outside of building trades apprenticeship programs (much harder to get into), can one get paid to learn new skills?

Then there's the longer-term promise that you will have good healthcare coverage if you end up with a service-related illness or injury or remain low-income. If you make the military a career, where else can you get a modest pension after twenty years? Either way, you'll have access to affordable higher education through the GI Bill.

Richard Ojeda, who grew up in the coalfields, sums up his own situation at age eighteen this way: "I had three choices in my corner of West Virginia—dig coal, sell dope, or join the Army ... the last choice was my one shot at breaking free." According to Ojeda, that's why thousands of other "young people from the hollers, the barrios, the farms, and the factory towns sign up—they want a way out, a way forward, and a chance to prove themselves."

As a result, the demographics of the US. military have changed since the mid-twentieth-century heyday of the "citizen soldier." Though the statistics vary by branch, the armed forces are ethnically and racially diverse, with people of color representing about 40 percent and women 17 percent of the workforce. When Donald Trump was elected president again in 2024, the military had become so "woke," in his view, that it even allowed forty-four hundred trans people to serve and paid for their transitions.

When Trump appointed Pete Hegseth to lead the Pentagon, the white nationalist from Princeton immediately banned the use of the slogan "our diversity is our strength," calling it "the single dumbest phrase in our military's history." (For more on what followed, see part 7 of this book.) In reality, the military has never been so "politically correct" that its young recruits—and even JROTC students—were spared various forms of workplace abuse, including sexual harassment and assault. After leaving the military, most former soldiers don't land high-paid jobs at Fox News or defense contractors or become a successful entrepreneur like former Navy SEAL Eddie Gallagher.

Too many service members are steered toward law enforcement agencies, a career choice critiqued below, and likely to become more common as hiring for "homeland security" is greatly increased to support Trump's clampdown on immigration. A disproportionate number of vets—almost all poor and working-class—end up in trouble with the law themselves, due to behavioral problems in the military or afterward. And now, as Ojeda notes, "Kids who joined for opportunity and service have been turned into enforcers for a tin-pot dictator" because the White House has federalized their National Guard units and sent them into US cities over the objections of multiple state governors.

1

ROTC Redux

How do campus foes of university complicity with the military build popular opposition to costly, disastrous, and unjust foreign wars? In any era, antiwar campaigners—from Gaza encampment organizers in 2024 to protesters against the Vietnam War more than fifty years before—need local targets of opportunity.

Then and now, students have focused on endowment funds invested in weapons manufacturers and military-related research. In the late 1960s and early 1970s, an even bigger organizing issue was military conscription affecting millions of draft-age males—even those with student deferments—and military training programs on campus.

During the Vietnam era, the much bigger personnel needs of the US armed forces were met by conscription, draft-driven enlistments, and volunteers. In the last category were graduates of West Point, other service academies, and private military colleges like the Virginia Military Institute or the Citadel. But the Department of Defense (DOD) needed far more first lieutenants than these institutions could produce. At two thousand public universities and private colleges around the country, DOD-funded military science departments played a critical role in generating the necessary newly commissioned officers.

When one of us (Steve) entered college in 1967, he joined 250,000 Reserve Officer Training Corps (ROTC) cadets drilling in uniform, firing guns at a rifle range, and studying military science that year. Two years before, at Middlebury College, that would not have been a matter of choice: Army ROTC enrollment was mandatory for all freshman and sophomore males. Foot-dragging by college trustees, administrators, and faculty members reluctant to cut ties with the military sparked an escalation of protest activity from peaceful picketing and sit-ins to more aggressive action.

ROTC buildings were trashed, bombed, or set on fire—most famously at Kent State University in May 1970. That arson attempt triggered a National Guard deployment by the Republican governor of Ohio that resulted in the fatal shooting of four students (one of them a ROTC cadet). Their deaths triggered the largest higher-education strike in US history, involving more than five million students.

Little-Known History

Opponents of ROTC during the Vietnam era were not well informed about previous campus- or community-based campaigns against military training in either high school or college settings. For more on that little-known story, present-day peace campaigners can now consult *Breaking the War Habit: The Debate over Militarism in American Education*, an essay collection compiled by Seth Kershner (a PhD candidate at the University of Massachusetts), Scott Harding (who teaches at the University of Connecticut), and Charles Howlett (a retired professor of education at Molloy College).

As their book shows, campus and community controversies over ROTC have been going on almost since its creation via the National Defense Act of 1916, part of the Wilson administration's preparation for US involvement in World War 1. By the mid 1920s, "nearly two-thirds of all universities hosting ROTC had made the program mandatory for at least some of its male students."[1]

In response, the national Committee on Militarism in Education (CME) was formed in 1925 to seek a congressional ban on compulsory military training "in any educational setting other than a military school." Even the conservative American Federation of Labor backed this effort. Organized labor warned that the United States would soon become a "militaristic nation" if the "propaganda of military sabre-rattlers" was allowed to "make goose-steppers [and potential strikebreakers] out of the schoolboys of America."[2]

Between the two world wars, the CME effectively debunked the notion that ROTC was an innocuous form of "citizenship training" and helped persuade "dozens of colleges and universities to abolish compulsory military instruction." Its "small cadre of committed individuals—pacifists, educators, socialists, and clergy—believed that, by opposing the militarization of education, they could prevent the formation of the military mindset capable of tipping the nation into another world war." But the climate for "peace education" was not very favorable in the late 1930s. Many of the CME's own "longtime allies began to view war as the only path to eliminate the threat of fascism" in German, Italy, and Japan. When conscription was reintroduced in 1940 by the Roosevelt administration, the group folded its tents and disbanded.[3]

In the post–World War II era, as the authors of *Breaking the War Habit* note, a victorious United States emerged "as the sole global superpower" but used its rivalry with the Soviet Union to justify the "largest peacetime military establishment in U.S. history." The resulting "repressive Cold War atmosphere constrained peace activism throughout the 1950s." All that had changed by 1967, when President Lyndon Johnson escalated US military intervention in Vietnam but did not want to call up the National Guard or reserve units to fight. His "decision to move nineteen-year-olds to the top of the draft list catalyzed the antiwar movement and sparked a much bigger wave of protest against on-campus military recruiting."[4]

By the spring of 1971, ROTC enrollment had shrunk to eighty-seven thousand, and the program had either been evicted from a number of colleges and universities or forced to shut down due to declining enrollment.

As the *Breaking the War Habit* authors point out, after US troops were withdrawn from Vietnam and the draft ended in 1973, "high schools became the answer to the Pentagon's manpower problems."[5] While the armed forces beat a strategic retreat from the Ivy League and some elite private colleges, enrollment in public high school Junior ROTC programs (JROTC) mushroomed. The DOD began targeting "under-resourced schools and low-income communities, where opportunities are limited and young people are susceptible to the military's promise of career advancement and college benefits."[6]

According to a *New York Times* analysis, "majority minority schools are nearly three times as likely as majority white schools to have a JROTC program." Nationwide, half a million teenagers now get military training in thirty-three public high schools throughout the country. About 40 percent of the cadets who spend three years in such programs end up enlisting after graduation. This makes JROTC a key component of the Pentagon's annual struggle to meet its "all-volunteer force" recruitment quotas.[7]

However, JROTC is not marketed as a pipeline to active duty. Rather, it's sold to teachers, parents, and school board members as an opportunity for additional adult mentoring, exposure to military discipline, and inculcation of civic values. Cadets get to drill in uniform, handle weapons, learn military ranks and history, and stand at attention when visitors come to their classes. Their instructors are military veterans certified by the DOD, although many states don't require them to have either teaching certificates or a college degree. In addition, the DOD leaves day-to-day monitoring of their classroom performance (and after-class behavior) to school administrators busy with many other responsibilities.

That lax oversight has had calamitous results. As the *Times* revealed in a major investigative piece, at least thirty-three JROTC instructors have engaged in sexual misbehavior with young women in the program between 2018 and 2023. And that JROTC rap sheet does not even include the "many others who have been accused of misconduct but never charged" or the inappropriate behavior that went unreported because cadets were afraid of jeopardizing their potential military careers.[8]

Adult Mentoring?

The front-page revelations sparked outrage from two House members with government oversight functions. In an August 2022 letter to Defense Secretary Lloyd Austin and the secretaries of the army, navy, and air force, US representatives Carolyn Maloney (D-NY) and Stephen Lynch (D-MA) called incidents of sexual harassment and abuse "completely unacceptable and an abject betrayal of the trust and faith these young men and women placed in the U.S. Military." The House members specifically demanded to know what action Pentagon leaders were taking in response to the reports, including whether additional oversight of JROTC instructors was being planned "to ensure the safety and well-being of cadets."[9]

If the DOD's past response to sexual harassment and assault of women in uniform by fellow soldiers is any guide, its efforts to protect vulnerable teenagers from pre-enlistment exposure to "military culture" will also fall short. The criminal behavior of so many "military science" instructors, implanted in public high schools by the DOD, may have two unintended consequences, however. First, it could give campaigners against such programs a new issue to organize around. Second, as

Maloney and Lynch note, negative publicity about JROTC could further dampen enthusiasm for military enlistment.

Even with the Pentagon dispatching some twenty thousand recruiters, spending $1.4 billion every year on fourteen hundred military recruiting stations, and gaining wide access to high schools throughout the country, only one in ten young people is considering military service. As Maj. Gen. Edward Thomas Jr., commander of the Air Force Recruiting Service, says of that polling result, "There are just lower levels of trust with the U.S. government and the military." By June 2022, for example, the army had only 40 percent of the fifty-seven thousand new soldiers it needed to sign up by last fall—so it began offering enlistment bonuses as high as $50,000.[10]

In addition, three-quarters of the seventeen-to-twenty-four-year-olds targeted by recruiters have disqualifying conditions like no high school diploma, a criminal record, chronic obesity, or some other physical or mental health problem that renders them ineligible to serve without a special waver. Among those in the last category are some of the damaged survivors of Junior ROTC. One, profiled by the *Times*, is Victoria Bauer from Picayune, Mississippi, who wanted to become a marine before she was sexually assaulted, at age fifteen, by her instructor. To this day, she still wants to know why those ostensibly responsible for defending the United States can't even protect their "own people."

Counter-Recruiting

Activists trying to spare other high school students the traumatic experience that plunged Bauer into depression and self-harm can learn much from the case studies in *Breaking the War Habit* and an earlier book by Kershner and Harding called *Counter-Recruitment and the Campaign to Demilitarize Public Schools* (Palgrave Macmillan, 2016). As anti-JROTC campaigners in Baltimore learned the hard way, challenging the "school to military pipeline for economically disadvantaged youth" in communities of color requires deft coalition-building. Despite persistent efforts, led by the American Friends Service Committee, foes of military training in Baltimore's inner-city schools "ultimately failed ... because their antimilitarist, ideological messages did not connect with pragmatic school board members and the local community."[11]

During an earlier phase of this struggle, Maryland peace activists got critical backing from US representative Parren Mitchell, a cofounder of the Congressional Black Caucus and the first African American elected to the House from his state. In a letter to the Baltimore school board, Mitchell acknowledged the need for programs that encouraged young people to stay in school, learn job skills, and stay out of gangs. But he strongly differed with those in the community "who believe that having military training for students … will dissipate underlying currents of unrest, anger or frustration" among African American youth. "This is a poor solution to a serious problem," Mitchell declared. "You do not solve the problems of our young people by teaching them to march and shout, 'Yes, sir!'"[12]

Like younger veterans involved in countering JROTC today, Mitchell had the street cred of past military service. Before becoming a local civil rights leader, he served as an infantry officer in World War II and received a Purple Heart after being wounded during combat in Italy. But voices like his—or that of the late congressman Ron Dellums (D-CA), a Marine Corps veteran critical of JROTC—are few and far between today. More typical is the boosterism of a nonveteran named Barack Obama, who used his 2011 State of the Union address to encourage more colleges and universities across the country to welcome ROTC back—which Harvard proceeded to do forty-two years after eliminating the program in response to a campus shutdown.

Two years later, the Department of Defense celebrated its return to the City College of New York, where ROTC had been ousted four decades earlier and student resistance to military training began in 1925. As the authors of *Counter Recruitment* note, strong opposition from the American Federation of Teachers–affiliated Professional Staff Congress, which represents thirty thousand City University of New York (CUNY) faculty members, did thwart the DOD at several other CUNY campuses, "a partial victory that was one of the few bright spots in an era marked by growing acceptance of ROTC."[13]

2

I Am Vanessa Guillén

In the summer of 2020, the city hall plaza in our new hometown, Richmond, California, was the scene of a protest vigil organized by Estefany Sanchez and her two sisters.[1] Estefany is a Richmond resident and an army veteran whose experience of sexual harassment in the military led her to identify strongly with the tragic case of Vanessa Guillén, a twenty-year-old soldier at Fort Hood in Killeen, Texas.

Guillén was sexually harassed by fellow soldiers at a base with one of the highest rates of sexual assault, sexual trafficking, suicide, and murder anywhere in the military. Her complaints to superior officers were repeatedly ignored before she was killed while at work in an armory on the base. Guillén's assailant, Aaron Robinson, then secretly moved, dismembered, and buried her body, with the help of a civilian accomplice. After escaping from military custody, Robinson became one of more than seventy suicides at Fort Hood since 2016.

The Sanchez sisters' local demonstration was part of a grassroots movement to challenge and change the toxic work environment that many young soldiers encounter, even if they are never deployed abroad or serve in a combat zone.

Protesters around the country demanded congressional action to better protect victims of military sexual assault and harassment. Some also angrily questioned the targeting of working-class communities by military recruiters, who encourage young people to enlist based on the promise of secure employment, job training, career advancement, and future access to affordable higher education through the GI Bill.

A Latina-Led Campaign

This Latina-led campaign for military justice reform is vividly recounted in a documentary called *I Am Vanessa Guillen*. Produced and directed by

Christy Wegener, the film takes its name from a now-viral hashtag created by Guillén's family to draw attention to her disappearance, which remained a mystery for several months, due to a bungled investigation by the army.

Studies have shown that one in four women in the military experience sexual assault, and this includes officers. Former US senator Martha McSally, the first female fighter pilot to serve in combat and a conservative Republican from Arizona, was raped by a superior officer.

An advocacy group called Protect Our Defenders found that 44 percent of the service members it surveyed about their sexual harassment complaints were encouraged to drop them. Another 41 percent said that no action was taken in response to such complaints. Despite the steady increase in sexual assault cases in the military, conviction rates plummeted by almost 60 percent between 2016 and 2022. In 2018–19, for example, there were 5,699 reports of sexual assault, but only 363 (6.4 percent) of those cases were tried by court-martial, and just 138 (2.4 percent) resulted in convictions.

I Am Vanessa Guillen shows how a vibrant young woman from an immigrant family became the human face of such statistics. She was part of a twenty-first-century influx of women into the armed forces that was initially lauded as an unqualified victory for gender equality. During the last two decades, three hundred thousand women were deployed to Iraq and Afghanistan, and female soldiers today comprise 16 percent of the active-duty military. Women are also the fastest-growing cohort of military veterans, representing about 10 percent of a total population of seventeen million.

Unfortunately, joining the military has proven to be more harmful than beneficial to many young women. Some who experience military sexual trauma have even been given "other than honorable" discharges, which can deprive them of VA healthcare coverage when they return to civilian life.

The popular uproar over Guillén's disappearance and death led Ryan McCarthy, then secretary of the army, to create an independent panel to determine whether Fort Hood was living up to the army's commitment to "safety, respect, inclusiveness, and diversity." Investigators interviewed more than five hundred female soldiers and found that ninety-three had credible accounts of sexual assault, but only fifty-nine had been reported.

The Fort Hood Scandal

McCarthy agreed there were "major flaws" in a command structure so "permissive of sexual harassment and sexual assault." The top officer in charge of the fifty-five thousand troops at Fort Hood was removed and disciplined along with twenty others. But despite DOD promises to crack down on harassment and discrimination, an internal survey found that nearly thirty-six thousand female service members reported unwanted sexual contact in 2021, a 13 percent increase over the year before and double the number in 2018.

Thanks to the tireless agitation of Vanessa Guillén's mother and her two sisters, Congress was also forced to confront the problem of local commanders covering up misconduct on their watch—a phenomenon long criticized by Rep. Jackie Speier (D-CA), an advocate for military justice reform for more than a decade.

By May 2021, sixty senators favored a bill cosponsored by Kirsten Gillibrand (D-NY) and Joni Ernst (R-IA), a ROTC program graduate who served in Iraq and spent many years in both the Army Reserves and the Iowa National Guard. This measure would have transferred decision-making power about a wide range of cases, including some hate crimes, to a specially trained team of uniformed prosecutors operating outside the chain of command.

In the Senate, two military veterans on the Armed Services Committee, Jack Reed (D-RI) and James Inhofe (R-OK), fought to narrow the scope of the legislation, limiting it to sexual assault cases only. In *I Am Vanessa Guillen*, Reed makes the factually challenged claim that "the basic instinct of the military is to protect your colleagues and subordinates, not to exploit them."

In late 2021, after similar pushback from Joe Biden's secretary of defense, General Lloyd Austin, Congress passed a watered-down version of military justice reform. Although it did empower a new cadre of "special victim prosecutors" to handle cases involving sexual assault, rape, murder, and domestic violence, court-martial authority was left in the chain of command.

Gillibrand criticized this legislative compromise as a "disservice to our service members" because "being able to offer discharges, deciding which evidence is allowed, which expert witness is called, and even just deciding judge, jury, prosecutor, and defense counsel—it's all still sitting with Commander So-and-So."[2]

She became a cosponsor of follow-up legislation called the Sexual Harassment Independent Investigations and Prosecutions Act. It was designed to transfer responsibility for handling sexual harassment cases from military commanders to the new special trial attorneys, who can gather evidence and decide what cases to pursue with less political interference. When the Democrats lost control of the Senate in November 2024, further military justice reform, of any sort, was no longer on the agenda.

That's because, just a few months later, former Fox News commentator Pete Hegseth became Lloyd Austin's successor as secretary of defense. Trump's nominee for that job was one of his most controversial picks. Hegseth was clearly no friend of female soldiers and someone who had behaved quite badly toward women in his own personal life.

One pivotal swing vote on his nomination—up for grabs briefly and performatively—was none other than Joni Ernst. The Senate's first female combat veteran told other participants in an annual "defense forum" at the Ronald Reagan Presidential Library that she was "a survivor of sexual assault, so I have worked very heavily on sexual assault measures within the military." Before supporting Hegseth, she wanted "to hear a little more about that," she said. "I'd like to hear about the role of women in our great United States military."

Ernst, a retired lieutenant colonel, proved to be no profile in courage when push came to shove. What she ultimately heard was a very real threat that any Senate Republican running for election who voted against a Trump cabinet nominee would face Republican primary opposition from a further-right MAGA loyalist backed by the White House. (Ultimately, Ernst decided to retire rather than face voters again in Iowa on any 2026 ballot.)

Three other Senate Republicans ignored that presidential pressure, so the initial vote on Hegseth's nomination ended in a fifty-fifty tie—which JD Vance, the former marine presiding over the Senate, as Trump's vice president, broke in the nominee's favor.

The late Vanessa Guillén would probably have expected as much from Vance. She would not have appreciated her betrayal by a fellow female service member. But that kind of treatment, at the hands of superior officers, would have been all too familiar to the young soldier who died, needlessly, at Fort Hood.

3

The Friends of Eddie Gallagher

Special operators in elite military units are the tip of the spear of US counterinsurgency campaigns around the globe.[1] Their exploits in Iraq, Afghanistan, and other fronts in the "Global War on Terror" have become fodder for scores of action films like *American Sniper* and tell-all memoirs by SEAL Team 6 members involved in the elimination of Osama bin Laden.

In the not-always-secretive world of special operations, few post-9/11 warriors have had a higher profile than Navy SEAL Eddie Gallagher. He was very fortunate to have a friend in the White House when accused by fellow SEALs of having executed a wounded Iraqi teenager and committing other war crimes.

In 2019, President Trump declared that he would "always stick up for our great fighters" like Chief Petty Officer Gallagher, who won an acquittal on all but a lesser charge (of taking a trophy shot of the dead ISIS soldier). And, true to his word, Trump blocked the navy's attempt to demote Gallagher and take away his Trident pin, the coveted symbol of SEAL Team membership.

Gallagher then retired after eight combat deployments and twenty years in the military. With much to say about that experience, he wrote an autobiography called *The Man in the Arena: From Fighting ISIS to Fighting for My Freedom*, coauthored with his wife, Andrea. Fortunately, a more objective account of his life and career was penned by David Philipps, the *New York Times* military correspondent whose reporting led to Gallagher's court-martial (and later unsuccessful defamation suit by Gallagher against him and his newspaper).

Read together, *Man in the Arena* and *Alpha: Eddie Gallagher and the War for the Soul of the Navy SEALs* constitute quite an indictment of a military subculture with a troubled past but a bright future under a second Trump administration.

Doing the Nation's Dirty Work

As Philipps recounts, the Navy SEALs are a direct descendant of the frogmen (Underwater Demolition Teams), who helped clear the way for beach landings in World War II. Their modern-day organizational ethos and mission were forged under less valorous circumstances in Vietnam, where they "stopped being combat swimmers and became jungle fighters."

Assigned to work with the Central Intelligence Agency on its notorious Phoenix Program, SEALs helped capture and kill civilian supporters of the National Liberation Front in peasant villages. As one army intelligence analyst testified at a later congressional hearing, Phoenix became "an indiscriminate murder program." In Philipps's words, it firmly established the SEALs as a commando group "created to go beyond what was officially sanctioned" and "do the nation's dirty work."

As the wars in Iraq and Afghanistan got "dirtier," Philipps explains, SEALs like Eddie Gallagher "got pulled into the muck." Eddie was a troubled teenager, raised in a devout Irish Catholic military family. He joined the navy in 1999, became a SEAL in 2004, and over the next decade "built a reputation as a seasoned badass" whose nickname was Blade. In the entirely male and overwhelmingly white SEAL Teams, "Donald Trump was a hero," Philipps reports, because of his 2016 campaign pledge to "knock the hell" out of ISIS after lifting any real or imagined Obama-era restraints on special operations.

Gallagher's last tour of duty, a year later, became a nightmare for his subordinates. The assigned role of his SEAL Team 7 Alpha Platoon was to support Iraqi forces during their liberation of Mosul while remaining a specified distance from the actual front lines. This mission was carried out in the face of suicidal ISIS resistance. Heavy US bombardment of the city resulted in many civilian casualties and widespread urban destruction.

Already much decorated for his past bravery, Gallagher insisted on joining the fray more directly, regardless of orders from above. As Philipps later learned from the navy's own investigative reports, "Gallagher had come unglued ... had put men in danger to build up his own glory, shot at women and children and crowds of civilians, and murdered a prisoner in cold blood."

An Alpha medic described his former platoon leader as "perfectly OK with killing anybody that was moving." According to a fellow sniper, Gallagher was a "toxic" influence; another Alpha member believed that his superior officer was just "freaking evil." Philipps attributes such alarming behavior, in part, to the combined influence of "steroids, stimulants, and opioids."

A Few Good Men

Gallagher's 2018 trial had more plot twists and surprises than the most popular movie ever made about a military court-martial. As scripted by Aaron Sorkin, *A Few Good Men* at least had a happy ending in the form of a Marine Corps officer (played by Jack Nicholson) being brought to justice for the needless death of a young soldier under his command. Unfortunately, the navy personnel prosecuting Gallagher for firing at unarmed civilians and killing an enemy prisoner did not have as much courtroom luck as the Marine Corps lawyer played by Tom Cruise.

Granted full immunity, a key prosecution witness changed his story on the stand. The witness took personal credit for what he now described as a mercy killing of the injured ISIS recruit, thereby absolving Gallagher of dispatching him. Other SEAL Team 7 veterans who bravely risked the wrath of other SEALs for testifying against their former leader did not succeed in convincing a jury of combat veterans that Gallagher had done much wrong. Nor was any higher-ranking SEAL in charge of supervising Gallagher held accountable in any other disciplinary proceeding.

According to Philipps, the Gallagher case showed how special operators, who started as "green-faced frogmen" in World War II, developed new protective covering, including a code of silence, during their many post-9/11 deployments in the Middle East. "Sheltered by secrecy, armored by public adoration, they built a tradition that celebrated brotherhood, rule-breaking, and blood. It morphed into a pirate culture ... where men were more loyal to the tribe than the nation they served. The culture hid under the halo of goodwill the SEALs created." Even a Special Operations Command internal review agreed that this organizational evolution was detrimental to "leadership, discipline, and accountability."

When "Killing Becomes an Addiction"

In Gallagher's own depiction of life and work in what he calls the SEAL community, there are no rogue operators engaged in barbaric behavior. There are only men like himself who derive "a sense of satisfaction from killing someone who is trying to kill you and your brothers."

"For some," he writes, "killing becomes an addiction, but I consider it a good addiction needed to win wars.... We aren't charity workers. Despite what the Pentagon upper brass says, our job isn't to win hearts and minds. SEALs are warfighters, trained [in]—and very good at—killing the enemy. Our country's wars are fought by one percent of one percent, and even a smaller percentage of those do the killing."

Late in his career, during the Obama administration, Gallagher detected an alarming "new emphasis on diversity and progressiveness" rather than maintaining high SEAL recruitment standards. "No longer recruiting those who wanted to go to war rendered the warfighter, the knuckle-draggers I came up with, obsolete; at worst, labelling us nuisances, casting us aside."

Among those guilty of ganging up on Gallagher were members of "a new softer and kinder generation of SEALs." *Man in the Arena* claims that the "little bitches" in his own platoon, who reported him to navy investigators, were trying to divert attention from their own active-duty failings. Other "bad actors in leadership positions" actively supported this "millennial mutiny," which turned Eddie into a sacrificial lamb on the altar of a newly woke military.

After his triumphant acquittal, won by high-priced civilian defense lawyers, Gallagher accused his former employer of leaking confidential documents about the case to Philipps, who then proceeded to "fabricate details" and "make false or misleading statements." Gallagher's defamation suit describes the Pulitzer Prize–winning Philipps as a "marginal journalist" who reinforced "negative and bigoted stereotypes" about combat veterans by depicting them as "damaged and violent." In reality, no reporter has done more than Philipps to blow the whistle on military training practices that do leave former service members badly damaged, even if they never served in a combat zone. (See, for example, his reporting on the case of Maine mass murderer Robert Card in chapter 12.)

Conservative Influencers

Now in his mid-forties, Gallagher appears to have landed on his feet, despite what he describes as "twenty years of beating the shit out of [his] body." His military service left him with two bulging discs, serious neck and shoulder pain, painkiller dependence, and traumatic brain injuries. As Philipps reports, Gallagher is now "modeling his own lifestyle clothing brand, endorsing nutritional supplements, and positioning himself as a conservative influencer." In collaboration with veteran-run companies like Nine Line Apparel and Black Rifle Coffee, he peddled T-shirts, hoodies, and drinkware marketed as "Salty Frog Gear." Some of his latest business collaborators include Precision Tactical Arms Company, We Kill Bad Dudes Merch, and Half Face Blades, a maker of "custom knives and axes for those who need to depend on their equipment." He conducts personal defense training courses, including one marketed as "Operator for a Day."

Gallagher's Instagram account has several hundred thousand followers, he's been invited to Mar-a-Lago by President Trump, and his book sold well. To help defend other soldiers or local law enforcement officers accused of wrongdoing, Gallagher and his wife launched a foundation called Pipe Hitter (military slang for special operations personnel).

One of Pipe Hitter's first beneficiaries was Marine Corps lieutenant colonel Stuart Scheller, a seventeen-year infantry officer who Gallagher believed was a fellow victim of "a military justice system corrupted by political correctness." According to the *Washington Examiner*, Gallagher helped raise more than $2.5 million for Scheller after he publicly criticized the chaotic US withdrawal from Kabul (marked by a suicide bombing that killed 13 service members and 170 Afghans).

Scheller's court-martial quickly became a Fox News cause célèbre—as Gallagher's own case was when Pete Hegseth used his perch there to denounce "overzealous prosecutors who were not giving the benefit of the doubt to the trigger pullers." Scheller's case was championed by Republican House members Marjorie Taylor Greene and Louie Gohmert, a former Judge Advocate General's (JAG) Corps attorney in the army. More than two dozen members of Congress protested the defendant's nine days of pretrial confinement.

In light of Scheller's otherwise "outstanding record," a military judge ended up giving him what the *Examiner* called "a slap on the wrist." The Camp Lejeune battalion commander forfeited $5,000 in pay and got a written reprimand after pleading guilty to "willfully disobeying a superior commissioned officer, dereliction in the performance of duties, and conduct unbecoming of an officer and gentleman." He also retired from the marines.

Scheller's real vindication came in early 2025. That's when the second Trump administration made him a DOD senior advisor on military personnel and readiness after Pete Hegseth praised Scheller's record at his own Senate confirmation hearing. In a social media post, Scheller lauded his new boss as the defense secretary that "warfighters deserve."

4

Trading One Uniform for Another

During the final year of Donald Trump's first term as president, more than fifteen million people participated in Black Lives Matter (BLM) protests around the country after the murder of George Floyd in Minneapolis.[1] Even as BLM supporters took to the streets to demand an end to police brutality, they were met in many places with dramatic displays of militarized policing in response to their own largely peaceful demonstrations.

Several hundred cities enforced curfews, fourteen thousand people were arrested, and nearly one hundred thousand troops from the National Guard and regular army were deployed in thirty states and the nation's capital. One peaceful downtown crowd in Washington, DC, was dispersed by the downward blast from the rotor blades of two low-flying Army National Guard helicopters, in a combat zone maneuver not unfamiliar to Afghanistan and Iraq War vets.

To one local observer, Georgetown law professor Rosa Brooks, this militarization of domestic law enforcement was a case of chickens coming home to roost. In her 2017 book, *Everything Became War and the Military Became Everything*, Brooks warned about the increasing convergence of post-9/11 "conceptions of war and warfighting" with day-to-day policing in US cities. Defenders of law and order, she wrote, "are increasingly trained to respond to threats that resemble war as much as they resemble crime, which has fueled their increased use of military weapons and tactics."

Loaded with cast-off gear from the Pentagon—body armor, bayonets, automatic rifles, grenade launchers, armored vehicles, and surveillance drones—local police converged on BLM protests like the latter were part of what Mark Esper, then secretary of defense, called "battlespace" in a widely reported June 2020 conference call with state governors.

When the Trump administration sent paramilitary units from the Department of Homeland Security and other federal agencies to Portland, Oregon, that summer, one "enemy combatant" they encountered was a white, middle-aged Naval Academy graduate. Despite posing no threat to his heavily armed assailants, Chris David was pepper-sprayed and beaten in an unprovoked assault later viewed seven million times on YouTube. In solidarity with David and other protesters at Portland's federal building, a "Wall of Vets," including some active and retired union members, joined the nightly demonstrations against militarized policing in that city for the next three months.

Kyle Bibby, an African American alum of Annapolis and former Marine Corps infantry officer, urged other veterans to stand against "Trump's authoritarian plan to use the military as his personal storm troopers to suppress dissent." A cofounder of the Black Veterans Project who served in Afghanistan, Bibby condemned the "use of force by uniformed police and a culture of violence that seeks to dominate communities rather than serve and heal them." Recalling his own past interactions with law enforcement, in and out of uniform, Bibby declared, "The police don't care that I've gone to war to protect this country—I could be the next George Floyd solely due to the color of my skin."

Supporters of the progressive vet group called Common Defense, including Bibby, launched a national campaign called "No War on Our Streets," against police department use of $7 billion worth of hardware obtained from the Pentagon. "It was our equipment first," Bibby said. "We understand it better than the police do.... It's important that we have veterans ready to stand up and say: 'These weapons need to go.'"

Two Pentagon to Police Pipelines

In 2020, even Common Defense was more comfortable focusing on the "Pentagon to Police" pipeline for military gear rather than the parallel one for personnel. Because nearly 20 percent of all law enforcement officers are ex-military—including Derek Chauvin, George Floyd's now-imprisoned killer, and Robert McCabe, who knocked a seventy-five-year-old protester senseless in Buffalo—that occupational overlap is part of the problem identified by Brooks.

Policing, including work for private security agencies, is the third-most-common post-military form of employment. It is an option widely encouraged by DOD career counselors and veterans' organizations like the American Legion. As a result, several hundred thousand veterans wear a badge of some sort. Thanks to Congress allocating $30 billion for the hiring of ten thousand more Immigration Control and Enforcement (ICE) officers between 2025 and 2030, many more ex-soldiers (and former prison guards) will join a paramilitary force with far less public oversight and accountability than any local police department.

When we were researching our book *Our Veterans*, two retired army officers, both graduates of West Point, expressed deep concern about the prevalence of policing, of any kind, as a post-military career for veterans already at risk for PTSD, substance abuse, and suicide.

As one, a Gulf War combat vet, told us: “To the extent that we’ve got a bunch of damaged young people, then maybe the last thing we want to do is put them in a job where they carry a gun in an environment that’s going to make things worse.” The other, a major who served in Afghanistan and Iraq noted that “When you leave the service, there’s no deprogramming.... They just load you up on meds and then you go straight to the police academy.” He added, “Military-style of policing is based on the notion that high-crime areas should be treated like occupied countries, [and] a guy can come back to Baltimore, Camden, or Detroit and function the same way we did when occupying Kabul or Baghdad.” (As noted in the epilogue, Jonathan Ross, the ICE agent who killed Renee Good in Minneapolis in January 2026, was an Iraq combat vet.)

Vets-Only Positions

Even during the Obama administration, the US Department of Justice (DOJ) was not listening to such knowledgeable insiders. Instead, the DOJ provided local police departments around the country with tens of millions of dollars to fund veterans-only positions.

As noted in a 2017 report by the Marshall Project, *When Warriors Put on the Badge*, this combination of special funding and preferential hiring mandated by state or federal law has made it harder to “build police forces that resemble and understand diverse communities.” The new hires benefiting most have been disproportionately white, because 60 percent of all enlisted men and women are not people of color.

The DOJ, during the first Trump administration, had little interest in tracking the later job performance of recently hired veterans or how their military background might affect their behavior vis-à-vis the public. As a former DOJ official told Marshall Project investigators, "I reject the notion that a returning veteran, who has seen combat, should cause concern for a police chief. I would even hire more if I could." By that time, however, the International Association of Chiefs of Police (IACP) had already raised some concerns about "the integration of military personnel" into law enforcement in the wake of 9/11.

In its own 2009 study, the IACP noted, "Veterans returning from the Vietnam War could easily distinguish between their combat environment—mostly jungle, farm, or open terrain—and their later urban or suburban policing environment. In the case of returning combat veterans from Iraq or Afghanistan, their combat environment and their policing environments may appear surprisingly similar." The police chiefs warned, "[Prior military service in the Middle East] may cause returning officers to mistakenly blur the lines between military combat situations and civilian crime situations, resulting in inappropriate decisions and actions, particularly in the use of less lethal or lethal force."

Cosponsored by the DOJ's Bureau of Justice Assistance, the report also noted that combat veterans who suffer from post-traumatic stress disorder and related "depression, anger, withdrawal, and family issues" may have "a low tolerance for civilian complaints" and greater propensity for the "inappropriate use of force." Some police chiefs interviewed reported that veterans under their command came back "ill-prepared for the civilian world" because their PTSD left them with "exaggerated survival instincts."

Officer-Involved Shootings

Veterans, of course, got high marks for their physical fitness, weapons-handling experience, habituation to discipline, and leadership qualities. Yet the report notes that some had trouble "readjusting to receiving rather than giving orders, trusting others, and changing the rules of engagement." According to 14 percent of chiefs surveyed, more citizen complaints are reported against officers with military experience than others without it, 28 percent of these law enforcement leaders noted that vets in their departments grappled with more psychological problems, and 10 percent found their performance marred by excessive violence.

Researchers at the University of Texas School of Public Health found that Dallas Police Department officers with military experience used their guns while on duty more than nonveterans. During a ten-year period, nearly one-third of more than five hundred cops involved in a shooting incident were veterans. Those who had been deployed overseas were nearly three times as likely to have fired their weapon; those who had not been deployed were still twice as likely to be involved in a shooting. The study concluded that some veterans employed by the Dallas Police Department lacked "critical thinking skills" when confronted with "high stress scenarios."

Similar findings were reported by the Marshall Project after it studied use-of-force complaints and fatal police shootings in several cities. In Boston and Miami, officers with military experience generated more civilian complaints of excessive force than nonveterans. Nearly one-third of the Albuquerque officers involved in a total of thirty-five fatal shootings between January 2010 and April 2014 were veterans. One of the officers sued after killing an unarmed motorist was an Iraq War veteran whose PTSD caused flashbacks, nightmares, and blackouts. As the Marshall Project discovered, he had been "assigned to patrol a high-crime area of town known as 'the War Zone.'"

Marshall Project researchers recommended clear and consistent departmental policies to "evaluate employees' mental and physical fitness" and thus "ensure public safety and guarantee a stable, reliable, and productive workforce." Yet local police department screening practices around the country remain far from standardized or effective. "Some agencies employ the use of administrative interviews and psychological evaluations to assess how veteran officers will perform the essential functions of their position, while other agencies revert to their department medical officer, or lack any policy at all."

Another Hazardous Occupation

An additional cause for concern about some veterans who end up in policing is their vulnerability to its well-known occupational hazards, which include substance abuse and suicide. In 2019, for example, far more cops (228) killed themselves than died in the line of duty (132), according to Blue Health, a mental health advocacy group for police officers and their families.

Some vets in law enforcement do discover, before it's too late, that preexisting mental health conditions can be exacerbated by the demands of another high-stress career. In Hawaii, we know a combat veteran who came back from Iraq with severe PTSD. He became a deputy sheriff but found the work made him more angry, irritable, volatile, and neglectful of his family. "I don't like gray areas," he told us. "If I'm in for a penny, I'm in for a pound. What that means is I can play cop, or I can play family man." When his wife finally threatened to leave unless he quit policing, he sought residential treatment and vocational training help from the Department of Veterans Affairs. The latter form of VA assistance enabled him to become a building trades worker instead.

Around the same time, to do research for her latest book, *Tangled Up in Blue: Policing the American City*, Rosa Brooks was moving in the opposite direction—by actually becoming a part-time police officer in Washington, DC, where she teaches law at Georgetown. In the District of Columbia, a citizen of good repute can become a reserve police officer. These reservists volunteer to take police academy courses and get field experience in a training program shorter than the one for new full-time officers. After Brooks met these requirements, she wore a badge, carried a gun, and had the authority to make arrests, albeit while working as few as three shifts per month.

Tangled Up in Blue

Brooks ended up spending hundreds of hours learning to be a cop, patrolling with more experienced officers, and responding to a wide range of citizen complaints and problems in Anacostia, "the poorest, saddest, most crime-ridden part of the nation's capital."

She discovered that her new colleagues "spent the vast majority of their time helping people who ask for their help." Via 911 calls, they end up serving as "protectors, social workers, mentors, and medics" who only rarely "used violence when needed to enforce the law." Brooks personally enjoyed "the social work aspect of the job," even if some coworkers grumbled about it.

In her new role as a uniformed "problem solver," she was soon "mediating family disputes and dealing with people who mostly need parenting classes, drug rehab, or psychiatric care, not police intervention." She concluded, "Over-policing of poor black urban communities is fueled by high demand for police services by members of those same communities. When other social goods and services are absent or scarce, police become the default solution to an astonishingly wide range of community problems."

According to Brooks, Metropolitan Police Department (MPD) interaction with low-income residents of the district was still dangerously fraught because of academy training and on-the-job socialization. "The chief lesson at the academy was this: Anyone can kill you at any time.... Week after week, we watched footage of cops getting attacked, injured, or killed. The world, it seemed, was a dangerous place for police officers; they were perpetually being stabbed, shot, punched, kicked, run over, drowned, poisoned by fentanyl, and bitten by savage dogs."

On the street, this same warning about "constant mortal danger" was transmitted from veterans to rookies, regardless of the race, gender, or ethnicity of either. According to Brooks, her fellow cops were left with an "exaggerated sense of risk" and related state of "hypervigilance." As one training officer told her during an introductory ride through Anacostia, "everyone you meet here would be happy to kill you." According to her white partner, "People here are different from you and me. We don't want to get in trouble or get hurt or go to jail. These people are so used to it, so they just don't care."

A City Out of Control?

In the summer of 2025, a new resident of the White House, recently moved back from Florida, began to describe Anacostia in similar dark and apocalyptic terms. President Trump was most triggered by an attempted carjacking and related assault on a young recruit to his Department of Government Efficiency. This crime victim was also a newcomer to a city long denied statehood because too many of its 750,000 residents were nonwhite.

The president referred to his law enforcement "surge" as a model for future crackdowns on any "crime emergency" elsewhere. (A month later, while addressing hundreds of generals and admirals ordered to assemble in Quantico, Virginia, Trump informed them that US cities would make good "training grounds" for the military.)

On August 21, 2025, Trump made his own heavily guarded, first-time visit to Anacostia, the long-troubled DC neighborhood once patrolled by Rosa Brooks when she wasn't teaching law students at Georgetown. In Trump's personal pep talk to his assembled troops, the commander in chief thanked everyone for being there. Then, in more familiar faux mob boss fashion, he told them: "You got to be strong, you got to be tough. You got to do your job. Whatever it takes to do your job."[2]

Trump decided to "rescue [the] nation's capital from crime, bloodshed, bedlam, and squalor" by taking over the MPD. It was already the nation's sixth-largest police force with twenty-three hundred "sworn officers" and six hundred civilian support staffers. The White House first summoned up reinforcements from various federal agencies under his direct command—like the FBI, DEA, and Secret Service. Then Trump went beyond his 2020 mobilization of the local National Guard to enlist a multi-state force of four thousand. This included troops sent by Republican governors in six states (all of which had a least one city with a crime rate higher than DC's).

Citizen Soldier Complaints

Some National Guard members—deployed far from their own homes, families, and regular work—quickly realized that doing their "new job" was totally FUBAR (fucked up beyond all recognition), as service members in World War II would say. One citizen soldier from somewhere out of town complained loudly to CNN about his twelve-hour-a-day stroll around Chinatown for no apparent purpose. A fellow malcontent reported, "We haven't gotten critically low on morale, but we're falling fast."

A National Guard critic of the deployment, who spoke to *Mother Jones* anonymously, was more emphatic about being used as a political prop. "I think people have hit their limit," he said. "This is an encroachment on everything we signed up for, and it feels like a violation. They just see us as little toy soldiers to put on the street to show some muscle. There's no clear mission or understanding of that mission."

When Brian Schwalb, the elected attorney general of Washington, DC, filed suit to end federal intervention in local policing, he echoed these rank-and-file complaints. "Deploying the National Guard to engage in law enforcement is not only unnecessary and unwanted, … it is also dangerous and harmful to the district and its residents," he asserted. "No American city should have the US military, particularly out-of-state military who are not accountable to the residents and untrained in local law enforcement, policing its streets." By December, 2025, two National Guard members from West Virginia were definitely harmed when a dangerous non-resident of DC—trained by the CIA as a death squad member in Afghanistan—drove from Washington state to open fire on them near a downtown Metro station. One soldier died and another was critically wounded.

The MPD's first Black female leader tried to put a positive spin on the military occupation when she talked to the media. Chief Pamela Smith claimed that all the additional traffic stops and foot patrols conducted by heavily armed federal agents and National Guard members in fatigues were really just part of crime-fighting strategies already employed by her department.

Mayor Muriel Bowser took a similar tack, suggesting that the district—if it could have afforded more personnel of its own—would have accomplished the same short-term crime rate reductions that the White House was claiming credit for. "Let me put it this way," she said. "If there were five hundred additional MPD officers, that same activity, arrests, and gun recoveries, would have likely been made."

Of course, hiring more cops would require the Trump administration and a Republican-controlled Congress to stop withholding $1 billion worth of federal funding for critical local programs. And Bowser's approach—if still pursued after Trump's escalation of militarized policing comes to an end—would not result in the much-needed reallocation of resources between police and social services long advocated by public safety reformers like Rosa Brooks.

5

Prisoners After War

Like old soldiers around the country, a group of former service members gathered in Crest Hill, Illinois, to remember fallen comrades on Memorial Day, 2024.[1] Several months later, the *Veteran*, a newspaper published by Vietnam Veterans Against the War, ran a photo of the event they attended. It shows a multigenerational, multiracial group standing at attention between two flags.[2]

In his dispatch to the newspaper, African American navy veteran Robert Maury explained why the Stateville Veterans Group was wearing government-issued clothing of a nonmilitary sort. As Maury wrote, "This was the first time in the history of Stateville, if not the first time in the history of the state of Illinois, that incarcerated veterans were allowed to organize a Memorial Day ceremony in a maximum-security prison."

There would not be another such event because the Illinois Department of Corrections would soon close this century-old facility. The Veterans Group was forced to disband, and its members were dispersed to other prisons around the state, where some hoped to plant seeds for future veteran-initiated programs

How did these vets and 180,000 others end up in a US prison population now numbering more than 1.2 million? And what can be done to keep other former service members out of prison in the future? These are questions explored by Jason Higgins, a Virginia Tech researcher, in his invaluable book *Prisoners After War: Veterans in the Age of Mass Incarceration*.

Higgins, along with John Kinder, an associate professor of history at Oklahoma State University, has also compiled an edited collection called *Service Denied*. That volume, with multiple contributors, offers a broader historical perspective on postwar mistreatment of former soldiers, including the hundreds of veterans who were born abroad, served in the US military, ended up in prison, and then were deported after their release.

Mass Incarceration

Higgins calls his own study a "social history of veterans in the age of mass incarceration." It links their experience in foreign wars and related problems transitioning back to civilian life to changes in the criminal justice system that put millions of men and women behind bars during an ongoing domestic crackdown on crime. Fifty years after the official end of US intervention in Southeast Asia, he reports, "Vietnam vets are still the single largest population of war veterans in prison, illustrating the profound and lasting impact of the 'war on crime' on their generation."

As Higgins notes, the broader US trend of "criminalizing and punishing people with behavioral and social problems"—due to their being nonwhite, unemployed, unhoused, and/or drug-dependent—led to a doubling in the number of vets in prison between the end of that war and 9/11. The author finds, however, that the "history of incarcerated veterans is not exclusively a story of racial injustice."

In *Prisoners After War,* we learn that white veterans are much more likely to go to prison than white nonveterans, while Black vets are slightly less likely than African Americans who never served. Overall, about one-third of all veterans reported having been arrested and booked into jail at least once in their lives, compared to less than one-fifth of the rest of the population.

Studies show that vets, on average, received longer sentences than nonveterans, despite the existence of a national network of Veterans Treatment Courts (VTCs). As Higgins documents in great detail, this "hybrid drug and mental health treatment system" offers access to counseling services, opportunities for housing, education, and job employment, and disability benefits through the Department of Veterans Affairs.

As a diversion program, VTCs have the lowest recidivism rates in the nation and, according to the author, "could serve as a model for greater criminal justice reform." But the effectiveness of their "reparative justice" approach varies from state to state, and the program is not available to vets charged with violent crimes, which disqualifies many defendants.

Betrayed and Abandoned

Higgins builds his book around personal stories he collected for the Incarcerated Veterans Oral History Project. He interviewed many former service members still imprisoned, some formerly imprisoned, police officers and judges, and other vets who have become VTC volunteers and helpers. One common theme among those who end up in legal trouble is the feeling of being betrayed and abandoned. That's because they've been denied the services and benefits—or opportunities for citizenship—promised by military recruiters, charged with filling the ranks of an "all-volunteer force" with poor and working-class youth since 1973.

Their exclusion from the perks of veteran status often occurred when preexisting mental health issues or service-related medical conditions led to misconduct while in uniform and resulted in military discipline. As Higgins notes, punitive discharges first became widespread during the Vietnam era, even before conscription was suspended. "Thousands of African Americans were excessively punished for minor offenses, behavioral issues, acts of resistance, and drug use," he writes. "As the military began to withdraw forces from Vietnam, a disproportionate number of Black soldiers received administrative discharges compared to whites, disqualifying them from VA care, disability compensation, and the GI Bill."

This left many Black combat veterans—more likely than others to suffer from PTSD—without access to much-needed treatment programs and disability pay. As one government study found in 1981, their resulting "readjustment difficulties increased the likelihood of incarceration."

More than three hundred thousand veterans who served at home and abroad after 9/11 also received less than "honorable" discharges. The Department of Defense often made such determinations in the absence of uniform disciplinary standards across military branches or even among individual commanders in the same branch. For the DOD, despite its more-than-ample $884 billion budget, getting rid of soldiers whose performance is adversely affected by PTSD, traumatic brain injuries, military sexual trauma, and/or drug or alcohol abuse is easier, quicker, and cheaper than treating them.

The Stigma of Bad Paper

Being drummed out of the military in this fashion, without even a court-martial, has lasting consequences. As civilians, "bad paper" holders aren't eligible for preferential treatment when applying for public sector jobs. The American Legion and Veterans of Foreign Wars won't even let them join. According to Swords to Plowshares, a San Francisco–based advocacy group, vets stigmatized in this fashion are more likely to have mental health conditions and are also twice as likely to commit suicide.

A Syracuse University study found that "minorities and women were disproportionately represented among veterans with bad paper" due to "racial inequities in the military's criminal justice system and the number of women who struggle with MST." Those who seek their own discharge upgrade face a long legal fight, which is why, in the waning days of the Obama administration, Vietnam Veterans of America (VVA) "called for the outgoing president to issue a full pardon for every veteran with a bad paper discharge."

More than most veterans' organizations, VVA has long been an advocate for vets unfairly discharged and in prison. In 2017, as Higgins reports, VVA helped win passage of the Fairness to Veterans Act, which reformed the individual appeals process for "bad paper veterans diagnosed with PTSD or a TBI [traumatic brain injury]." Unfortunately, Barack Obama left office without acting on VVA's appeal for broader clemency. After Joe Biden became commander-in-chief in 2020, he pardoned a few of the many LGBTQ service members court-martialed and kicked out of the military before the DOD's "Don't Ask, Don't Tell" policy was repealed in 2011.

With time running out on Biden's presidency, Swords to Plowshares, Minority Veterans of America, the Black Veterans Project, and two veterans' legal clinics sent a letter to the White House in December 2024, urging similar action on behalf of "bad paper" holders. They argued that past "administrative separations and resulting denial of critical veterans' benefits" are "a life sentence" that can result in greater risk of substance abuse, joblessness, homelessness, incarceration, and self-harm. But Biden, like Obama before him, ignored their pleas to erase the stain of bad paper from the records of the many vets who tried to serve honorably but got fired from their jobs in the military with little or no due process, and with lasting adverse consequences.

Biden did grant clemency to fifteen vets, who were among fifteen hundred other people who got pardons or commutations the same day because they had "turned their lives around." This small group of former service members were mainly officers and NCOs aged forty-six to seventy-nine, who had received military decorations and honorable discharges but were later convicted of nonviolent crimes, including drug offenses in the distant past.

Members of the Stateville Veterans Group—no matter how old, infirm, or well rehabilitated—did not see their names on any additional presidential pardon lists before January 20, 2015. For them, the Democratic president's claim that America "was built on the promise of possibility and second chances" sounded like the spiel many got from military recruiters who signed them up as teenagers and put them into their first government-issued uniform.

Joe Biden did remember to pardon his own son, Hunter, who was drummed out of a direct commission officer program after one month when he failed a drug test in 2013. Hunter's continued use of cocaine contributed to other behavior that resulted in multiple federal criminal convictions during his father's term in office. He avoided spending time in prison thanks to last-minute presidential intervention on his behalf.

Soon thereafter, when Donald Trump marched into the White House for a second time, he was very quick to pardon or commute the sentences of sixteen hundred MAGA supporters who stormed the Capitol building on January 6, 2021. Among the beneficiaries of that executive action were quite a few former service members but not the kind behind bars for less serious crimes and without a merciful benefactor in either major party.

PART II

VETERANHOOD AND ITS DISCONTENTS

What turns some combat veterans, even highly decorated former officers, into critics of war and militarism? The chapters in this section are a salute to all those who have served in the military, in the United States or elsewhere, and then become, in the words of the Quincy Institute, advocates for "a world where peace is the norm and war is the exception." Let the voices of such veterans, past and present, be a reminder that their personal pathways to antiwar activism were often very difficult—due to the risk of social ostracism by friends, family, and former comrades—and in some cases involved courts-martial leading to imprisonment.

6

A Gangster for Capitalism

Haiti's tragic descent into the condition of a "failed state" is usually chronicled in mainstream media reports about its extreme poverty, political corruption and instability, and lack of public safety due to growing gang violence.[1] A front-page series in the *New York Times* in 2022 was notable for providing historical context usually lacking from such coverage.[2]

The *Times* series recounted the role of the US Marine Corps in creating the conditions for more than a century of foreign domination and exploitation of Haiti. The accompanying photos showed marines in battle dress, boarding a ship in Philadelphia headed for Port-au-Prince in 1915, forming a skirmish line in the jungle, and posing with the bodies of Haitians killed while resisting the US overthrow of their government. As the *Times* reported, one highlight of this mission was the brazen theft of $500,000 in gold from Haiti's national bank and its transfer to the vault of a bank on Wall Street.

One of the officers who departed from Philadelphia to help oversee this brutal, murderous, and Wall Street-inspired occupation was Smedley Darlington Butler. He was the son of a US congressman and the product of a wealthy family from West Chester, Pennsylvania. who belonged to the Religious Society of Friends. If Butler's name sounds familiar, it's because no critic of the US military has been more frequently quoted by antiwar veterans, over the years, than the "Fighting Quaker."

Five years before Butler's death in 1940, this two-time Medal of Honor winner penned a best-selling pamphlet titled *War Is a Racket*. In a follow-up piece for a socialist magazine, *Common Sense*, he famously summed up his personal role in this "racket": "I spent thirty-three years and four months in active service as a member of our country's most agile military force—the Marine Corps. I served in all commissioned ranks from a second lieutenant to Major-General. And during that period, I spent most of my time being a high-class muscle man for Big Business, for Wall Street, and for the bankers. In short, I was a racketeer for capitalism."

The rest of that much-quoted passage took readers on a tour of all the battle-scarred places, including Haiti, where Butler and marines under his command had helped defeat nationalist insurgents and install US-friendly puppet governments to preserve a favorable investment climate for bondholders, plantation owners, or oil refiners.

A True Believer

What led to Butler's transformation from a leading warrior for the US empire—in Central America, Mexico, Cuba, the Philippines, and China—to his brief but memorable period of 1930s antiwar campaigning? In his 2022 biography *Gangsters of Capitalism: Smedley Butler, the Marines, and the Making and Breaking of America's Empire*, journalist Jonathan Katz retraced Butler's footsteps in all his foreign postings in order to answer that question.

Before his late-in-life conversion, Butler was a staunch Republican, with often racist opinions and a fervent belief in America's imperial mission. He enlisted in the marines before he turned seventeen, in 1898, just in time to join a seemingly righteous crusade "to end Spanish tyranny and imperialism in Cuba," a war that his own father voted against in Congress. In Cuba, the Marine Corps, including Butler, wrestled control of Guantánamo Bay from the Spanish—a local land grab with lasting consequences. In the short term, US occupiers made sure that Cuban "independence" did not interfere with J.P. Morgan and United Fruit Company gaining control of the nation's sugar, tobacco, railroads, mining, and utilities.

Shipped off to the Pacific next, First Lieutenant Butler battled Filipinos opposed to replacing Spanish colonial rule with US control of their country. His next stop was China, the target of a full-scale invasion launched by the McKinley administration without congressional approval. There, as part of an allied expeditionary force, Butler and his marine detachment helped suppress the Boxer Rebellion, a conflict that took the lives of one hundred thousand Chinese people but financially benefited all the foreign powers involved. Back in Central

America, Butler helped secure the US Canal Zone and the surrounding, newly created Republic of Panama after it was carved out of Colombia.

As a marine battalion commander in 1910–12, he then helped "pacify" Nicaragua, where he first began to see more clearly: "The whole game of these degenerate Americans down here is to force the United States to intervene and, by doing so, make their investments good." The year 1914 found Butler meddling in the Mexican Revolution on behalf of US-based oil companies. This time he won a Medal of Honor for his role in a seven-month military occupation of Veracruz, which resulted in thousands of civilian casualties. Soon thereafter, Butler was in Haiti crushing the armed resistance of the Cacos, rebels who opposed the system of forced labor imposed on the Haitian poor during the Wilson administration.

He also trained and led a repressive local constabulary force known as the Gendarmerie d'Haiti (a warm-up, of sorts, for his unhappy two-year stint as Philadelphia's director of public safety, during a leave of absence from the marines in the mid-1920s.) Before leaving the island of Hispaniola, Butler led a flying column of two hundred marines and Haitian gendarmes across the border into the Dominican Republic to help install a US-friendly government there. Butler's final overseas command, in 1927, landed him back in China two weeks before the Nationalist Chinese massacre of their Communist Party rivals in Shanghai. As Katz reports, "he ordered his men not to interfere," since their mission was to protect the city's foreign residents and their commercial property.

A Bonus March Awakening

Butler's retirement from the military in 1931 left him with time to reflect on his blood-stained career. "Like all members of the military profession, I never had an original thought until I left the service," he explained. "My mental faculties remained in suspended animation while I obeyed the orders of the higher-ups."

One post-retirement turning point was how "the higher-ups" in the Hoover administration responded to jobless World War I veterans, who were seeking promised bonus payments. In 1932, these poverty-stricken protesters created a huge encampment along the banks of the Anacostia River, not far from the US Capitol. This crowd of twenty thousand "bonus marchers" included women and children and was multiracial in an era when both the military and veterans' organizations were still segregated. Roy Wilkins, who covered the protest for an African American newspaper and later led the National Association for the Advancement of Colored People (NAACP), was so impressed that he "saw it as a model for integration in the United States."

President Herbert Hoover, a conservative Republican, refused to meet with Bonus March leaders, red-baited them in the press, and rejected their main demand. His position was backed by the Senate, which adjourned and left town without passing House-approved legislation authorizing immediate cash payments to veterans entitled to them. In late July 1932, Butler visited the veterans' encampment to rally the flagging spirits of the protesters in the face of an impending military assault. Eight days later, Hoover ordered active-duty troops—led by future World War II generals Douglas MacArthur, George Patton, and Dwight D. Eisenhower—to eradicate this threatening display of working-class veteran solidarity. Using cavalry, tanks, tear gas, and fixed bayonets, regular army troops drove the veterans out of Washington, killing two and wounding nearly one thousand.

Campaigning for the election of Franklin Roosevelt four months later, Butler told a crowd in Queens, New York, "When the war is over, the soldier comes back, is given a march up Fifth Avenue and, as soon as he is disbanded at the end of the march, the capitalists say, 'to hell with him.'" By 1936, Butler was even disillusioned with Roosevelt and voted for Socialist Party presidential candidate Norman Thomas instead. In the intervening years, as Katz reports, the retired marine blew the whistle on a shadowy cabal of right-wing industrialists who were plotting a coup against the Roosevelt administration and made the mistake of broaching the subject with Butler. This "Business Plot" involved key figures in the anti–New Deal Liberty League and became the subject of Butler's explosive testimony before the House Committee on Un-American Activities. There Butler warned Congress that wealthy American admirers of European fascist leaders were trying to mobilize disgruntled veterans, using the same Depression-era scapegoats (Bolsheviks and Jews).

Butler's patriotic efforts were not appreciated by the institution he had served so loyally for so long. According to documents cited by Katz, informants for the military closely tracked Butler's left turn. They filed regular reports on his public appearances, like a speech in Cleveland where "he shared the stage with radical journalists, an antifascist rabbi, official members of the Communist Party, and the poet Langston Hughes." The Marine Corps informant who attended that meeting heard Butler urge Americans to "lay aside all religious and racial feeling and stand together" against fascism and war. His confidential report concluded with the observation that "the General appeared to be either insane or an out-and-out traitor." As Katz also discovered, librarians at Marine Corps Base Quantico in Virginia are careful to keep Butler's antiwar tracts hidden away from other volumes, which provide laudatory accounts of his active-duty exploits as a Medal of Honor winner and former commandant of the base.

Even after he died, in a navy hospital in 1940, Butler could not escape controversy. He was buried without military honors after a private service, which included tributes by a speaker from his hometown Friends Meeting. As Katz notes, the congregation had defended him for years against complaints from other Quakers that "an admitted mass murderer was allowed to call himself a member in good standing." Butler's eulogist gave that personal contradiction the best possible spin: "Although General Butler was, for thirty years, in the military service of his country, he hated war. There can be no doubt that his preaching produced results and carried his peace message to places and peoples that would not have been reached and influenced otherwise."

7

Pathways to Dissent

One frequent casualty of war is the confident belief shared by many new soldiers that their cause is just and worthy of great personal sacrifice.[1] After Al-Qaeda downed four civilian airliners and caused nearly three thousand deaths on September 11, 2001, US military recruiters were flooded with eager volunteers. Patriotic fervor, coupled with an urge for revenge and a desire to make the world a safer place, motivated many young men and women to enlist.

As the reality of simultaneous interventions in Iraq and Afghanistan began to sink in, many participants—like Vietnam veterans before them—became angry, embittered, and disillusioned. Some of them have turned to memoir-writing that debunks the whole costly and disastrous $8 trillion project known as the "Global War on Terror." Three such book-length reflections on military training, socialization, and combat duty in the Middle East definitely won't end up on the reading lists of college-level or junior ROTC programs or even the US service academies (now being purged of dissenting voices by the second Trump administration). But many civilian readers will benefit from the policy critiques and personal insights found in Erik Edstrom's *Un-American: A Soldier's Reckoning of Our Longest War* (Bloomsbury, 2020), Lyle Jeremy Rubin's *Pain Is Weakness Leaving the Body: A Marine's Unbecoming* (Bold Type Books, 2022), and *Paths of Dissent: Soldiers Speak Out Against America's Misguided Wars* (Metropolitan Books, 2022), an edited collection compiled by Andrew Bacevich and Daniel A. Sjursen, both of whom became historians while serving as career army officers.

Like Bacevich and Sjursen, Edstrom attended West Point. Afterward, he served as an Army Ranger, an infantry platoon leader and Bronze Star winner in Afghanistan, and a member of Barack Obama's Presidential Escort Platoon. The grandson of a World War II veteran and product of a middle-class upbringing in a Boston suburb, he was part of the first post-9/11 crop of applicants to West Point, where one "couldn't help but get excited at the prospect of shooting, bombing, and invading." His second thoughts about soldiering started when his first-year class was immediately "isolated, separated from families and support networks" so that, during their "initial indoctrination," they would be "sheltered from anything that could temper or make [them] question military dogma."

Pray and Spray

As part of the process of getting "all-American swimmers, pious altar boys, cauliflower-eared wrestlers, nerdy class treasurers, and Eagle Scouts" ready for eventual deployments in Iraq and Afghanistan, West Point cadets were marched in cadence to this edifying chant: "Left, right, left, right, left, right KILL! ... I went to the mosque, where all the terrorists pray, I set up my claymore, AND BLEW 'EM ALL AWAY ... I went to the store where all the women shop, pulled out my machete, AND I BEGAN TO CHOP! ... I went to the playground where all the kiddies play, I pulled out my Uzi AND BEGAN TO SPRAY!"

At the academy, Edstrom reports, "I was taught to think about how to win my small part of the war, not whether we should be at war." Sent to Afghanistan, he soon discovered that "fighting terrorism" was a confounding task for soldiers up and down the chain of command. Many of his local foes turned out to be "teenagers or angry farmers with legitimate grievances ... people tired of our never-ending occupation of their land and contemptuous devaluation of Afghan lives. When I searched my own soul, I couldn't blame them for fighting back. Had I been in their shoes, I would have done the same."

Rubin took a more unusual route to becoming a junior officer disillusioned with his own "forever wars" involvement. As we learn in *Pain Is Weakness Leaving the Body*, Rubin was a fervent Zionist in high school and a "pro-war activist" while a Young Republican in college. Skipping service academy training and ROTC at Emory University in Atlanta, Rubin first experienced the Marine Corps as a failed Officer Candidate School contender who became a boot camp grunt. This gave him considerable insight into what he calls the "lance corporal underground" and "camaraderie of the enlisted ranks that adds up to a latent class solidarity."

As enlisted marines are fond of remarking, they represent the majority of the military that "works for a living." The USMC officer corps, on the other hand, is made up of "strivers, who've learned to compete at an early age and [end up] pitted against other in a cutthroat peer-review process and promotional system that follows." Rubin adds, "In contrast there was an earnestness to the enlisted existence, a conviction of collective duty and sacrifice, however barbaric its realizations, that was never allowed to congeal among the brass."

Rubin was eventually tapped to be a first lieutenant doing signals intelligence work in Afghanistan. This followed a two-month stint at the National Security Agency (NSA) headquarters in Fort Meade, Maryland, where he was briefed on a surveillance system "designed to make kill-or-capture missions as user-friendly as possible." As part of his training, Rubin learned about the NSA's "pattern-of-life analysis of random Afghans at a top-secret watch floor," where it was hard not to feel suffused with a "god-like omniscience."

Real-Time Targeting

As Rubin discovered later in the field, the US military's ability to "eradicate anyone holding an earmarked SIM card" did not prevent tech-savvy Taliban commanders from "switching out their cards as a regular security precaution." The same "real-time" targeting capability was used thousands of times during his deployment "to finish off alleged enemy combatants, many of whom investigative reports have now concluded were civilians." At the time, however, "battle damage assessments listed virtually all military-aged males as the enemy."

The disconnect between War on Terror propaganda and the reality of meddling in the affairs of a country long resistant to foreign occupation took a painful toll on Edstrom and Rubin. On his return to the United States as an army captain, Edstrom received "thudding back slaps and free beers from well-meaning civilians" for whom the war had become "elevator music." Meanwhile, he had to live with the memory of soldiers killed and maimed under his command and the knowledge that terrorism—in the form of "targeted assassinations, bombings, drone strikes, secret 'black site' prisons, torture, and wanton civilian murder"—was central to the "counterterrorism" mission. All Rubin wanted to do, after coming home, "was stop the war. And short of that, commiserate with those who, at the very least, could see it."

The fifteen contributors to *Paths of Dissent* shared that desire as well and often helped create organizational platforms for educating and agitating against US foreign and military policy. In his essay for the book, Jonathan Hutto describes his path from Howard University to the navy, where he became a key organizer of the "Appeal for Redress." This 2006 statement, backed by several thousand active-duty, reserve, and National Guard troops serving in ten countries around the world, called on Congress to end the occupations of Iraq and Afghanistan.

Following their military service abroad, both Joy Damiani and Vincent Emanuele found their way to Iraq Veterans Against the War and Veterans for Peace. With their guidance and encouragement, Damiani "learned more and more of the truth," whose surface she had "barely scratched as a miserable, demoralized soldier" assigned, as an army public affairs specialist, to "making PR look like news and an unwinnable war look like a victory." A marine who refused a third combat deployment to Iraq, Emanuele took his criticism of the war to Capitol Hill, where he testified in 2008 about mistreatment of prisoners and about rules of engagement that endangered noncombatants.

Truth, Lies, and Propaganda

Among the other notable voices in this outstanding collection is that of Matthew Hoh, a dissenter in the Pentagon and the State Department who resigned in protest in 2009, continued his antiwar activism, and even ran for US Senate as a Green Party candidate from North Carolina. In another chapter, "Truth, Lies, and Propaganda," former minor league baseball player Kevin Tillman recalls how he and his brother Pat, a National Football League star, became Army Rangers deployed to Iraq and Afghanistan. Pat Tillman's death during a 2004 firefight in Afghanistan was infamously covered up by the Pentagon. As his brother recalls, "the Bush administration didn't like the optics of a high-profile soldier like Pat being killed by friendly fire ... So, the government lied to us—his family—and to the American people with a manufactured story about dying by enemy fire and then used him to promote more war."

In addition to coediting *Paths of Dissent*, retired army colonel and former Boston University history professor Bacevich and retired army major Sjursen both helped launch new vehicles for influencing public opinion about military intervention abroad. Bacevich cofounded the Quincy Institute for Responsible Statecraft, a Washington, DC–based think tank critical of military intervention abroad and the political influence of major arms manufacturers.

Like Quincy, the nonprofit Eisenhower Media Network (EMN), started by Sjursen and funded by Ben & Jerry's cofounder Ben Cohen, is dedicated "to educating Americans about the social, political, and financial destructiveness of the military industrial complex." By making well-credentialed antiwar speakers available to podcasts, TV and radio shows, national magazines, and newspapers, the EMN is trying to reach "broad cross-partisan audiences," rather than already like-minded ones. Its roster of military vets who can offer media outlets an alternative perspective often missing from mainstream reporting and commentary on "defense issues" includes Erik Edstrom and his fellow *Paths of Dissent* contributors Hoh and Dan Berschinski.

Cohen's latest and overlapping initiative, launched in mid-2025 and called Up in Arms, is mapping out a planned four-year public education and advocacy campaign to expose the fact that "Congress has sold us out to weapons manufacturers, war profiteers, and endless wars," regardless of who is in the White House. Up in Arms has a distinguished roster of supporters, including retired colonels Ann Wright and Lawrence Wilkerson, the latter a professor at the College of William and Mary and fellow at the Quincy Institute. As Bacevich told us when the Quincy Institute was launched in 2019, "I'm optimistic that we're going to make a dent at least in the foreign policy consensus. That won't necessarily send the military-industrial complex fleeing or surrendering, but it will have some impact."

8

A Working-Class Veteran for Peace

Every four years, voters looking for substantive differences between Democratic and Republican presidential candidates on issues related to US foreign and military policy are invariably disappointed.[1]

In 2020, for example, Joe Biden pledged to ensure that "we have the strongest military in the world," promising to "make the investments necessary to equip our troops for the challenges of the next century, not the last one." During his unsuccessful reelection campaign, Donald Trump used some of the same anti-interventionist rhetoric that won him votes four years earlier against a seemingly more hawkish Hillary Clinton, who had backed open-ended warfare in Iraq and Afghanistan. In a May 2020 graduation address at West Point, Trump recycled applause lines from 2016 about "ending an era of endless wars" as well as America's role as "policeman of the world."

In reality, the first Trump administration made no significant reduction in the US military presence abroad. As Andrew Bacevich noted at the time: "Endless wars persist (and in some cases have even intensified); the nation's various alliances and its empire of overseas bases remain intact; U.S. troops are still present in something like 140 countries; Pentagon and national security state spending continues to increase astronomically."

When the National Defense Authorization Act for the next fiscal year came before Congress in 2020, Sen. Bernie Sanders proposed a modest 10 percent reduction in military spending so $70 billion could be redirected to domestic programs. Then Rep. Barbara Lee (D-CA) introduced a House resolution calling for $350 billion worth of DOD cuts. Neither proposal gained much support, even among President Trump's putative opponents on Capitol Hill during his first term. Instead, members of the Democrat-controlled House Armed

Services Committee voted fifty-six to zero to allocate $740.5 billion for the Pentagon for the following year, prefiguring the outcome of final votes on the matter by the full House and Senate.

By the time Trump got reelected four years later, US military spending had—on Joe Biden's watch—ballooned to nearly $1 trillion a year, despite US withdrawal from Afghanistan. In her failed bid for the presidency, Vice President Kamala Harris pledged that, as commander-in-chief, she would ensure that "America always has the strongest, most lethal fighting force in the world"—as if having a bigger national defense budget than the next nine-largest military spenders in the world hadn't already accomplished that goal.

Her opponent's presidential platform declared, in contrast, "The Biden administration's weak Foreign Policy has made us less safe and a laughingstock all over the World. The Republican Plan is to return Peace through Strength, rebuilding our Military and Alliances, countering China, defeating terrorism, building an Iron Dome Missile Defense Shield, promoting American Values, securing our Homeland and Borders, and reviving our Defense Industrial Base. We will build a Military bigger, better, and stronger than ever before.... Republicans will ensure our military is the most modern, lethal and powerful Force in the World."

By late 2025, under the new DOD secretary profiled in part 6 of this book, the second Trump administration was well on its way to spending even more on military operations, at home and abroad, including Israel's genocidal assault on Palestinians in Gaza (which the Biden administration funded as well).

In the Zinn Tradition

Clearly, the valiant efforts of the US peace movement and allied initiatives like the Quincy Institute and Up in Arms need more ground troops to overcome the bipartisan consensus in favor of militarism and war. Pentagon critics with military credentials bring much-needed credibility and moral authority to this uphill fight. Daniel Sjursen, a forty-two-year-old veteran of combat in Iraq and Afghanistan, has been one such valued campaigner.

Inspired in part by the much-published Bacevich, Sjursen's latest book is called *Patriotic Dissent: America in the Age of Endless War* (Heyday Books). It's a short volume, just 141 pages, but it packs the same kind of punch as Howard Zinn's classic 1967 polemic *Vietnam: The Logic of Withdrawal*. Like Zinn, who eventually became a popular historian after serving as a World War II bombardier, Sjursen skillfully debunks the conventional wisdom of the foreign policy establishment and the military's current generation of "yes men for another war power hungry president." His powerful voice, political insights, and painful personal reflections offer a timely reminder of how costly, wasteful, and disastrous our post-9/11 wars have been.

Sjursen's appeal to the conscience of fellow soldiers, veterans, and civilians is rooted in the unusual arc of his own eighteen-year military career. He graduated from and later taught at West Point, an institution that produces few political dissenters. He grew up in a firefighter family on working-class Staten Island. Even before enrolling at the US Military Academy at age seventeen, he was no stranger to what he calls "deep-seated toxically masculine patriotism." As a newly commissioned officer in 2005, he was still a "burgeoning neoconservative and George W. Bush admirer" and definitely not, he reports, any kind of "defeatist liberal, pacifist, or dissenter."

Sjursen's initial experience in combat—vividly described in his first book, *Ghost Riders of Baghdad: Soldiers, Civilians, and the Myth of the Surge* (University Press of New England)—"occurred at the statistical height of sectarian strife" in Iraq. "The horror, the futility, the farce of that war was the turning point in my life," Sjursen writes in *Patriotic Dissent*. When he returned, at age twenty-four, from his "brutal, ghastly deployment" as a platoon leader, he "knew that the war was built on lies, ill-advised, illegal, and immoral." This "unexpected, undesired realization generated profound doubts about the course and nature of the entire American enterprise in the Greater Middle East—what was then unapologetically labeled the Global War on Terrorism (GWOT)."

A Professional Soldier

By the time Sjursen landed in Kandahar Province, Afghanistan, in early 2011, he had been promoted to captain but "no longer believed in anything we were doing." He was, he confesses, "simply a professional soldier—a mercenary, really—on a mandatory mission I couldn't avoid. Three more of my soldiers died, thirty-plus were wounded, including a triple amputee, and another overdosed on pain meds after our return."

Despite his disillusionment, Sjursen had long dreamed of returning to West Point to teach history. He applied for and won that highly competitive assignment, which meant the army had to send him to grad school first. He ended up getting credentialed, while living out of uniform, in the "People's Republic of Lawrence, Kansas, a progressive oasis in an intolerant, militarist sea of Republican red." During his studies at the state university, Sjursen found an intellectual framework for his "own doubts about and opposition to U.S. foreign policy," and he completed his first book, *Ghost Riders*, which combines personal memoir with counterinsurgency critique. Amazingly enough, it was published while he was still on active duty in 2015, with "almost no blowback" from superior officers.

Before retiring as a major four years later, Sjursen pushed the envelope further by writing more than one hundred critical articles for TomDispatch and other civilian publications. He was no longer at West Point, and that body of work triggered "a grueling, stressful, and scary four-month investigation" by the brass at Fort Leavenworth, during which the author was subjected to "a non-publication order." At risk were his career, military pension, and benefits. He ended up receiving only a verbal admonishment for violating a Pentagon rule against publishing words "contemptuous of the President of the United States." His "PTSD and co-occurring diagnoses" eventually made him eligible for a medical retirement.

Sjursen then gave up his identity as a soldier, which he said was the only identity he had known in his adult life, trading it "for that of an antiwar, anti-imperialist, social justice crusader," albeit one who did not attend his first protest rally until he was thirty-two years old. With several left-leaning comrades, he started *Fortress on a Hill*, a lively and informative podcast about military affairs and veterans' issues. He became a frequent, funny, and always well-informed guest on progressive radio and cable-TV shows, as well as a contributing editor at Antiwar.com. and a contributor to a host of mainstream liberal publications.

In *Patriotic Dissent*, Sjursen not only recounts his own personal trajectory from military service to peace activism. He also shows how that intellectual journey has been informed by reading and thinking about US history, the relationship between civil society and military culture, the meaning of patriotism, and the price of dissent.

Reframing Dissent

Sjursen contrasts Marine general Smedley Butler's anti-interventionist whistleblowing in the 1930s with the silence of high-ranking twenty-first-century veterans after nearly two decades "of ill-advised, remarkably unsuccessful American wars." Among friends and former West Point classmates, he knows many still serving who "obediently resign themselves to continued combat deployments" because they long ago "stopped asking questions about their own role in perpetuating and enabling a counter-productive, inertia-driven warfare state."

Sjursen looks instead to groups like Veterans for Peace and About Face (formerly Iraq Veterans Against the War) and Bring Our Troops Home, the latter a network of veterans influenced by the libertarian right. Each in its own way seeks to "reframe dissent, against empire and endless war, as the truest form of patriotism." But, the author believes, taming the military-industrial complex will require "big-tent, intersectional action from civilian and soldier alike" on a much larger scale. One obstacle to that is the societal divide between the "vast majority of citizens who have chosen not to serve" in the military and the "1 percent of their fellow citizens on active duty," who then become part of "an increasingly insular, disconnected, and sometimes sententious post 9/11 veteran community."

Not many on the left favor a return to conscription. But Sjursen makes it clear there's been a downside to the United States replacing "citizen soldiering" with "a tiny professional warrior caste," created in response to draft-driven dissent against the Vietnam War, inside and outside the military. As he observes: "Nothing so motivates a young adult to follow foreign policy, to weigh the advisability or morality of an ongoing war as the possibility of having to put 'skin in the game.' Without at least the potential requirement to serve in the military and in one of America's now countless wars, an entire generation—or really two, since President Nixon ended the draft in 1973—has had the luxury of ignoring the ills of U.S. foreign policy, to distance themselves from its reality."

At a time when the US "desperately needs a massive, public, empowered antiwar and anti-imperial wave" sweeping over the country, we have instead a "civil military" gap that Sjursen believes has "stifled antiwar and anti-imperial dissent and seemingly will continue to do so." That's why his own mission is to find more "socially conscious veterans of these endless, fruitless wars" who are willing to "step up and form a vanguard of sorts for revitalized patriotic dissent."

Readers of Sjursen's book—either new recruits to that "vanguard" or longtime peace activists—will find *Patriotic Dissent* to be an invaluable educational tool. It should be required reading in progressive study groups, high school and college history classes, and book clubs across the country. Let's hope that the author's willingness to take personal risks, rethink his view of the world, and then work to change things for the better will inspire many others, in uniform and out.

9

Leaving the Soldier Box

Military service in the United States and the UK promised more than it ever delivered for many post-9/11 volunteers.[1] As sociologist and Vietnam vet Jerry Lembcke observes, "This generation of veterans went off to Iraq and Afghanistan with more hoopla than any generation since World War II. But a lot of them, particularly the men, came back deflated and disappointed with the experience they had. It did not live up to the mythology of what war is supposed to be, because there is no glory in these ... wars."

Adding insult to moral injury, hundreds of thousands of today's veterans developed long-term medical or mental health conditions that were service related. If these afflictions affected their job performance while still on active duty, the Department of Defense thanked many of them for their service by drumming them out in punitive fashion. Depending on their discharge status, many became ineligible for free healthcare provided by the Department of Veterans Affairs or access to free higher education via GI Bill benefits. Under the rules of most old guard veterans' organizations, they were not even welcome at their local post of the American Legion or Veterans of Foreign Wars.

Close readers of Joe Glenton's *Veteranhood: Hope and Rage in British Ex-Military Life* (Repeater Books, 2021) will be surprised to learn that any Brit who served for even a single day is considered a veteran. Medical care is, of course, less of a concern to former military personnel in a nation where a VA-style National Health Service covers everyone, plus higher education remains far more affordable than in the United States. And even someone like Glenton—who went AWOL to avoid a second tour of duty in Afghanistan and then was court-martialed for it—later received a package in the mail which welcomed him to the brotherhood and sisterhood of former squaddies. It included, he reports, "one of the small enamel veterans' badges widely worn among the ex-forces community and a bundle of brochures about getting on in post-military life."

This UK peculiarity aside, Glenton's account of how post-9/11 veterans in his country are "getting on" in civilian life reveals many striking parallels with the readjustment problems of their counterparts in the United States. Now a freelance military affairs correspondent for the *Guardian*, the *Independent*, and other papers, Glenton first wrote about his experience in uniform and afterward in *Soldier Box: Why I Won't Return to the War on Terror* (Verso, 2013). In the book, he confesses that his own enlistment decision was made by "a chump ready made for the army, indifferent, apolitical, and working class." In rural Yorkshire, he says, "life was hard, we were poor, and this took its toll." Teenage drinking, drug use, housing insecurity, and minimum-wage work were widespread.

After Al Qaeda recruits toppled the twin towers in Manhattan, Tony Blair's Labour government rallied to the side of the Bush administration. For Glenton and many other working-class lads on both sides of the Atlantic, this terrorist attack was "the call to arms of the age; of my age." As his recruiting station officer promised, "[I] would be paid and there would be 'three meals a day and a roof over [my] head' and girls would queue to swoon over me and my soldier friends." There would be other opportunities as well, including one stressed on a "leaving card" from his coworkers on his last day in a restaurant job: "Make sure you kill some ragheads!"

Invaders, Not Guests

During Glenton's subsequent year-long deployment in Afghanistan, he never got a chance to kill anyone, confined as he was to a "logistics park" at Kandahar Airport. As an ammunition store man in the Royal Logistics Corps, he doled out Hellfire missiles and other high explosives "at an astonishing rate" to fellow soldiers who were not being welcomed as "peacekeepers." Even through Glenton had limited contact with Afghan nationals, the nature of the war began to sink in. "We were not guests, but invaders. We were not friends of the Afghan people, we were occupiers... Insurgencies of the scale we were seeing cannot happen without popular support. I did not have to be a general to recognize this."

Three years into his military career and recently promoted to lance corporal, Glenton found himself back in England but resolutely opposed to doing another tour in Afghanistan. "I had joined the army half meaning to help people, to do something to improve the conditions of other people's lives, not to occupy other people's countries under the pretext of securing my own." To avoid another combat deployment, he went into exile in Australia. Returning home after two years away, he faced charges of desertion, which carried a prison sentence of ten years or more.

The rest of Glenton's first book tells the story of how his court-martial backfired on the Ministry of Defense. While awaiting trial but initially not confined to the brig, he became a high-profile peace campaigner. He spoke at Stop the War Coalition meetings, did TV, radio, and newspaper interviews, and personally delivered a letter to then–prime minister Gordon Brown, at 10 Downing Street, which called for the withdrawal of all British troops from Afghanistan. As part of a deal with the prosecution, Glenton eventually pleaded guilty—to the lesser charge of going AWOL—and served four months of a nine-month sentence in a military prison.

On his first night there, "alone and locked in a single cell," he nevertheless felt liberated. He had found his calling as "an anti-imperialist activist," and after his release he completed university studies that helped him become a journalist, filmmaker, and award-winning author. In *Veteranhood*, Glenton returns to the subject of how ending up in the "soldier box," as he calls it, can have a lasting personal and political impact. In the UK, as in the United States, military training "discourages critical thought" and "promotes antagonism" between those who serve and the vast majority of civilians who don't. Even the author finds himself straddling the resulting "civilian-soldier" divide. After a decade of involvement in left-wing politics, including general election campaigning for Jeremy Corbyn, Glenton still finds "dealing with civvies" a trial, he says. "In moments of regression, they appear to me as ponderously slow, indecisive, dithering, governed by unmanly levels of self-doubt."

Such estrangement didn't exist to the same degree during the heyday of mid-twentieth-century "citizen armies," which included many volunteers and draftees with higher levels of class consciousness. Glenton notes, "The modern British military has little in common with the military of WWII. Structurally, technologically, ideologically, and morally, these are two different organizations. One was a vast conscript army built … to fight fascism. The other is a small, rather backwards, and culturally separatist professional force." Veterans of World War II "were far more likely to come from communities with a powerful sense of their role in the economy, with traditions and experiences of class solidarity and trade unionism."

Some even participated in the so-called "Cairo Parliaments," organized by active-duty British troops stationed in Egypt. Before being shut down by the brass, these left-influenced meetings debated and voted on proposals for postwar reforms like nationalizing banks and mines, increasing pensions and access to higher education, and building four million affordable homes. In contrast, modern-day British vets exist in a world shaped by Thatcherism and individualism, "in which traditional working-class organizations and communities have been diminished and replaced with a kind of warrior-ideal-meets-neoliberalism." As a result, too many ex-soldiers "cling to the only strong identity they have—that of the veteran." And, as Glenton documents, that's "an identity concocted by the very institutions that have wronged them."

Blazers or Something Better?

The resulting form of "identity politics" manifests itself in often negative but also some positive ways across the spectrum. In his own book-writing quest to find "a better way of being a veteran," Glenton bridles at the facile assumption that his former comrades constitute a solid "right-wing bloc whose politics do not extend much beyond braying racism and lagged-up squadrismo." Instead, his journalistic portrait of the more than two million UK citizens who served in the military reveals them to be "a divided, fractious, and politically divergent group."

The author does acknowledge that "far right gatherings always seem to include military veterans—bitter men, wraiths in berets," like those who joined the militant defense of Whitehall statuary about to be targeted by Black Lives Matter protesters. Seven months later, ex-military personnel were disproportionately involved in storming the US Capitol to prevent Donald Trump from being toppled. As Glenton observes, that event—which featured former soldiers stacking up in tight formation to breach the building—became "an upscaled and vastly more lethal American version of our July 2020 anti-BLM riot."

Glenton devotes a whole chapter to critiquing what he calls "Blazerism"—mainstream vet culture, with its hosts of "sartorial signifiers—berets, medals, regimental ties, and blazers." While Blazers may be vocally antisocialist and antiliberal in their social media barrages and voting patterns, they are, as Glenton reveals, quite collectivist within their own "ex-forces community." For example, many are devoted to British Legion–backed charitable work, while always ready "to play homeless ex-serviceman off against migrants and civilian rough sleepers," who are not among the deserving poor. The century-old Legion soldiers on "as a monolithic, highly political corporate charity and ultimate custodian of Remembrance." At the other end of the spectrum, Glenton lauds the public education and organizing activity of Veterans for Peace UK. With far fewer foot soldiers, VFP-UK tries to counter "the revanchist nostalgia of Blazerism" by fostering a veteran identity based on broad leftist values. According to the author, members of the group also tap into what one ex-military nurse calls the "positive experience of their service—the camaraderie, being part of team, and having a sense of purpose."

Playing the Veteran Card

Glenton is a fierce and hilarious critic of special operators who have turned themselves into celebrity vets. Special Forces veteran Ant Middleton is among those, on both sides of the Atlantic, who have "monetized" their military service by peddling books, apparel, or other products under a newly acquired personal brand. Thanks to his second career as a television personality, best-selling author, and "positivity guru," Middleton raked in four million British pounds in 2021 alone, according to the *Sun* (which employed him as its "Ask Ant" columnist). As Glenton asks: "Are the people who lost the wars in Iraq and Afghanistan really the people to dish out life advice? Can they supercharge your Bitcoin scam? Can former Navy SEAL Hank McMassive's ten-point warrior code get you through a long shift at a Nottingham call center? Should you buy their new brand of Predator Drone Coffee?"

The author's answer is a resounding No! But that hasn't stopped major parties in Britain and the United States from marketing more veterans themselves as a new breed of politician, somehow better than the rest. The distinct brand of these "service candidates" is their unassailable patriotism and demonstrated past devotion to a cause greater than themselves. Nevertheless, as Glenton reports, "the ex-military people who have found their way into Parliament are mostly conservative former officers." Among them, until his reelection defeat in 2024, was Captain Johnny Mercer, a banker's son and Sandhurst graduate. This Afghan war vet was "the sullen personification of a failed officer corps" who served as Tory minister for veterans affairs but then parted ways with Prime Minister Boris Johnson over the latter's failure to provide sufficient legal protection for ex-soldiers facing prosecution for killing civilians in Northern Ireland in the 1970s.

Mercer's now governing party counterparts can be found in "Labour Friends of the Forces." Resurrected in 2020 by Keir Starmer, before he became prime minister, this group, according to Glenton, provides little counterweight to "reactionary ex-servicemen's dominance in public life" because it is essentially "a stage prop for the Labour Right."

Glenton faults New Labour for initially importing the "American model of soldier-worship." When Glenton joined the army in 2004, "soldiers were not popular and veterans were barely mentioned in the press." In the period since then, the British state, its generals, MPs, the media, and military charities have engaged in what Glenton calls "a conscious campaign to repopularize the military." This "militarization offensive" was necessary because millions of UK citizens were not big fans of the disastrous foreign interventions backed by Tony Blair, prime minister from 1997 to 2007. Labour's response to that domestic opinion problem was outlined in a 2018 paper, "Report of Inquiry into National Recognition of Our Armed Forces," which included a foreword by then–prime minister Gordon Brown. According to Glenton, the report became "an instruction manual for militarists looking to secure public support for war or reduce, to a tolerable level, active public opposition to military occupations" of Iraq and Afghanistan.

The fruits of this long-term project—embraced even more wholeheartedly by the Tories—are often on display. They included mandatory professions of support for the troops by "any parliamentarian broaching a defense topic; the *Sun*'s cretinous annual military awards and Turbo-Remembrancing; the careful positioning of uniformed service personnel at sports matches; and ardent poppy nationalism."

Arrayed against this mainstream celebration of "veteranhood" is the small cohort of "critical veterans" championed by the author. Those interviewed by Glenton and profiled in his book remain engaged in various forms of leftist activism—BLM, the climate movement, tenants' unions and trade unions, the Northern Independence Party, Irish and antimonarchical Republicanism, antifascism, and advocacy for Scottish independence. If nothing else, he concludes, they are helping to inform the left's own "outsider perspectives on war, the military, and veterans" by dispelling harmful but popular myths about all three.

PART III

WOUNDS OF WAR

Our friend Rick Weidman, a longtime political director for Vietnam Veterans of America, spent much of his lobbying career in Washington explaining to legislators that "the military is a collection of very dangerous occupations even for those serving in non-combat roles and far from any battlefield."

Consider, for example, the post-9/11 expansion of drone warfare as a military specialty. In his book *Dirty Work*, journalist Eyal Press interviewed "joystick warriors," operating from bases in the United States, who carried out targeted assassinations via Hellfire missile strikes in Iraq and Afghanistan, on the other side of the world.[1]

Some discovered that remote killing, no less than direct combat, can be a later source of stigma, shame, PTSD, and moral injury. Heather Linebaugh, a US Air Force veteran involved in drone operations for three years, took to the pages of the *Guardian* to describe the "depression, sleep disorders, and anxiety" that she and other drone surveillance analysts experienced.[2] Two of her former colleagues committed suicide, but others were able to get mental health treatment, like the soldiers profiled in chapter 2 of this section.

As for troops on the ground, the Department of Defense has often failed to protect them in very basic ways. In the earliest stages of the US occupation of Iraq, many soldiers died or suffered brain damage unnecessarily because existing armored vehicles offered insufficient protection against improvised explosive devices.

Others experienced head injuries and long-term hearing loss because the helmets they were issued did not fit properly, and a product manufactured by 3M, the Minnesota-based Fortune 500 company—Combat Arms Earplugs Version 2 (CAEv2)—proved to be defective.

(For more on that costly example of contractor fraud and resulting class action litigation, see our previous book, *Our Veterans*.)

When hundreds of thousands of troops were shipped off to newly built bases in the Middle East (or former Soviet ones in Afghanistan or Uzbekistan), the soil and air itself became a daily hazard.[3] A well-connected Pentagon contractor called KBR (formerly Kellogg, Brown & Root) was paid billions of dollars to handle combat zone waste disposal. On several hundred bases in the Middle East, the company known during the Vietnam War as "Burn & Loot" used open-air burn pits to dispose of hundreds of thousands of tons of toxic materials.

As ex-marine and Gulf War veteran Joseph Hickman documents in *The Burn Pits: The Poisoning of America's Soldiers*, these bonfires violated not only Environmental Protection Agency (EPA) air quality standards but the Pentagon's own regulations as well. They "were supposed to be used only as a temporary measure, until trash incinerators would be put in place," but "the Pentagon quickly approved their use ... for the entire course of the wars." Soldiers regularly exposed to this never-ending "siege of smoke and ash" found that their only periods of respite occurred "when high-ranking generals or politicians came to visit their bases" and base commanders would put a temporary stop to the burning.[4]

And now, as described in the next chapter, the major commitment made by Congress in 2022 to address the long-term impact of such toxic exposure may become just another broken promise to veterans if the Trump-Vance administration has its way with the VA.

10

The PACT Act and Its Problems

When Joe Biden endured Republican jeers and boos during his third State of the Union address, one of the few lines that received bipartisan applause referenced congressional action in 2022 on what Biden called the "most significant law our nation ever passed to help millions of veterans."[1]

That legislation—called the Honoring Our Promise to Address Comprehensive Toxics (PACT) Act—committed the federal government to spend $280 billion, over ten years, on expanded healthcare and disability benefit coverage for former service members harmed by toxic substances. An estimated 3.5 million service members had been exposed to noxious fumes from open burn pits and other chemical hazards during three Middle Eastern wars since 1991.

Many PACT Act beneficiaries developed long-term health problems during the Vietnam War, Cold War weapons testing in the Pacific, or just training to become soldiers on bases at home. The DOD now acknowledges that the groundwater at 126 US military installations, active or closed, "contains potentially harmful levels of perfluorinated compounds, which have been linked to cancers and developmental delays for fetuses and infants."[2]

Fort McClellan, a major army training site for eighty years, has been called "the most contaminated place in the United States."[3] Among other confirmed sources of contaminated drinking water are Marine Corps bases in North Carolina, including Camp Lejeune, a major source of post–PACT Act disability claims.

Veterans' organizations fought long and hard for federal recognition of a devastating array of service-related ailments now better covered by the PACT Act. And, in the home stretch of their membership mobilization and lobbying campaign in 2022, disabled vets got much help from Jon Stewart, a high-profile Hollywood booster of their cause.

The filmmaker and *Daily Show* host was particularly effective in his public shaming of Senate Republicans like Patrick J. Toomey (R-PA). A former Wall Street banker who never served in the military, Toomey was not alone in initially voting against the PACT Act because, he claimed, it contained a "budget gimmick" that would trigger $400 billion in future spending "unrelated to veterans care."[4]

Toomey did not run for reelection, but most of the forty other Republicans who voted the same way are still senators today. As noted below, they—along with the Trump-Vance administration—are resorting to budgetary tricks of their own to curb PACT Act–related expenditures as stealthily as possible.

VBA Claims Processing

The PACT Act directed the VA to consider twenty-three conditions ranging from bronchial asthma to a series of rare cancers as presumptively related to burn pit exposure and other environmental hazards. By January 2023—less than six months after the act's passage—the VA-run Veterans Benefits Administration (VBA) had received about 278,000 PACT Act claims, processing nearly 40,000 of them with an 85 percent approval rate.

With a workforce of more than thirty thousand, the VBA processes claims for healthcare coverage and disability benefits for service-related conditions. One immediate, Biden-era obstacle to the fastest possible implementation of the PACT Act was the fact that overall VA functioning during the previous eight years had been increasingly impaired by understaffing, costly and wasteful outsourcing, and other organizational problems inherited from the first Trump administration and Barack Obama's second term as president.

As a result, too many disabled vets continued to experience what Paul Sullivan, a Gulf War veteran and expert on the VBA, called "an adversarial, complex, and burdensome claims nightmare." This bred anger and frustration over delayed disability payments and healthcare access. When Denis McDonough became Joe Biden's VA secretary in February 2021, he inherited a huge backlog of unresolved claims, including those filed by burn pit victims whose denial rate, before the PACT Act, was 78 percent. Military.com reported in January 2023, "The

[VBA's disability] claims backlog, defined as claims older than 125 days, has grown by roughly fifty thousand since September to 200,140."[5]

To reduce that caseload, the PACT Act authorized the Biden administration to hire and train nineteen hundred new VBA employees to help veterans navigate the byzantine and time-consuming process of getting a "disability rating." These ratings are necessary to qualify for financial compensation for service-related conditions and for healthcare coverage, which some veterans receive based solely on their low income or recent active duty in a combat zone.

AFGE Survey Results

According to a 2023 survey of more than one thousand VBA and VHA staff represented by the American Federation of Government Employees (AFGE), short staffing, inadequate training, bad management, and unnecessary outsourcing continued to plague their agency—halfway through Biden's presidency.[6]

It took the White House two years to nominate a permanent VA undersecretary for benefits, the appointee in charge of the VBA. Nearly 80 percent of VBA staffers reported caseload quotas that limited their ability to help individual veterans with confusing paperwork or complicated claims. One of their biggest concerns was the Biden administration's continued use of private contractors to evaluate veteran healthcare conditions. Most compensation and pension exams, as they are called, were once handled by VHA clinicians with specialized knowledge of military culture and the signature wounds of particular wars.

During the first Trump administration, thousands of VHA positions were left unfilled, so these medical examinations were outsourced on a larger scale than ever before. Private sector doctors working for the VBA were even permitted to assess complex conditions like military sexual trauma, traumatic brain injury, and Gulf War Illness.

According to a 2021 Government Accountability Office (GAO) report, about 1.1 million of the 1.4 million exams completed in fiscal year 2020 were handled by outside physicians, who were projected to receive more than $6.8 billion for this work over a ten-year period. Unfortunately for veterans, the GAO found that "exam reports for selected complex claims were returned to [outside] examiners for correction or clarification at about twice the rate that exam reports were returned overall."[7]

This faulty work results in additional claims processing delays and makes it even harder for overburdened VBA staff to assign fair and accurate disability ratings, which are themselves subject to further administrative and legal appeals, often dragging on for years.

Healthcare Capacity?

On the healthcare side of the agency, 95 percent of the AFGE members who responded to the survey conducted by the Veterans Healthcare Policy Institute (VHPI) reported shortages of frontline clinical staff. Nearly 60 percent of all VHA respondents complained that management was not recruiting to fill vacant positions at their hospitals or clinics.

In southern West Virginia, AFGE Local 2198 president Melissa Miklos warned that her medical center had become seriously understaffed. And it was slated to lose funding for already approved and scheduled construction projects because 65 percent of its patients were now getting outside appointments, whether they wanted them or not. So regional managers told Miklos there was no way they could now justify adding "another square foot to the Beckley VA."

Because of this, Miklos worried that patients with respiratory problems—newly enrolled in the VA thanks to the PACT Act—would have trouble accessing needed care inside or outside her facility. The Beckley VA Medical Center has only one pulmonologist, and he would be "unable to handle the new patient load." In the "medical desert" of southern West Virginia, with its long wait times for any kind of care, getting an appointment with a specialist like a pulmonologist takes six to eight months.

Members of National Nurses United (NNU), which represents about sixteen thousand RNs at the VHA, were not included in VHPI's 2023 survey. But Irma Westmoreland, a nurse at the VA medical center in Augusta, Georgia, who serves as a national vice president of NNU, agreed that her employer needed to hire more staff to cope with an influx of new PACT Act patients.

One obstacle to doing that was Secretary McDonough's botched overhaul of the agency's human resources department. "You can't get in touch with an HR person in a local facility," Westmoreland told us. "You call, and no one returns your calls. It's taking months to hire a doctor or nurse. Nurses aren't going to wait for months for a VA job when they can get one at a private-sector hospital or sign up with a temp agency and earn thousands and thousands more than at the VA. We want these patients, but there are not enough people to take care of them."

Here again, the Biden administration inherited an HR "modernization" initiative from the first Trump administration that made the VA's notoriously cumbersome hiring process worse, not better. That failed experiment centralized control over new hiring, reduced the role of local HR staff, and replaced person-to-person contact with an online system that McDonough continued to employ after he took over the agency.[8]

Biden's VA secretary was, of course, far more labor-friendly than his Trump-appointed predecessor and even more antiunion Republican successor (profiled in part 6). Yet McDonough's inaction on this and other critical fronts was a source of much frustration among frontline caregivers throughout his four years as their boss at VA headquarters. "We know that the VA delivers care that is far superior to the private sector, particularly when it comes to emergency care. So why," asked Jim Martin, an ER doctor and AFGE activist in Chicago, "are we sending so many patients out to the private sector? Why is my job caring for them becoming harder?"

Ultimately, the Biden administration did succeed in helping five hundred thousand veterans gain medical coverage for the first time; about a million vets are now in a "priority group" that gives them quicker access to care. The VA conducted 6.3 million toxic exposure screenings, 2.5 million veterans filed a disability claim under the PACT Act, and more than 1.9 million claims (or about 74 percent) were approved.[9]

The Return of Trump

Shortly after Joe Biden left office, the "Trump administration hit the brakes" on PACT Act implementation, as one observer put it. "Many of the features of the PACT Act required specialized services provided under contract with private-sector suppliers." But, in early 2025, new VA secretary Doug Collins tried to be a good soldier for Elon Musk's Department of Government Efficiency.

With little scrutiny of their actual worth or purpose, Collins canceled nearly six hundred federal contracts, including those which "provided the necessary personnel and resources to conduct outreach to eligible veterans, screen applicants, and process claims—cutting the heart out of the PACT Act."[10]

Critics of Collins, like Sen. Mazie Hirono (D-HA), who opposed his confirmation as VA secretary, accused the White House of "hiding the truth from Congress" about staff cuts and contract cancellations that would adversely affect benefit claimants under the PACT Act.[11] By then, the Republican House majority had already tipped its hand about further implementation of a Biden administration legislative accomplishment. By a party-line vote in March 2025, the House authorized a $22.8 billion reduction in funding allocated just three years before to care for more burn pit victims. With the 2026 midterm elections in mind, the Republican-controlled Senate was less eager to follow suit.[12]

Another "big tell" was Secretary Collins's VA funding request for the 2026 fiscal year. He sought congressional approval for shifting more than $11 billion in VA discretionary spending from direct care to reimbursement of private doctors who don't know the difference between a burn pit and a barbecue pit. Meanwhile, Collins proposed a $12 billion (or 17 percent) reduction in funding for VA caregivers like Melissa Miklos, Irma Westmoreland, and Jim Martin, who know that they are doing and have been doing it for years.

Paul Sullivan, the Gulf War veteran who helped thousands of other vets qualify for VA benefits before and after the PACT Act, watched such developments from his retirement refuge in rural Virginia with growing horror. "These political signals are extraordinarily ominous for veterans who depend on the VA for care and benefits," Sullivan says. "Literally, Trump is betraying us and pulling the rug out from under our feet."

11

Invisible Storm

Post-traumatic stress disorder (PTSD) is an often-hidden wound of war, but it can be no less debilitating than service-related conditions resulting from toxic exposures. About 18 percent of returning Afghanistan and Iraq vets have been diagnosed with PTSD. Their struggle to deal with it is well described in *Invisible Storm: A Soldier's Memoir of Politics and PTSD*, a book by army veteran Jason Kander, and a related documentary called *HERE. IS. BETTER.*, directed by Emmy Award winner Jack Youngelson. The film follows Kander and three fellow patients getting VA treatment for anger and depression, substance abuse, suicidal ideation, or past military sexual trauma.

Kander's title is his way of describing what makes holding a job, getting an education, finding a place to live, and maintaining personal relationships very difficult for some veterans, even years after leaving the military. Youngelson and his film crew followed all four PTSD sufferers during their interaction with family members, other participants in group therapy or peer counseling sessions, and their work with staffers of a VA-run residential treatment center in Cincinnati and the Veterans Community Project in Kansas City, which provides transitional housing and support services for homeless vets.

Not Feeling Disabled

While varying in age, gender, and ethnicity, all the vets in the film were reluctant to seek professional help. In Kander's case, he felt that his brief tour of duty in Afghanistan as an army intelligence officer hardly qualified him to be a disabled veteran. "I didn't feel like I did enough to earn it," he explains. "I was just some jerk who went to meetings. To even consider I had PTSD felt like 'stolen valor' [the phenomenon of veterans or nonveterans claiming military laurels they were not awarded]."

After all, some soldiers who served in the same combat zone came back with traumatic brain injuries, amputated limbs, or spinal cord injuries that left them paralyzed for life. After he was discharged, Kander's only problem was "bad dreams," not even troubling enough to keep him from reading books or watching movies about war.

The other veterans who tell their stories in HERE. IS. BETTER.—on a first-name basis only—similarly ignored or minimized their symptoms while experiencing, like Kander, a considerable amount of survivor's guilt. We meet Teresa and Tabitha, both post-9/11 war veterans, and John, a draftee in 1968 who won a Silver Star for his role in a firefight that killed 170 North Vietnamese and Americans. A helicopter door gunner in Vietnam, John returned home with traumatic memories of jungle warfare that he managed to suppress for fifty years until he couldn't find a way "to move beyond them."

Teresa was an army heavy equipment operator who never recovered from the impact of an improvised explosive device that rocked her convoy in Iraq. Recruited at age eighteen, Tabitha was sexually assaulted during her Marine Corps training, like many other women in the military. She managed to complete tours of duty in Iraq and Afghanistan, but the scars of military sexual trauma troubled her later civilian life as a single mother of two young children.

A High-Profile Crash

Kander's own mental health crisis is recalled movingly in both the film and *Invisible Storm* but with more humor in the latter. When he entered the Kansas City VA Medical Center as a walk-in patient, the Georgetown Law School graduate and former army captain was still a rising star in regional and national politics. He had been a state legislator, served as Missouri's secretary of state, and in 2016 ran a highly competitive campaign for the US Senate against a Republican incumbent.

After that narrow defeat, he formed a voting rights group called Let America Vote and went on a speaking tour that took him to forty-six states in a single year, including appearances in Iowa and New Hampshire. The grueling schedule—plus Barack Obama hailing him as the future of the Democratic Party—fueled speculation about an eventual presidential campaign. Kander's next stepping-stone in that direction was supposed to be the city hall in Kansas City. By late 2018, based on polling and fundraising, he was far ahead in the mayoral race.

Then he suddenly dropped out. He informed supporters and the media that he had called a VA hotline, tearfully confessed to having "suicidal thoughts," and checked himself into a VA hospital. As a new patient, Kander pulled a baseball cap down to hide his face because "the one place where you don't want to be famous is in a psych ward." Dressed in hospital scrubs, sitting in a bare room with the psychiatric resident assigned to take his medical history, Kander confessed everything he'd spent years hiding from the world: "My night terrors, my consuming fear of someone hurting me or my family, my ever-present anger, my unrelenting guilt and punishing shame, my inability to feel joy, and my increasing dislike of myself."

Not recognizing his patient or knowing anything about him, Kander's doctor asked him if his post-military career was particularly stressful. "I'm in politics," Kander explained, referencing both his Kansas City mayoral campaign and his eventual plan to run for the White House with Obama's blessing. The disbelieving young shrink sat back in his chair, tapped his notebook a few times with his pen, and then pursed his lips. "Barack Obama told you that you could run for president?" he asked. "How often would you say you hear voices?"

Blue-Collar Backgrounds

The personal struggles of the other veterans profiled in HERE. IS. BETTER. are more representative of what most service members, from blue-collar backgrounds, experience in civilian life.

After much prodding from her husband, Teresa joined an all-female cohort of veterans enrolled in a "last chance program," as one participant calls it. They begin their seven-week stay at a VA residential treatment center beset with dark thoughts and doubts about its effectiveness. "I sat in my fucking shit for a lot of years, making it hard to be a wife and mother," Teresa tells the group. Likewise Tabitha reveals why she was in the program: "[I was] a horrible person and a horrible mother [who just] wanted to die." We learn that, after her sexual assault, she was "yelled at for being a whore" and transferred to another Marine Corps unit, while her attackers, per usual, went unpunished.[1]

As the story of John, the Vietnam vet, unfolds, we find out that he first tried to get help from the VA in the early 1970s. At the time, it was underfunded, understaffed, and unprepared for a huge influx of new patients, thanks to the Nixon and Ford administrations. "There was nothing there then," he says. John was able to find stability in his job and marriage but rarely discussed his combat experience with anyone, even his wife of thirty-six years. "What I saw, what I did, the loss ... it all still plays on my head," he confesses in the film.

After John retired and was nearing age seventy, he attended a retreat for older veterans, facilitated by a clinical social worker from the VA. This time he found that he was not "alone in this search for a little more peace in our lives." At the retreat and follow-up peer counseling sessions, he reconnected with one aspect of his long-ago military service that was more positive—namely, the mutual aid and strong sense of camaraderie that was essential to individual survival in Vietnam.

Among those shown caring for John, Teresa, Tabitha, and Kander are clinical social workers, psychologists, psychiatrists, and peer support specialists. In that last job category—but others as well—are fellow veterans, since about one-third of all VA healthcare staff served in the military themselves. This helps foster a unique institutional culture of empathy and solidarity between patients and providers that has no counterpart anywhere else in the US healthcare system.

In addition, every VA employee is trained how to better recognize and assist patients who are suicidal. Thousands of its mental health providers learn to use and then employ the latest evidence-based treatments for PTSD; outside the VA, studies show, only 30 percent of private sector providers employ such treatments.

In HERE. IS. BETTER., one in-house VA caregiver says her biggest treatment challenge is "how to create hope." The filmmakers report that participants in the residential program that Teresa and Tabitha completed have a 70 percent success rate, leading them to suggest that the model of "trauma-informed care" used by the VA could also help the millions of other Americans with a PTSD diagnosis.

The VA has long been a source of innovation in many areas of clinical practice, as well as developing new treatment tools—including the nicotine patch, the first implantable cardiac pacemaker, and the shingles vaccine—that now benefit all patients who need them. Numerous research studies also show the VA does a far better job treating patients with varied and complex conditions than private medical practices and for-profit hospital chains do. Nevertheless, the VA's direct care delivery capacity, medical research functions, and major teaching hospital role have all been jeopardized by incremental privatization under Presidents Obama, Trump, Biden, and now Trump again.

Every year, tens of billions of dollars are diverted from the VA's budget to pay for costly and unnecessary outside referrals. As a result, an exemplary system of integrated and coordinated care is continually weakened and disrupted. Outsourcing may eventually lead to the VA system being dismantled, leaving patients without access to the highly skilled suicide prevention specialists and group therapists we meet in HERE. IS. BETTER and *Invisible Storm*.

Advocates of privatization often point to the work of groups like Kander's own community-based program for homeless vets as examples of how VA patients—in need of housing, healthcare, or emergency assistance—are better served by private sector initiatives than a big government bureaucracy. Yet the thousands of nonprofit and for-profit entities now vying for an ever-larger share of the VA budget invariably lack the institutional scale, resources, and experience necessary to meet the complex needs of veterans like those profiled in HERE. IS. BETTER and *Invisible Storm*.

In his memoir, Kander confesses that he never dreamed during his political career of becoming a "poster child" for what he calls "post-traumatic growth." Let's hope that this former supporter of single-payer healthcare in the Missouri state legislature will use his continuing "platform and influence" to help save the nation's best working model of socialized medicine. It was that healthcare system that changed his life for the better, along with the lives of many others who left the military, never expecting to have personal problems or career challenges due to the "invisible storm" that later overtook them.

12

Suicide by Rental Truck

On New Year's Day 2025, headline-making events in two of America's most party-hearty cities sent us back to our well-thumbed copy of *Touching the Dragon*, a 2018 memoir by James Hatch.

Never heard of Hatch? Well, maybe that's because he spent much of his military career as a Navy SEAL "warfighter" always "close to the enemy" in Bosnia, Africa, Iraq, and Afghanistan but never seeking headlines. A survivor of 150 combat missions, Hatch returned home in bad mental and physical shape; in fact, his crippling wounds of war ended his career. Then insult was added to injury. "I was forced to ... reintegrate into a society that I had spent two decades defending, but in which I didn't feel I had a place."

In his insightful and prophetic book, Hatch warned about what his generational cohort of "special operators," who experienced a similar "volume of fighting," was now facing: "A serious volume of aftermath. Marriages falling apart. Alcoholism. Guys getting kicked out of their houses. Guys drowning in opioids. The real recoil hasn't even hit yet."

The dozens of civilians left dead or injured in Las Vegas and New Orleans during the last missions of US Army sergeant Matthew Livelsberger and army veteran Shamsud-Din Jabbar were definitely victims of that "real recoil." But why would two much-saluted young men—who served their country so honorably at home and abroad, for a combined total of thirty-three years—both rent trucks in the same holiday season week and turn them into deadly weapons.

In notes left behind, Livelsberger, a decorated Green Beret combat veteran, insisted that his action "was not a terrorist attack" but rather "a wake-up call" necessary because "Americans only pay attention to spectacles and violence." His declared goal was "to cleanse my mind of the brothers I've lost and relieve myself of the burden of the lives I took." Jabbar, a former information technology specialist, left video messages announcing that he had switched sides in the "war between the believers and the disbelievers" and had become a follower of ISIS.

Asymmetrical Warfare

The two soldiers had spent a total of four tours of duty in Afghanistan, where only one set of combatants had B-52 bombers, fighter jets, helicopter gunships, long-range artillery, and tanks. As a result, both Jabbar and Livelsberger were familiar with key tools of the "asymmetrical warfare" waged by the Taliban (suicide vests, improvised bombs, and speeding vehicles packed with explosives).

Back home, they geared up in equivalent fashion and became domestic terrorists, but their actions were definitely not without precedent. According to the University of Maryland's National Consortium for the Study of Terrorism and Responses to Terrorism (START), "A U.S. military background is the single strongest individual-level predictor of whether a subject ... in the PIRUS (Profiles of Individual Radicalization in the United States) data is classified as a mass casualty offender." A record of military service, START explains, is an even more reliable predictor than mental health problems or a criminal history.

Consider the long list of those who preceded Jabbar and Livelsberger down the same path. In 1995, Gulf War veteran Timothy McVeigh parked his Ryder truck, with a homemade bomb, outside the federal building in Oklahoma City. He lit fuses, drove off in a getaway car, and soon 168 people were dead and 680 injured, a crime for which he was executed in 2001.

Jabbar, who contemplated murdering his own estranged family, seemed to be channeling the murderous energy of another quiet Texan, Charles Whitman. A former Eagle Scout and marine sniper, Whitman killed fifteen people and injured thirty-one during a 1966 shooting spree conducted from the clock tower of the University of Texas at Austin. (On his way to campus, he fatally stabbed his wife and mother).

More recently, in 2009, at Fort Hood, Texas, Maj. Nidal Hasan, an army psychiatrist, murdered twelve soldiers and one civilian, and injured thirty others, a crime for which he is now on death row. In March 2018, Albert Wong, who saw combat in Afghanistan (where Hasan was headed before his killing spree), shot himself and three caregivers at a veteran's clinic in Yountville, California. That same year, ex-marine

Ian David Long, decorated for his service as a machine gunner in Afghanistan, killed twelve people at a country-and-western bar in Thousand Oaks, California. In October 2023, Army Reservist Robert Card slaughtered eighteen of his neighbors at a bowling alley and bar in Lewiston, Maine, while wounding thirteen others. (Both Card and Long killed themselves to avoid capture.) In two separate incidents, within the same twelve-hour period in late September 2025, a total of seven people died and sixteen were injured when two ex-marines, Nigel Edge and Thomas Sanford—both Iraq War veterans—opened fire at a waterfront bar in North Carolina and a Latter-Day Saints church in Michigan, respectively. Edge was captured, and Sanford, who rammed his truck into the church before opening fire on its congregation, was fatally shot by police.[1]

If readers are noticing a pattern here, it's because there is one. While veteran advocates correctly point out that the majority of former service members are certainly not mass murderers, it is also true that a tiny subset of veterans have been responsible for a disproportionate number of mass shootings and other violent attacks.

Military Socialization

One big factor behind that data point is their military training and indoctrination. As retired army lieutenant colonel David Grossman explains in his book *On Killing: The Psychological Cost of Learning to Kill in War and Society*, the cultivation of anger and aggression is critical to overcoming normal human resistance to killing other people. This becomes part of the socialization of all military recruits, even those who never see combat. For those who do, the battlefield deaths of close friends and comrades can, according to Grossman, further "enable killing."

As clinical psychiatrist Jonathan Shay reported in his 1994 study "Achilles in Vietnam," "replacement of grief by rage has lasted for years and become an entrenched way of being" for many sufferers of combat-related PTSD. Researchers at the VA Puget Sound Health Care System in Seattle, found that, among Iraq and Afghanistan veterans, anger was "independent from, albeit related to, PTSD." Veterans who had been diagnosed with PTSD or "subthreshold PTSD" reported increased levels of anger, hostility, and physical aggression, particularly in their intimate relationships.

If service members have a history of behavioral problems before enlisting, being in the military can make them worse. Albert Wong suffered from PTSD, which is why he was a patient of Pathway Homes (the Northern California treatment center made famous in the 2017 feature film *Thank You for Your Service*). But, like Ian David Long, his mental health issues predated his active duty.

Both Wong and Long were troubled children and adolescents. Wong was raised by a series of friends and foster parents and had difficulty in high school. Long's friends and neighbors did not report their concerns about his aggressive behavior as a teenager because they didn't want to spoil his dream of enlisting to "kill for his country."

Better screening of recruits like Wong and Long might have kept them out of the military. Unfortunately, when both signed up—thanks to simultaneous wars in Iraq and Afghanistan—the US military was suffering from a "serious recruitment crisis." As a result, screening and drug testing standards were relaxed, and even a felony conviction was not necessarily disqualifying. In 2017, the army even waived a previous ban on signing up young men and women with a history of "self-mutilation, bipolar disorder, depression, and drug and alcohol abuse."

Traumatic Brain Injury

Service-related traumatic brain injury can be a toxic affliction of former soldiers with past combat exposure, like Livelsberger, and even those, like forty-year-old Robert Card, who never served abroad. Dave Philipps's investigative reporting in the *New York Times* has revealed how Card, an experienced Army Reserve grenade instructor, was subject to repeated blast injuries that seriously damaged his brain. The result was increasingly erratic and ultimately very deadly behavior.

Philipps's reporting has focused on Livelsberger's blast exposure in training and when deployed. An army nurse and former girlfriend, Alicia Arritt, had no trouble recognizing his symptoms—anger, aggression, depression, and inability to concentrate—because she had encountered them before among her patients still on active duty (as Livelsberger was until his wake-up call in Las Vegas).

The Department of Defense tends to downplay such links, at the time and after the fact. In the Card case, it took an independent commission, appointed by the governor of Maine, to confirm that Card's superior officers had failed to heed warnings about him from fellow soldiers, concerned family members, and mental health clinicians. During his treatment at a civilian psychiatric hospital three months before his rampage, Card was found to be experiencing psychosis and having homicidal thoughts. He even had a hit list.

Two years after the Lewiston massacre, one hundred survivors and relatives of those who died sued for damages over what they claim was "one of the most preventable mass tragedies in American history—a mass shooting that could and should have been stopped by the United States Army." As one of their lawyer's asked, "How many other Robert Cards are out there right now, suffering from mental illness, with ready access to assault weapons?"

Fortunately, as part of the National Defense Authorization Act passed in December 2024, Congress has finally required the DOD to set limits on blast exposure, consider its impact on the brain in designing new weaponry, and "standardize and improve the detection, treatment, and reporting" of blast injuries. These harm reduction measures won't make medical detection any easier because imaging techniques don't always confirm the impact of blast injuries. That's why friends, family members, and caregivers for service members or veterans need to better understand and be alert for symptoms like those displayed by Livelsberger and Card. Among the documented shortcomings of outsourced care is the fact that most doctors in private practice are not familiar with links between blast injury and depression or PTSD and related anger and aggression.

Dr. Harold Kudler, a Duke Medical School professor, is a skilled caregiver who does recognize those symptoms based on years of experience with VA patients. He told us: "It's important to remember that ... PTSD, traumatic brain injury, moral injury, depression or even schizophrenia are not likely to make you a mass shooter. That said, these recent events in Las Vegas and Louisiana, like so many others, make it clear the burden that so many of our veterans bear."

Without a properly functioning healthcare system of their own, too many former soldiers will be left to carry that burden themselves. If they crack under the strain of doing so, the consequences can be devastating—not only for their friends, family, and former comrades but also for everyone else on the receiving end of a "mass casualty "event.

13

Workplace Wellness, as Delivered by Amazon?

The persistent problem of veteran suicide has provided big companies with an opportunity to demonstrate their patriotic concern for the health and well-being of former military personnel, including those they employ.

Brown University's Cost of War Project estimates that the total suicide toll among veterans and service members during the past several decades is more than thirty thousand. According to a VA study, veterans are 1.5 times more likely to die by suicide than nonveterans, while female veterans are 2.2 times more likely to die by suicide than civilian women. Four times as many men and women who have served in the US military have died by suicide than were killed in post-9/11 wars.

When vets enter the civilian job market, their pay, benefits, and treatment by supervisors can have a major impact on their emotional and financial stability. With this in mind, the US Chamber of Commerce Foundation joined forces with the first Trump administration to promote a suicide reduction initiative called Prevents. Its stated objective was building "a public/private partnership to strengthen emotional well-being in the workplace."

Major corporations were solicited to sign a "Hiring Our Heroes Challenge Pledge" and then employ "best practices for strengthening mental wellness and preventing suicide." The reason for the latter commitment is that "employee populations," including veterans, may have certain risk factors, such as "financial stress, emotional stress, and substance use and abuse." The signatory firms agreed to "promote a safe, inclusive work environment and leverage employee resource groups" to "create communities of support."

Among the first twenty-five "forward-looking employers" to sign up was Amazon, along with equally antiunion firms like Walmart,

Starbucks, Comcast, Sprint, and T-Mobile. The $2.4 trillion company founded by Jeff Bezos, the world's second-richest man, pledged to hire twenty-five thousand more veterans and military spouses—a goal later increased to one hundred thousand.

All these new hires are encouraged to join the company's officially approved workplace-based "affinity group," known as Warriors@Amazon. Its ranks extend from the warehouse shop floor all the way to Amazon's board of directors. That body includes a "warrior" who has received over $1 million in total compensation for his part-time work for the company—retired general Keith Alexander, a multimillionaire former director of the National Security Agency. Bezos likes being around vets so much that he also created a Super PAC called the With Honor Fund. Its wealthy donors seek out centrist Democrats and conservative Republicans who served in the military and promise, if elected to Congress, to join "a cross-partisan veterans caucus." During the 2018 election cycle, Bezos gave $10 million to With Honor during the same week that Super PAC critic Bernie Sanders introduced a bill in the Senate called the Stop Bezos Act.

A Revolving Door?

The goal of Sanders's legislation was to force Amazon to reimburse the federal government for the cost of public benefits, like Medicaid or food stamps, that thousands of its workers are eligible to collect because their pay is so low. Sanders's attempt to hold the company accountable was not successful, in part because Congress already has too many members like the ones Bezos helps run for office while playing the veteran card.

At a town hall meeting hosted by Sanders—to aid union organizing at Amazon—the socialist from Vermont invited navy veteran Seth King to assess Amazon's commitment to providing fair wages and "workplace wellness." King described Amazon's employment model as "a revolving door of just bodies that they're throwing at the floor."

Telling a now-familiar warehouse worker tale, he recalled working long hours under the pressure of demanding productivity standards, with few chances to sit down or take a bathroom break. As King drove to work every day, he was already tired. "It was exhausting just thinking about having to come in and start another ten-hour shift, being on my feet the whole time." At a company supposedly sensitive to risk factors for suicide, King felt himself moving in that direction. "I didn't want to be alive anymore if that was the future that I had to look forward to. I was in the navy for eight years, and there wasn't a single day that I felt as miserable or isolated as I did at Amazon." He quit after three months, which was typical for a worker at Amazon, which has a startling annual turnover rate of 150 percent.

Even veterans hired to be supervisors have made similar unfavorable comparisons between military job conditions and civilian life at Amazon. One officer, still active in the reserves, reported that his warehouse was understaffed and overheated due to insufficient air conditioning. When mistakes occurred, he said, he would usually get chewed out by one of his bosses. "I didn't get treated as bad ... in basic training," he said. "You screw up—it's a screaming, cussing, yelling tirade on the floor." This supervisor faced pressure to end his role as a part-time soldier because, as one higher-level manager informed him, he would be unable to advance at the company if he continued to serve both the military and Amazon.

The Uniformed Services Employment and Reemployment Rights Act (USERRA) supposedly protects service members from such job discrimination or denial of promotions due to their absence from work for military commitments. When a media outlet queried Amazon about its compliance with USERRA, the company denied any violations. Amazon once again proclaimed its commitment "to supporting our military and veteran employees and providing opportunities for their long-term career growth and success."

Reporting by the *New York Times* has found, however, that Amazon actually "intentionally limits upward mobility for hourly workers," both veterans and nonveterans. It is Bezos's personal belief that hourly workers who stay too long at the company become lazy, disgruntled, and entrenched, putting Amazon on what he calls "a march to mediocrity." So top executives torpedoed one proposal from Amazon's HR department to "create more leadership roles for hourly employees, similar to non-commissioned officers in the military." Instead, as the *Times* reported, "guaranteed wage increases stopped after three years and Amazon provided incentives for low-skilled employees to leave."

Pandemic-Related Changes?

During the COVID-19 pandemic, Amazon again tried to burnish its tarnished reputation as an employer by highlighting how many vets it was hiring who had lost their jobs at other firms that were not profiting from a huge increase in online order filling. Management announced what proved to be a temporary wage hike for warehouse workers, whose starting pay at the time was fifteen dollars per hour. The company also modified its leave policy to permit employees with virus symptoms to stay home for up to two weeks with pay. Workers later complained that this policy was not fairly or consistently implemented.

By the 2020 holiday season, Amazon was acting like the pandemic was over, according to Courtenay Brown, a warehouse worker in New Jersey. Bezos, she noted, had "made $70 billion since March when the pandemic started," but the company still "canceled the measly $2 bonus back in June." Brown was not happy about it. "Amazon calls us heroes in their commercials, they call us essential, but it feels like we are expendable." She was among the Amazon workers who joined forces with Walmart employees in a national campaign called "Five to Survive." As Brown explained, its five demands included "five dollars per hour in essential pay, safety on the job, and real protections from retaliation if they [spoke] out about working conditions or health hazards."

Unfortunately, as former Amazon vice president Tim Bray pointed out in a newspaper opinion piece, the company's "productivity targets" continued to make the "already stressful work of those who sort, package, and deliver Amazon goods even worse." According to Bray—an unlikely advocate for unionization—only workplace organizing will ensure better treatment of the company's hourly workers, including the forty-five thousand veterans, military spouses, and part-time military personnel currently among them.

One function of any labor organization that wins bargaining rights at Amazon, now or in the future, will be negotiating contract language that creates job safety and health committees. Those are needed, along with better enforcement of the Occupational Safety and Health Act, to help reduce the company's high job injury rate, which is twice that of any warehousing rival. According to the labor-backed Strategic Organizing Center, as many as forty thousand Amazon employees are injured on the job every year. And the rate of serious injuries has been as high as 6.8 for every 100 warehouse workers on its payroll.

Vet-on-Vet Surveillance

As Amazon workers from Bessemer, Alabama, to Staten Island, New

York, have discovered, one deterrent to joining an unapproved "affinity group"—like a union—is management's pervasive workplace surveillance. As the Open Markets Research Institute found, the giant firm "uses navigation software, item scanners, wristbands, thermal cameras, security cameras, and recorded footage to surveil its workforce in warehouses." These tools are designed both to boost output and to closely monitor employee involvement in any workplace organizing activity.

Amazon's worldwide system of in-house spying has, in the United States, even pitted military veterans against each other. In job postings for positions in Amazon's Global Security Operations (GSO) and Global Intelligence Program (GIP), the company solicited applications from veterans able to keep its union-busting lawyers well informed about "sensitive topics that are highly confidential, including labor organizing threats against the company." If hired, their role would be to "track funding and activities connected to corporate campaigns (internal and external) against Amazon, and provide sophisticated analysis on these topics."

It's not clear whether informing on fellow Warriors@Amazon, who work on the shop floor, will also require some actual heavy lifting (while undercover) or just operating surveillance equipment and writing voluminous Stasi-style reports. Either way, these newly hired "heroes" will be adding little luster to whatever laurels they might have earned during past uniformed employment with the DOD, other national security agencies, or local police departments.

14

A Real Culture of Solidarity

In an increasingly corporatized and profit-driven US healthcare system, patients now have something in common with purchasers of products from Amazon or any other major corporation. They are treated as "customers" in a competitive marketplace for goods and services.

The emphasis of management is on speed of delivery—time-studied down to the last second—and use of automation to reduce human labor. In the context of healthcare provision, such well-documented trends are not positive or healthy for people already sick or their caregivers, particularly when the latter become totally stressed out by job speedup or burnt out by understaffing.

As explored further in part 5 of this book, the commodification of healthcare has become so widespread that even our best-working model of socialized medicine is now threatened by its congressionally mandated use of "VA-purchased care" from private sector providers.

Advocates for privatization tell veterans and their families that care, inside and outside the VA, is interchangeable. That is not true. One of the unique features of the VA is its culture of empathy, solidarity, mutual aid, and support.

When one of us (Suzanne) closely observed patients and staff at the VA over many years, a real community of care—which is not reproducible in a "fee for service" world—was clearly on display. Close to a third of the VA's healthcare workforce—about one hundred thousand people—served in the military themselves. So, at VA hospitals and clinics around the country, veterans are taking care of other veterans, and they're doing it as doctors, nurses, therapists, and support staff.

A Therapeutic Community

Veterans say they value the VA because it's *their* healthcare system, it was created for them, still belongs to them (for the time being), and provides multiple opportunities for social connection that VA patients truly value and cannot find anywhere else.

Patients in VA waiting rooms, cafeterias, lobbies, and hallways not only acknowledge each other but also talk to each other, all the time. The VA's hospitals and clinics are not just the scene of medical checkups, procedures, and trips to the pharmacy. The interactions between patients and providers are very human and relational. There is a sense of belonging and camaraderie that is both poignant and inspirational, with therapeutic value of its own.

Socialized by the military to "embrace the suck," some veterans avoid getting much-needed mental health therapy for many years. Vets are more apt to end up eventually at the VA because it's a well-known, nonjudgmental "safe space" where they can reconnect with other veterans. "They don't want to come for an appointment," one VA doctor once told us, "But they want to come and see their buddies. So that means they come and see me too."

Lest anyone think that such valorization of the VA, based on mere anecdotal evidence, is just another thinly disguised form of single-payer propaganda, the prestigious *Journal of the American Medical Association* (JAMA) has confirmed the observations above. On April 15, 2025, JAMA published an article titled "Camaraderie Among US Veterans and Their Preferences for Health Care Systems and Practitioners," coauthored by eight practitioners with extensive, hands-on experience treating veterans. The purpose of their study was to "more formally determine whether the desire to affiliate with other veterans, herein referred to as 'camaraderie,' influences veterans' choice of health care systems and practitioners."[1]

The authors asked a series of questions about cultural factors, VA patients' level of trust in their VA caregivers, and "a scenario-based question to ascertain whether veterans would choose VA or private health care if cost and distance were equivalent." Most of the 652 respondents reported that camaraderie was very important to them. Overall, about 52 percent of those surveyed rated being around other veterans that way; this increased to 75 percent among veterans aged eighteen to thirty-four years and to 65.35 percent for those aged thirty-five to sixty-four years. When VA users were asked whether they would choose in-house care over outsourced care—assuming cost and travel distance were equivalent—nearly 70 percent preferred to stay with the VA.

In their JAMA article, the authors explained why they believe camaraderie is important to veterans. Starting in basic training, military personnel learned the importance of "unit cohesion"—not just to achieve their superior officers' goal of peak "operational performance." Looking out for each other is the basic survival tool of fellow foot soldiers in any army.

Transitioning to Civilian Life

Such camaraderie is also an important factor in transitioning from military service to civilian life—a change that can be alienating, jarring, and very difficult in ways never explained to an eighteen-year-old by a friendly military recruiter. The JAMA researchers found that when "military social networks are ruptured," veterans can face huge problems—with "employment, finances, housing insecurity, and health issues"—all of which can "contribute to substance abuse and suicide."

Just as the absence of camaraderie can produce multiple physical and mental health problems, so too its presence can be a "protective factor" against them. According to the authors, "cohesive social networks have been shown to be a protective factor for those in recovery. Among veterans with PTSD, those who expressed satisfaction with their social networks were less likely to have suicidal ideation and behaviors. A study of 128 male veterans with PTSD suggested that veteran friends were more important sources of support than nonveteran friends."

The JAMA article contains this timely reminder for policymakers on Capitol Hill: "The value of veteran social support, camaraderie, and military or veteran culture is typically not considered when weighing the benefits of the VA healthcare system. Our findings suggest that veterans value camaraderie and the ability to affiliate with other veterans, and that these factors contribute to their propensity to choose VA, especially younger veterans. With over 80 million outpatient visits each year, VA uniquely creates opportunities for veterans to engage with each other, experience camaraderie, and sustain social relationships that may be beneficial."

In a bid to make the best of a deeply flawed but very bipartisan privatization project, the chroniclers of "Camaraderie Among U.S.

Veterans" threw one final Hail Mary pass. They suggested that, "by creating preferred provider networks, VA could facilitate veteran access to a selected group of community practitioners who have demonstrated higher quality, greater cultural competency, and a willingness to proactively share data with VA to enhance veteran care coordination." This might also enable some community-based practitioners to care for a sufficient volume of veterans to create veteran outpatient environments or inpatient units that enable veteran affiliation and camaraderie. VA's existing partnerships with academic institutions could be the foundation for such a preferred network.

Insufficient patient volume is likely to make this idea unworkable, even if Trump administration appointees at the VA cared enough about the quality of its outsourced care to organize its "preferred providers" in the fashion recommended. Even in areas where the VA's nine million patients have greater local density, veterans overall represent just a sliver of the adult patient population, about 3 percent. So the clinical environment described above is not easily replicated outside the VA system, even under the best imaginable circumstances.

Camaraderie—at least the real kind on display every day at the VA—cannot be found at the nearest "doc-in-a-box" or most of the 1.7 million private sector providers siphoning away billions of dollars a year from the VA budget.

PART IV

VETERANS IN LABOR

One of us (Steve) has appreciated the role of veterans in the labor movement since his first union job, as a seasonal worker in an A&P grocery store on Cape Cod in the late 1960s. The Retail Clerks International Association (RCIA)—later to become part of the United Food and Commercial Workers (UFCW)—was a largely invisible representative of cashiers, shelf stockers, and truck unloaders. RCIA initiation fees were collected by the store manager, and it had no shop-floor presence.

Over in the meat department, however, A&P workers had a strong craft union, the Meat Cutters (also now part of UFCW). Its steward was a stocky, middle-aged World War II vet who charged into the manager's office whenever one of his dues-payers had a beef (so to speak) and sorted things out very quickly.

In subsequent decades, amid many organizing and strike committees, stewards' meetings, union rallies, and picket lines, it was never hard to find former service members with similar pugnacity and grit, now fortunately deployed in the cause of labor rather than management. (Ex-military types who become factory supervisors are another story.)

As recommended in this part of the book, unions need to be on the lookout for members, new and old, with military service on their resume. Veterans in the workforce often have relevant leadership skills, organizational experience, and training in the importance of teamwork. Their past experience with collective activity, in a different context, can be put to good use in a strike situation, as noted below, or in a nonunion workplace where organizers must be resourceful and brave to stand up against a union-busting employer like Amazon or Walmart.

Historically, the postal service has been one major way that men and women could trade one uniform for another and provide a vital public service for their community. About 110,000 postal workers represented by the American Postal Workers Union (APWU), the letter carriers and mail handlers, are veterans. The postal service is a key source of employment for African American vets, and it provides public sectors job with decent benefits and pay—and, until recently, good job security.

As noted in this section, veterans in the postal service have been rank-and-file leaders in the fight against privatization of their agency, just as vets employed by the Department of Veterans Affairs have been campaigning to "Save Our VA" with active support from Veterans for Peace, Common Defense, and other veterans' groups.

Since some union members also have ties to the National Guard, the experience of the Military Caucus of the Texas State Employees Union (TSEU), described below, has more relevance than ever, amid growing abuse of Guard members by the Trump administration. TSEU's forty-year record of building a membership-based union—without ever being able to legally negotiate a single state worker contract—provides a blueprint for the survival of federal labor organizations stripped of their bargaining rights in 2025, for however long that condition lasts.

15

When Soldiers Become Workers

In the United States, seventeen million people, across multiple generations, have a shared personal identity based on past service in the military. Mainstream media outlets often notice them only on Veterans Day or Memorial Day, when they show up in vet organization caps at commemorations for former soldiers, young and old, alive or dead. Easily forgotten is the less visible role that veterans from working-class backgrounds have played in key labor and political struggles since the mid-twentieth century.

In the heyday of industrial unionism in the 1950s and 1960s, tens of thousands of World War II veterans could be found on the front lines of labor struggles in the auto, steel, meat-packing, mining, trucking, and telephone industries. Today about 1.3 million former military personnel work in union jobs, with women and people of color making up the fastest-growing cohorts in their ranks.

According to the AFL-CIO, veterans are more likely to join a union than nonveterans. In at least six states, 25 percent or more of working veterans belong to unions. David Van Deusen, a longtime union rep in Vermont and former president of its state labor council, views veterans as "an underutilized resource for the labor movement," particularly in high-profile organizing campaigns. No one, he believes, is better positioned to "expose the hypocrisy and duplicity of 'veteran-friendly' firms like Amazon and Walmart, who wrap themselves in the flag, while violating the rights of working-class Americans who served in uniform and the many who did not."

In her widely read advice about worker organizing and strike preparation, the late author and consultant Jane McAlevey urged her labor clients to follow the example of industrial unions in the post–World War II era. In that period, she pointed out, organized labor better appreciated the "strategic value" of former soldiers in strike situations because of their past "experience with discipline, military formation, and overcoming fear and adversity." In addition, the high social standing of military veterans in many blue-collar communities was an important, if underused, PR asset for unions trying to generate popular support for their contract fights.

An OCAW Role Model

Brooklyn-born Tony Mazzocchi was a leading figure in that postwar generational cohort. A combat veteran of the Battle of the Bulge, he became a catalyst for change within the Oil, Chemical and Atomic Workers (OCAW) and the broader labor movement for five decades.

In the early 1970s, Mazzocchi coordinated labor's campaign for the Occupational Safety and Health Act (OSHA), which now provides workplace protections for 130 million Americans. He also championed civil rights, nuclear disarmament, environmentalism, and single-payer healthcare. In the 1990s, the OCAW leader helped found a union-backed Labor Party because the business-friendly Democratic Party was such an unreliable friend of labor and right-wing Republicans even more hostile to its agenda.

While Mazzocchi was lobbying for passage of OSHA, union members in another hazardous industry—coal mining—had similar safety and health concerns, which fueled a rank-and-file rebellion. Among them were Vietnam veterans who returned home, went to work in the Appalachian coalfields, and became dissidents in the United Mine Workers of America (UMWA). In 1972, their reform movement overthrew the corrupt, murderous old-guard union leadership. This helped inspire similar insurgencies, later in the seventies, in the United Steel Workers and the International Brotherhood of Teamsters.

At their Miners for Democracy (MFD) convention in 1972, four hundred rank-and-filers and retirees adopted a thirty-four-point union reform platform. They nominated Arnold Miller from Cabin Creek, West Virginia, as their candidate for national union president. Miller was a disabled miner, leader of the Black Lung Association, and a former GI whose face was scarred by injuries suffered during the D-Day invasion. His MFD slate included another military veteran, forty-one-year-old Harry Patrick, a voice for younger miners, who served during the Korean War era.

Cecil Roberts was one of those Vietnam veterans who got jobs in the mines and backed the MFD in 1972. Roberts later became UMWA president for thirty years and used his position to rally the union's members and their families against a resurgence of black lung disease due to coal and silica dust exposure among underground miners. In the mid 1970s, Roberts's home turf—UMWA District 17—was the epicenter of a huge wildcat strike movement that landed Skip Delano, a Vietnam vet (and later Veterans for Peace activist) in jail for violating federal court injunctions in West Virginia.[1]

The PATCO Strikers

Fifteen years after that rank-and-file uprising, former service members who became federal air traffic controllers paid an even bigger price for their union militancy. Members of the Professional Air Traffic Controllers Organization (PATCO) were unlikely martyrs. In 1980, their national union broke with most others when it endorsed conservative Republican Ronald Reagan, a former leader of the Screen Actors Guild, for US president.

This proved to be a major miscalculation. During his first year in the White House, Reagan fired twelve thousand PATCO members for engaging in an illegal nationwide strike. The strikers remained under a lifetime presidential ban from federal employment as controllers until 1993, when the Clinton administration finally allowed a trickle of them to return to their old jobs. As part of its crushing defeat, PATCO was decertified and replaced in 1987 by the National Air Traffic Controllers Association, an organization then composed of many striker replacements.

Georgetown University professor Joe McCartin, an ally of federal workers to this day, wrote the definitive account of that turning point for labor. In *Collision Course: Ronald Reagan, the Air Traffic Controllers, and the Strike that Changed America*, McCartin noted that the vast majority of PATCO strikers were "suburban-dwelling military veterans" who went directly from the service into "the rigid, hierarchical culture of the FAA."

"Although they were breaking federal law in an unprecedented effort to shut down the nation's air travel, they were hardly radicals," McCartin observed. They were extremely well-organized and disciplined, with an elaborate, military-style blueprint for their work stoppage that contrasted sharply with the far-sketchier strike plans of many other unions, before and since. As McCartin revealed:

> In April 1980, PATCO had distributed a fifty-five-page strike-planning booklet to members. In the months that followed, the union prepared as though it was going to war. Strike planners developed "clusters" of locals that could coordinate their activity during the anticipated strike independent of national direction should PATCO's leaders be arrested. Clusters had established secret "safe houses" from which local strike efforts could be directed in the event that union headquarters were raided. Strike planners urged local clusters to set up decentralized calling trees to pass information and recommended that members use phone booths or friends' phones when communicating vital strike information.[2]

Where PATCO strike planners fell short was in laying the groundwork for sufficient labor and community support, which would have required building better ties with the airline industry's private sector unions and the broader labor movement, before walking out. The coauthors of this book were among the thousands of PATCO supporters who raised money and organized events to support local leaders of the strike (including three in Boston) who were indicted by the Justice Department.

In unions like Communications Workers of America (CWA), one major takeaway from the PATCO strike was the need for building broader public support for strikes—in part, by more clearly articulating how bargaining demands might benefit other workers and members of the public. One successful post-PATCO example of that approach was a four-month fight against contract concessions by sixty thousand workers at NYNEX, a 1989 strike victory during an otherwise dark decade of contract give-backs, lockouts, and failed walkouts.[3]

CWA Veterans for Social Change

One veteran of that and other strikes by CWA and the International Brotherhood of Electrical Workers (IBEW) was telecom technician Chris Shelton, whose father was a union member before him as a New York City transit worker. Shelton served in the air force and then became a shop steward, CWA rep, regional vice president, and then national union leader. In that last role, Shelton viewed Donald Trump's election in 2016 as an even bigger threat to labor than the previous attacks of Ronald Reagan and both George Bushes.

So, while serving as CWA president, Shelton started a rank-and-file program called Veterans for Social Change. Why was this needed? As he explained, active-duty service members, and military families "are constantly exploited by politicians and others who seek to loot our economy, attack our communities, and divide our nation with racism and bigotry so they can consolidate more power amongst themselves."[4] CWA has tried to counter this political threat by "developing and organizing a broad base of union activists who are veterans and/or currently serving in the military." Their mission is to engage in grassroots campaigns with community allies and increase awareness of veterans' issues in CWA, like the need for a strong, fully funded veterans' healthcare system.

To help train and support these local union activists, CWA partnered with Common Defense and began sending promising recruits to weekend-long sessions of its Veterans Organizing Institute (VOI). These face-to-face (and, during the COVID-19 pandemic, virtual gatherings) have brought together hundreds of younger veterans. They learn from each other about how to fight big money in politics and make politicians more accountable to poor and working-class people.

At one of first VOI training sessions attended by CWA members, shop stewards and local officers from swing states like Ohio, Arizona, North Carolina, and Texas shared organizing experiences and learned new skills useful in electoral campaigning and day-to-day advocacy for fellow workers and other vets. Four months after he participated in VOI training, Frank Cota, a Marine Corps veteran and vice president of CWA Local 7026 in Tucson, was in Washington, DC, as part of a group of CWA vets urging Congress to pass the PRO Act, legislation that would strengthen private sector organizing and bargaining rights.

"VOI provides a great introduction to getting a grassroots movement started and getting veterans, labor, and the community all working together," says John Blake, a member of Electrical Workers (IBEW) Local 400, who attended the same training. Blake chairs the veterans' committee of a local Central Labor Council and a similar group in his own local, which represents construction electricians. Blake tries to make the union's brand "more appealing to vets coming out of the service," which Local 400 does by participating in community events like "Operation Ruck It," an annual fundraising walk to raise awareness about veteran suicide.

Third-Generation Union Member

In some unions and central labor bodies, such veterans' councils or committees are sadly just a hollow shell. In CWA, a former marine who became an AT&T customer service tech in Texas has played a big role in making sure that Veterans for Social Change maintains its grassroots focus. CWA Local 6215 leader David Marshall in Dallas has also helped thirty staffers of Common Defense around the country—almost all fellow vets—become card-carrying union members too, as new recruits to Local 6215.

Marshall was born and raised in southern West Virginia. He is the son and grandson of coal miners; his grandmother Molly Marshall was active in the same Black Lung Association that helped propel Arnold Miller into the presidency of the UMWA. During his own twenty-five-year career as a CWA member, Marshall has served as a safety committee member, national union convention delegate, and now executive vice president of his local.

Marshall is also a member of CWA's Minority Caucus, the Coalition of Black Trade Unionists, and the NAACP. Along with Britni Cuington, an air force vet, Howard University graduate, and Local 6215 activist, he went to a founding meeting of Common Defense's Black Veterans Caucus at the Highlander Center in Tennessee. During the first year of Donald Trump's second term, Marshall joined Common Defense lobbying in Washington, DC, against Trump-Vance cuts in VA staffing and services, calling them "a betrayal of a promise to care for us."

Marshall was also a fiery and effective speaker at a "No Kings Day" rally in Dallas on June 14, 2025. "We've seen peaceful protesters met with riot gear, and we've heard the threats to deploy active-duty marines against American citizens," he told a crowd of ten thousand. "Let me be clear: using the military to silence dissent is not strength; it's tyranny. And no one knows that better than those who have worn the uniform."[5]

Labor Notes Troublemakers

Another important organizational home for vets in labor is Labor Notes. Its every-other-year national conferences now attract young, diverse crowds of five thousand, with even more rank-and-file militants attending its local "Troublemakers Schools" around the country.

At the 2024 Labor Notes conference in Chicago, one plenary speaker was Keturah Johnson, a VA user who went to work for Piedmont Airlines in 2013 as a ramp agent and then become a flight attendant. A decade later, she became the first queer woman of color and combat veteran to serve as international vice president of the fifty-thousand-member Association of Flight Attendants (AFA)-CWA. She says, "it is an honor to represent so many [in the airline industry] and to work to make these spaces safe and supportive for all people, including immigrants, trans people, Black and Indigenous people, and the LGBTQIA+ community so that every person ... has a voice."[6]

Another Labor Notes conference regular is Adam Pelletier, a white working-class vet from upstate New York. After returning from Iraq and leaving the marines, Pelletier used the GI Bill to finish college. In his early thirties he got a job working for the Social Security Administration in Albany, where he and his coworkers assisted retired and disabled Americans who depend on federal benefits. Pelletier first became an American Federation of Government Employees (AFGE) shop steward. Then he was elected local president, while also serving as a leader of the Troy Area Labor Council."

He later worked as an organizer for the AFSCME-affiliated Civil Service Employees Association and then became a federal union activist again as a field agent for the National Labor Relations Board, which has its own independent labor organization.

Pelletier has been active in the labor-community campaign to "Save the VA." He helped bring together fellow VA patients and their unionized caregivers at a Labor Notes conference workshop to discuss better cross-union cooperation and information sharing. He became a valued advisor to the Veterans Healthcare Policy Institute, a Bay Area-based research group that works with AFGE and Veterans for Peace (which Pelletier belongs to, along with Democratic Socialists of America).

At town hall meetings in upstate New York, Pelletier has challenged members of Congress from both parties about their complicity with VA privatization. "Congress continually votes to outsource VA services, pushing people into more expensive and less effective care," he says. "They do this instead of adequately funding the VA and looking at it as the model by which we could all someday enjoy universal health care. We must mobilize to stop it!"

A Blue-Green Alliance Builder

In Tony Mazzocchi's OCAW, now part of the United Steel Workers, a military veteran named B.K. White has become a key Northern California intermediary between refinery labor and environmental groups. As vice president of USW Local 5, White helped lead a ten-week strike against Chevron in Richmond, California, in 2022, the longest walkout by refinery workers there in forty years.

A twenty-seven-year Chevron refinery operator, local contract negotiator, and longtime advocate for tougher refinery safety rules, White faced post-strike retaliation by management and was fired along with four other USW members. While continuing to contest his dismissal, White took a new job as public policy director for Richmond mayor Eduardo Martinez, a leader of the Richmond Progressive Alliance and frequent critic of Chevron.[7]

In his new role, White works on "just transition" planning and workforce development issues. At several recent Labor Notes Troublemakers Schools in Oakland, he has strategized with other union activists about conducting strikes, creating good union jobs less dependent on fossil fuel, and dealing with Big Oil. "I understood that there would be repercussions from taking a position, representing my people, and fighting such a big company," White says. "Big corporations don't like being challenged."

But wherever corporate America is challenged—on the job, in the community, or in electoral politics—one can safely assume that vets in labor will be there, as in the past, helping to lead the charge.

16

The GI Bill, Then and Now

Twenty-five years ago, a terminally ill Tony Mazzocchi was promoting a Labor Party campaign called "Free for All." As noted above, one of organized labor's best-known radicals was a World War II vet who personally benefited from the original GI Bill. Mazzocchi had read and was much inspired by *When Dreams Come True*, historian Michael Bennett's account of how the Servicemen's Readjustment Act of 1944 was enacted and the social impact it had. As his own biographer, Les Leopold, writes, the former OCAW leader decided to "reintroduce free higher education into the national political agenda."

Like Bennett, Mazzocchi believed that the GI Bill was "one of the greatest pieces of legislation ever enacted," because it gave millions of returning veterans like himself a "sabbatical," a much-needed government-paid chance to retool for the civilian job market. Mazzocchi argued that a twenty-first-century version of this program could similarly plant the "seeds of the good life" for millions of Americans by allowing them to attend public universities and graduate schools without accumulating ruinous personal debt.

When potential supporters balked at the $23 billion price tag for his proposal, Mazzocchi noted that a congressional study in 1988 found that the original GI Bill "had paid for itself six times over." When veterans' groups, in their usual fashion, questioned why everyone should qualify for this benefit without "earning" it through military service, Mazzocchi brushed aside those objections too. "We all need to participate in continuing education," he insisted. "It should be part of our work-life and it should be free."[1]

Fourteen years after Mazzocchi died, his old friend and political ally Bernie Sanders finally succeeded in making this old Labor Party idea part of the national political conversation—in the first of his

Democratic presidential primary campaigns. In his 2019–20 run for the White House, Sanders's candidacy pushed the eventual nominee, Joe Biden, to announce that, if elected, he would make public colleges and universities free for students from families earning less than $125,000 per year.

Later, during the economic crisis created by COVID-19 (and after Sanders suspended his second campaign), Biden unveiled a "a student debt forgiveness plan." The *New York Times* reported in April 2020, "[It] would eliminate student debt for low-income and middle-class people who attended public colleges and universities, and other institutions that serve students of color—[but] does not go as far as Mr. Sanders's plan to cancel all student debt."[2]

An Obstacle to Enlistment?

One reason the Biden administration and most members of Congress balk at taking that step is its likely impact on military recruitment. Former Army Ranger and Veterans for Peace member Rory Fanning points out, "If college were free, then the pool of potential military recruits would plummet—and that fact scares elected officials to death. Roughly 20 percent of the one hundred eighty-four thousand people who sign up for the military each year come from households that make less than $40,000 a year. It's hard to find a college education that costs less than that amount."

Fanning was among the many young men and women who enlisted partly to pay off college loans. If he had been debt-free, his decision might have been different, he says. Erasing college debt would be "a huge threat to the U.S. war machine," he told us, because "thousands of soldiers would lose their incentive to stay in the military."

Will Fischer, another prolabor vet, served as a marine in Iraq before becoming the second person in his family "to graduate from college and do so without the yoke of student debt." Later he became director of the AFL-CIO's Unions Veterans Council and governmental affairs director for VoteVets. Like Sanders, Fischer would like to see student debt canceled and public higher education, including vocational schools, made tuition-free because all working-class people "would benefit, without question, from such legislation."

Like Fanning, he also believes that limiting GI Bill–type benefits to veterans confronts too many young people with an unacceptable choice: "put on a uniform and participate in never-ending U.S. wars or take on crushing debt."

The Specter of Postwar Unrest

Long before education benefits were beefed up as a key recruitment tool for our today's "all-volunteer army," the original GI Bill was developed in response to a different threat, from a returning "citizens' army." As Michael Bennett describes it bluntly: "If the twelve million veterans of World War II had been dumped off the boats like the nearly four million from the previous world war and given only $60 and a train ticket home, with neither educational nor economic opportunity waiting when they got back, violent revolution might have easily been sparked."

Key backers of the Servicemen's Readjustment Act of 1944, like American Legion national commander Henry Colmery, were aware that angry veterans had become shock troops for the right and left in Germany and Russia after their experience of combat in World War II. In the United States, postwar social unrest among veterans culminated in a march on Washington by thousands of them in 1932—and the clashes with the Hoover administration described earlier in this book.

To avoid similar upheavals after World War II, Congress and the Roosevelt administration authorized what Bennett calls "first-class education benefits"—covering tuition and fees up to $500 a year at a time when Harvard and other top schools were charging $400. By 1947, veterans comprised nearly 50 percent of total student enrollment of 2.3 million. Nearly half of all World War II veterans using the GI Bill went to private colleges and universities, including Ivy League institutions; under the less-generous educational benefits provided after subsequent wars in Korea and Vietnam, about 80 percent of the veterans using the program opted for public higher education instead.

The original GI Bill was egalitarian in another important way. As Bennett notes, it enabled many leading figures in the 1960s civil rights movement to attend college or professional school, along with future political leaders like Ron Dellums, John Conyers, and Charles Rangel and cultural figures like Harry Belafonte and Ossie Davis.

In the aftermath of World War II, it also provided unemployment insurance for Black veterans that was equal to the benefits for whites (a GI Bill provision that southern segregationists in Congress fiercely opposed and tried unsuccessfully to block).

From Soldiers to Citizens

In her book *Citizen Soldiers: The GI Bill and the Making of the Greatest Generation*, Cornell University professor Suzanne Mettler assesses the broader impact of free higher education for veterans. Prior to World War II, she notes: "advanced education had been largely restricted to the privileged, especially to white, native-born, elite Protestants. The social rights offered by the GI Bill broadened educational opportunity to veterans who were Jewish or Catholic, African American and immigrants, as well as those whose families had struggled in the American working class for generations."

In Mettler's view, the GI Bill provided "social opportunity but also promoted more active citizenship," making the "political system more inclusive and egalitarian during the middle decades of the 20th century." Mettler cites studies showing that the 7.8 million beneficiaries of the original GI Bill participated in civic and political organizations to a greater degree than nonveterans and veterans who did not use their educational benefits.

In the late 1940s, of course, existing veterans' groups like the American Legion and Veterans of Foreign Wars experienced a huge membership increase. But, according to Mettler, they were not the only vehicle for community engagement and organizational leadership development among veterans. Both as members and leaders, veteran participation greatly increased in "cross-class fraternal groups" like the Elks, Eagles, Knights of Columbus, and Shriners, in labor unions, civil rights and religious organizations, and in political parties, which ran many candidates for public office who were GI Bill–educated veterans. (Tony Mazzocchi, then an OCAW local president and Democratic Party reformer on Long Island, was one of them; in 1964, he briefly launched a campaign for Congress.) Across the country, other veterans served in disproportionate numbers on civic boards and commissions.

As Mettler notes, even the "sub-college training benefits" of the GI Bill "played an important role in democratizing the nature of organizational leadership." Because vocational training benefits also increased the skills and expanded the confidence of veterans who ended up in blue-collar jobs, they also "were more likely to hold office or serve on a committee for a civic organization."

The scope of the original GI Bill was wide indeed, reaching nearly 5 percent of all Americans. But even before the draft ended and the United

States switched to an "all-volunteer force" in 1974, later iterations of the Servicemen's Readjustment Act of 1944 provided educational opportunity to far fewer disadvantaged citizens. "The version of the law established for Vietnam veterans in 1967 was more restrictive than those for either World War II or Korean War veterans," Mettler notes. It reached only 1.5 percent of the population, although veterans using their less generous benefits during the Cold War accessed higher education at a higher rate than those who served in World War II.

The For-Profit College Threat

As Department of Defense officials started building a "professional army," they quickly discovered that education benefits were cited as a major factor in the enlistment decisions of nearly 80 percent of those recruited for it. In 1984, Congress passed the Montgomery GI Bill (named after its congressional sponsor from Mississippi, Rep. Gillespie Montgomery), which created the modern-day framework for making higher education affordable for many veterans who might not have been able to pay for it themselves.

Since the military is much smaller today—comprising just 1 percent of the total population—the program's potential for expanding social opportunity is far more limited than eight decades ago. Nevertheless, since 2008, more than a million men and women who served in the military have used the GI Bill to obtain postsecondary degrees or certificates, which has made them more employable in the civilian job market they have returned to.

One problematic feature of the current educational landscape is the existence of so many for-profit institutions, which are now vacuuming up nearly 40 percent of GI Bill tuition and fee payments in recent years.[3]

Over the last two decades, the big post-9/11 increase in veteran use of GI Bill benefits has not been accompanied by effective regulation of educational service providers. As the Student Veterans of America (SVA) and others have warned, the risk of fraud, waste, and abuse is "exceptionally high at for-profit schools," which have left too many veterans with worthless degrees, course credits they can't transfer, exhausted GI Bill benefits, and student debt that their military service was supposed to help them avoid.[4]

Obama administration appointees did establish a GI Bill complaint system and an online tool for easier consumer comparisons of schools wooing veterans. Obama's new Consumer Financial Protection Bureau (CFPB) also created an office dedicated to protecting service members, veterans, and military families from predatory lenders. In 2016, the CFPB fined for-profit Bridgepoint Education, Inc., $8 million and directed it to discharge $23.5 million in student loans because of its deceptive practices. Before leaving office in 2017, Obama promised that tens of thousands of student vets would get some measure of debt relief after his Department of Education determined that such deception was widespread.[5]

The election of Donald Trump in 2016 and his appointment of fellow billionaire Betsy DeVos as secretary of education made a bad situation worse. With industry insider help, DeVos began "eviscerating student protections and quality controls," according to the SVA.[6]

This left a whole generation of student veterans, often from communities of color, at the mercy of firms more concerned about private profit than quality education.

DeVos issued a new federal rule, effective July 1, 2020, that required debt relief applicants to file a claim within three years of any alleged deception and supply more evidence of how they were personally misled and financially harmed. On the eve of its implementation, veterans' groups won broad congressional support for a resolution calling on the Trump administration to rescind DeVos's proposed new rule. As American Legion commander James W. Oxford reminded the White House, "this type of deception against our veterans and service members has been a lucrative scam for unscrupulous actors."[7] President Trump ignored such appeals and vetoed the House-Senate resolution.

During Trump's first four years in office, other Obama-era initiatives were thwarted with less public outcry. Among them was a 2012 executive order requiring closer collaboration between the Departments of Defense, Veterans Affairs, and Education on ways to better measure educational outcomes for student veterans. The CFPB was gutted, which left its office serving veterans and active-duty military personnel understaffed and suffering from high leadership turnover. Crippling the CFPB limited its consumer education function and weakened enforcement of the Military Lending Act, which caps interest rates for active-duty service members.

In 2017, the Trump administration even found a way to make legal challenges to consumer fraud more difficult. Vice President Mike Pence broke a Senate tie and was the deciding vote to repeal a CFPB rule that facilitated class action litigation against financial predators. As advocates for veterans and active-duty personnel pointed out, forcing plaintiffs in uniform to instead pursue individual arbitration cases when they have few personal financial resources and are often deployed abroad guarantees that fewer claims will be filed.

During the first Trump administration, the VA was similarly reluctant to use its own regulatory powers to sanction educational institutions guilty of deceiving veterans. In 2018, the VA's inspector general estimated that, if oversight was not ramped up significantly, $2.3 billion in GI Bill funds could be funneled to potentially ineligible academic programs over the next five years, putting the educational outcomes of more than seventeen thousand student veterans at risk.[8]

Trump's reelection in 2024 ensured that federal regulation and oversight of programs for student veterans would go back to the same troubled state they were in when he first left office. Only this time the resulting damage to the CFPB, the US Department of Education, and the VA was even wider, leaving consumers of publicly funded education and healthcare for vets at greater risk.

17

Can the National Guard Be Organized?

When a group of Texas workers started discussing job problems and what to do about them a few years ago, their list of complaints would have been familiar to Starbucks baristas, Amazon warehouse employees, or restive young journalists at new and old media outlets alike.[1]

With little notice, their employer changed work schedules and transferred employees to a new job location. Some of those adversely affected applied for hardship waivers, based on family life disruption, but many requests were denied. Meanwhile, access to a major job benefit—tuition assistance—was sharply curtailed, and paychecks were no longer arriving promptly or at the right address. When a few brave souls called attention to these problems, management called them "union agitators" and accused them of trying to mislead their coworkers.

In mid-April 2022, those ringleaders—members of the Texas State Guard and the state's Army National Guard and Air Force National Guard—declared themselves to be the Military Caucus of the Texas State Employees Union (TSEU), an affiliate of the Communications Workers of America. Taking direct aim at Republican governor Greg Abbott, who had recently ordered thousands of them to police the US-Mexico border, these new TSEU dues-payers called for greater legislative oversight of such open-ended missions so that Guard members would only be called up to "provide genuine service to the public good, not posturing for political gain."

Hunter Schuler, a Texas Army National Guard member and medic who helped initiate this unusual organizing effort, was one of those labelled an "agitator" for doing so. "None of us would be unionizing if our jobs didn't suck and without all the negative aspects of the mission," he explained. "There's not great mechanisms for getting problems to the attention of the top leadership any other way."

The union's mission statement, crafted by Schuler and his fellow soldiers, declared they would meet with legislators, the governor's office, and the Texas Military Department. Their demands included a guaranteed end date for all Guard members on state active duty at the time, full restoration of tuition assistance slashed by Abbott, and immediate access to the same healthcare coverage as other state employees, along with state subsidized coverage for their families "while on Texas military state mobilization."

To achieve these objectives, they pledged to build a strong union ("which gets stronger with every new member we sign up") and coordinate with other state employees who have a "proud history of organizing" as part of the eight-thousand-member TSEU, which has functioned as a union for forty years in a state that prohibits collective bargaining by state workers.

A Relevant Model for Today?

TSEU's Military Caucus and a parallel effort by the American Federation of State, County, and Municipal Employees (AFSCME) in Connecticut, also launched during the COVID-19 pandemic, proved challenging to sustain, given the part-time workforce involved. But these creative attempts to give citizen soldiers a collective voice—when their Guard service was turned into a Republican political stunt or their pandemic-related relief work was performed alongside other public employees with union representation—provide a valuable model for similar organizing work on a broader scale today.

When even former National Guard generals start criticizing the Trump administration for its "detestable" practice of using the Guard to "intimidate the local population" in Los Angeles, Portland, DC, and other cities, you can be sure that many enlistees are thinking the same way.[2]

According to former Army Ranger and About Face member Rory Fanning, so many rank-and-file Guard members view "Trump's deployment orders negatively" that morale will eventually collapse.[3] Like those who joined the Military Caucus of TSEU and its Vietnam-era forerunners, more of these disgruntled soldiers may eventually turn to collective action, in various forms—if they get the necessary outside encouragement and support.[4]

Sixty years ago, what some on the left call "the soldiers' revolt" helped shorten US military intervention in Southeast Asia and end mass conscription.[5] It also included a workplace organizing component, which took the form of groups like the Movement for a Democratic Military (MDM), started by former members of the Black Panther Party, and the American Servicemen's Union (ASU), formed by draftees and enlisted men during the Vietnam War. Among MDM's demands were "the right to collective bargaining" and "wages equal to the federal minimum wage." Among ASU's radical demands was the right to elect officers and reject what soldiers might deem to be illegal orders issued by their superiors.

The ASU issued membership cards, formed local chapters on military bases and on naval vessels, and published a national newspaper. Among its organizational models were already existing soldier associations in Sweden, Norway, Denmark, Belgium, West Germany, and the Netherlands (where a union of conscripts had won higher pay and reforms of the military penal code). As part of its broader repression of political dissent in the ranks of active-duty GIs, the army twice court-martialed ASU cofounder Andy Stapp while he was a private serving at Fort Still in Oklahoma during the late 1960s.

Sidestepping a Post-Vietnam Ban

Sensing an opportunity for membership growth and using a more moderate approach, the American Federation of Government Employees (AFGE)—which already represented civilian workers at the DOD and other federal agencies—voted in 1976 to amend its constitution to permit the recruitment of active-duty service members. This triggered action by Congress the following year to prevent any further threats to "good order and discipline" in the ranks. Senators Strom Thurmond (R-SC) and Joe Biden (D-DE) joined forces in a bipartisan effort to ban membership in any "military labor organization," making the penalty for that new felony five years in jail.

During Biden's term as president over forty years later, AFSCME was one of four public employee unions that obtained a Justice Department opinion that this ban on unionization by uniformed DOD employees does not apply to Guard members when operating under state control (as opposed to their recent Trump administration call-ups). After receiving that ruling, Jodi Barr, a veteran of the Connecticut National Guard and director of AFSCME District Council 4, began signing up new members like Christopher Albani.

As a member of the 103rd Civil Engineer squadron, Albani had helped his home state respond to natural disasters, public health crises, and other emergencies. During the pandemic, the squadron was involved in setting up field hospitals and distributing medical supplies. But, as Barr explained, "they were not able to bargain over necessary safety precautions, even though state employees they worked directly alongside were able to have a voice in COVID-19 testing and similar workplace protocols."

Operation Lone Star

It is often said in the field of labor relations that unions don't organize workers: bad bosses do. While the validity of that old saw is questionable, it's certainly been true of a bad boss named Greg Abbott. In 2021, with an eye toward his reelection campaign the following year, Governor Abbott launched Operation Lone Star. This expensive attempt to police the US-Mexico border with Texas Guard members ($2 billion a year) was necessary, he claimed, because the Biden administration was failing to do so with the Border Patrol.

Viewed by many as a political stunt, Abbott's sudden mobilization of ten thousand Guard members took them away, with little notice, from their regular jobs or shorter-term duty in pandemic relief efforts. Nearly one thousand applied for hardship waivers, citing family responsibilities or their civilian work as first responders, and a quarter of these requests were denied. As one Army National Guard veteran explained, "For this mission, if you had a warm pulse, they were sending you to the border. They didn't care what your issues were."

Adding insult to injury was the seemingly pointless nature of border duty. Its main initial risk was COVID-19 outbreaks among troops packed together in trailers in groups of thirty each. TSEU noted, "Members reported being assigned to twelve-hour shifts, which they spent sitting in a Humvee or walking around near an observation post, waiting for something to happen." One soldier assigned to a post near Brownsville explained, "If someone comes up, we ask them to stop and wait, we call the Border Patrol. If someone runs, we call the Border Patrol. We're basically mall cops at the border."

In the spring of 2022, Abbott's mission resulted in its first fatality. On a treacherous stretch of the Rio Grande, Spc. Bishop Evans saw several migrants struggling in the water. The twenty-two-year-old

African American from Arlington, Texas, stripped off his body armor and dove in to save them. They survived, but Evans, without proper training or equipment, was swept away while trying to do what a local mayor called a "good deed." (A year later, after TSEU lobbying of state representatives from both parties, the Texas legislature voted to establish an assistance payment for survivors of any Guard member who died while on state active duty). At least seven other deaths—suicides—were reported among soldiers whose mental health problems or financial pressures were exacerbated when they were sent to the border or awaited open-ended deployment there.

A Tuition Assistance Cut

Meanwhile, Abbott's administration sharply reduced one of the main incentives for young Texans to join the Guard. While the governor was boasting about Operation Lone Star on Fox News and fending off a Republican primary challenge from two other right-wing Republicans, he cut the budget for tuition assistance for Guard members from $3 million to $1.4 million. Previously Guard members, working full-time toward a graduate or undergraduate degree, were eligible for tuition reimbursement amounting to $4,500 per semester. That award was reduced to $1,000, and it was only paid to about 714 Guard members.

In addition, as then–TSEU organizing coordinator Missy Bolbecker explained, the state's involuntary, yearlong call-up order was highly disruptive for soldiers trying to be part-time students. Some were forced to withdraw from classes in mid-semester; others had to pay out of pocket for courses or take out loans.

When TSEU's Military Caucus was created and signed up about fifty members, Hunter Schuler's civilian day job was serving as deputy clerk for the Supreme Court of Texas. Schuler has a master's degree in statistics and was planning to enroll in a doctorate program in that field at Southern Methodist University. "I don't really have any prior experience with unions," he told us at time. "Ideologically, I think of myself as pretty conservative, leaning to the right."

In that respect, he had much in common with other "young, adult males who join the military" and "are pretty unfamiliar with unions in Texas." As a recruiter for TSEU, Schuler had to reassure some new dues-payers that the union was "not just a bunch of Democrats who want to get Beto O'Rourke elected." (However, TSEU did endorse O'Rourke's

2022 election challenge to Abbott and, during his campaign for governor, the Democratic candidate met with Military Caucus members).

One of the things that makes Guard recruitment a particular challenge is the nature of military service and the degree of management control over this group of state employees. "The Texas Military Department is not like a 9-to-5 employer," Schuler notes. "When soldiers are on state active duty, TMD controls every aspect of your life. Even if they don't do something that's obviously retaliatory, there's a lot of things they can do to make your life miserable, without overtly breaking the law or demoting you."

So it was difficult to build and sustain a durable network of union stewards and representatives. Yet, by forming a statewide solidarity network and generating much favorable publicity, Schuler and others clearly demonstrated that military-style teamwork and esprit de corps can be put to better use than the border guard duty that led them to organize. "The idea [of unionizing] started as joke," he told Military.com. "But now we have a real opportunity to make the lives of soldiers better."

More Controversial Guard Roles

In Texas and other states, the Guard has often been called out, with much popular applause, to help with disaster relief efforts or public health emergencies. On other occasions, it gets drawn into policing—the very treacherous terrain that the Trump administration has put Guard members on with increasingly frequency and insufficient training, and without the approval of Democratic governors, who are normally in charge of their own state Guard units (but prone to misusing them too).

In 1986 Minnesota, for example, the state's Democratic-Farmer-Labor (DFL) governor sent Guard members to protect strikebreakers at the Hormel meat-packing plant in Austin. Thirty-four years later, another DFL governor in the same state—future vice presidential candidate Tim Walz—deployed Guard members in Minneapolis and St. Paul during Black Lives Matter protests over the killing of George Floyd. And during the 2021 trial of former police officer Derek Chauvin, the Guard was again posted on Twin Cities street corners, along with local police, in anticipation of renewed civil unrest triggered by any acquittal of Floyd's murderer.

When CWA Local 7250 president Kieran Knutson learned that one unit, with fifty soldiers and fifteen armored vehicles, was operating out of the St. Paul Labor Center during that latter deployment, he decided, "Our union hall should have no place in those militarized efforts against the Black community, activists, and working-class people." A group of concerned trade unionists from CWA, the Minnesota Nurses Association, and United Brotherhood of Carpenters quickly gathered at the labor center to demand that the Guard members leave. According to Knutson, they spoke one-on-one with the soldiers based there, who were mainly white and from rural areas of the state.

Knutson has friends, relatives, and fellow CWA telephone workers who serve in the Guard, the reserves, or active-duty military. One such CWA member, Andrew Wolfe, was called away from his job at Frontier Communications in West Virginia to police Washington, DC, in the fall of 2025 as part Donald Trump's contested National Guard deployment there. This led to Wolfe being critically wounded and a fellow soldier being shot to death by a CIA-trained Afghan veteran relocated to the US after the Taliban victory in 2021.

When Knutson worked as a Teamster at UPS in Chicago twenty-five years ago, he recalls Vietnam veterans who belonged to IBT Local 705 strongly supporting a resolution against the war in Iraq, introduced by left-wing activists in the local. So, drawing on that experience, he and other activists urged the Guard members in the St. Paul Labor Center "to break ranks and join the antiracist movement sparked by murders of Black people by the police."

Guard officers quickly ended the fraternization by ordering that the unit's armored vehicles be loaded up and the labor center evacuated. Nevertheless, Knutson said, "We need to engage with people in the National Guard, because who they are and the role they play is different than full-time police officers and prison guards even when they are called out to defend the status quo." He even expressed the hope that unionization efforts like TSEU's might lead to "more potential solidarity between the Guard and people on the street or on strike."

A Union Without Collective Bargaining

In Texas, TSEU has long been a vehicle for solidarity among state workers of all types, and its efforts have not been not limited to legally defined "bargaining units" of the sort found in states where public sector unionists can engage in formal contract negotiations. Formed forty-two years ago, TSEU was a pioneering "non-majority union" in the open-shop environment of the South and Southwest.

TSEU members learned to build workplace organization, based on voluntary payment of membership dues and rank-and-file activism, long before the US Supreme Court, in its 2018 *Janus* decision, put all public sector unions to that new stress test. Both white-collar and blue-collar state workers of any rank can join—workers in any state department, agency, or Texas University System campus. When longtime progressive activist and writer Jim Hightower was Texas agriculture commissioner, an elected position, he was a card-carrying TSEU member. More recently the TSEU has rallied around Tom Alter, a tenured associate professor at Texas State University, who was summarily dismissed in September 2015 for comments he made during an online socialist meeting. The labor historian was targeted by a right-wing website, Texas Scorecard, which claims to provides "real news for real Texans" and said that he had called for "the violent overthrow of the U.S. government."[6]

Alter's case was yet another reminder of the importance of bringing all types of workers together under the same roof and making an injury to one an injury to all. As the late Jim Branson, a longtime left activist and much beloved TSEU lead organizer, once explained:

> We have a voice on the job because we are an active and growing movement that puts a lot of emphasis on organizing. We have lots of agency caucuses, made up of union activists, who meet regularly to formulate goals and plan actions for winning those goals. From time to time, members of the caucus will meet with agency heads to discuss our goals, and when the legislature is in session, caucus members will speak directly to lawmakers.... If a united group of workers act like a union, they can have a voice on the job. It's not easy, but it can be done.

18

Defending, Not Defunding, Public Service Jobs

One of the biggest employers of veterans is the now 250-year-old US Postal Service (USPS), which delivers mail to 163 million homes and businesses.[1] The USPS workforce is one-fifth Black, employs more than 110,000 veterans (many of them people of color), and counts military service as prior employment. As William Burrus, the first Black president of the American Postal Workers Union (APWU) has pointed out, "the post office has permitted millions of African Americans to better themselves" in jobs with good benefits and job security. In 2025, the average annual salary for a postal worker ranged from $42,000 to $72,000, depending on job title, location, and level of experience.

Keith Combs, president of APWU's fifteen-hundred-member Detroit local, comes from a military family and joined the Postal Service after serving as a marine. In his view, "military values like hard work, showing up on time, and taking pride in your work set you up perfectly for postal jobs." In addition to the preferential hiring treatment veterans get when they apply, veterans who are disabled, like many Combs works with in Detroit, are eligible for Wounded Warriors Leave. "This is separate from regular USPS sick leave and enables vets with a VA disability rating of 30 percent or more to take time off, at full pay, to undergo medical treatment for a service-related condition."

After Donald Trump's electoral college victory in 2016, Combs and other postal union activists faced an administration eager to reduce staff and services through automation and outsourcing. Republicans' ultimate goal was to force the agency into bankruptcy and then sell it off, in pieces, to private corporations, thereby enriching investor-owned businesses at the expense of the public and forcing customers to rely on FedEx or UPS. As Combs warned at the time: "They want to eliminate our collective bargaining rights, which would jeopardize all those benefits we've won for veterans and other employees. They also want to cut delivery days, close local post offices, and raise prices, which would hurt customers." Such cuts would disrupt census taking and mail ballot voting (viewed as favorable to Democrats).

For the next four years, and into the Biden administration, the APWU, the National Association of Letter Carriers, and their community allies waged major defensive battles against Louis DeJoy. A conservative businessman from North Carolina worth $110 million, DeJoy left his logistics company to become postmaster general after donating millions to Trump and other right-wing Republicans.

Save the Post Office Coalition

Coming together as the Save the Post Office Coalition, members of three hundred advocacy groups mounted successful protests against DeJoy's attempt to cut service and slow mail delivery in 2020, a presidential election year. After Democrats regained control of the White House and the Senate, Congress passed the Postal Service Reform Act, which put the agency on a sounder financial footing. Since the USPS is formally independent of the executive branch, its top official serves at the pleasure of a nine-member board of governors and cannot be sacked by the president like a cabinet member.

Despite mounting calls for DeJoy's resignation, he remained postmaster general throughout the presidency of Joe Biden, who moved too slowly with new appointments to create a board majority willing to fire the Trump administration holdover.[2] This gave DeJoy plenty of time to develop and roll out a ten-year consolidation plan calling for a massive change in mail sorting and delivery that would initially impact two hundred facilities nationwide.

Under DeJoy's plan, instead of sorting mail in neighborhood post offices, tens of thousands of mail carriers are now driving to large centralized regional sorting centers, located far away from their delivery routes. Labor critics of this reorganization pointed out that bad working conditions, like understaffing and long hours, were already causing many letter carriers to take early retirement. The retention rate for new hires is 30 percent, a number likely to drop if the job soon entails longer and more costly commutes.

Post offices losing their "back-end" delivery units have fewer clerks and shorter retail hours. So they end up becoming candidates for closure, helping DeJoy meet his announced goal of reducing the USPS workforce by fifty thousand. In response to this threat, an activist network called Communities and Postal Workers United urged all post office customers to sign protest petitions, contact their members of Congress, and speak out at a USPS Board of Governors meeting, stressing the adverse economic impact it would have on postal workers and the communities they serve, particularly in rural areas.

Back to the Future?

Two months after Trump began his second term as president, this and many other battles resumed, with renewed intensity. APWU and NALC mobilized members in five hundred locations for two separate days of action in March 2025. A month later, the cause of saving the postal service was embraced by a national coalition of organizations—including MoveOn, Indivisible, 50501, and others—that turned out millions of people for "Hands Off" protests directed at Elon Musk and his Department of Government Efficiency (DOGE).

The already existing Save the Post Office Coalition swung into action by collecting two hundred thousand signatures on a petition against Trump's second-term appointees to the USPS Board of Governors, which helped trigger the withdrawal of their nominations. Meanwhile, having lost the confidence of the man in the White House who appointed him, DeJoy stepped down. A DOGE-inspired early retirement offer, directed at APWU bargaining unit members, drew ten thousand volunteers, which did help DeJoy reduce headcount on his way out the door.

Trump's nominee for new postmaster general was David Steiner, a FedEx board member and former CEO of Waste Management. In the latter role, he boasted about how he cut in half the number of workers represented by the Teamsters and other unions.[3] NALC president Brian Renfroe said Steiner's appointment wasn't just a conflict of interest: "It's an aggressive step toward handing America's mail system over to corporate interests. Private shippers have been waiting to get USPS out of parcel delivery for years. Steiner's selection is an open invitation to do just that." APWU president Mark Dimondstein likened Steiner's new role to hiring a "fox to guard the hen house."[4]

A few months later, in the fall of 2025, Dimondstein retired as president and passed the torch, after a membership vote, to Jonathan

Smith, APWU's longtime New York City leader, who is "totally against the ten-year plan" left behind by DeJoy. For years, Dimondstein had barnstormed around the country, warning APWU members that privatizers of any popular public service had to pursue that goal, step by step, with as much stealth as possible. Their game plan always employed what he called "the Four Ds." Step one: Defund the service involved, to begin its slow financial strangulation; then Degrade the service so that people who can afford private sector alternatives choose them instead; next, Demonize the workers who provide the service for its shortcomings; and finally Dismantle and privatize the service.

On the anniversary of D-Day in 2025, when thousands of veterans in in the labor movement" rallied in Washington, under the banner of the national AFL-CIO, Dimondstein, a longtime dissident on its executive council, was not a speaker. But his prescient warning about how privatization plays out—not all at once but instead incrementally, at various federal agencies—was echoed by other officials on the platform, some of whom began studying the Trump playbook rather late in the game.

19

Labor and Vets, Unite and Fight

June 6 of Donald Trump's first year back in the White House, after his four-year exile in Florida, was a pretty irresistible date for scheduling a labor rally about veterans' issues. Eighty-one years before, US soldiers and their allies stormed ashore in Normandy, establishing a critical beachhead in the military campaign to defeat Adolf Hitler and fascism.

In the aftermath of World War II, hundreds of thousands of injured veterans were treated back home in a nationwide network of hospitals run by the federal government. During the decades that followed, the VA-run Veterans Health Administration (VHA) had its ups and downs. These were invariably dependent on whether Congress and the White House—after launching later, much less popular wars did sufficient planning for the resulting postwar increase in VA patients and properly funded their care.

During Trump's first term, a bipartisan coalition in Congress made the corporate donor–influenced decision to double down on Barack Obama's embrace of more healthcare "choice" for post-9/11 veterans. After passage of the VA MISSION Act of 2018, Trump's second VA secretary, Robert Wilkie—a right-wing southern Republican—declared that partial privatization of the VA would produce "more patient satisfaction and predictability, more efficiency for our clinicians, and better value for taxpayers." Using D-Day as a protest peg, a few vets and their caregivers began to challenge this outsourcing trend back in 2019. Members of the American Federation of Government Employees, National Nurses United, and Veterans for Peace organized protests on a "National Day to Save the VA."

Their collective turnout for rallies, informational picketing, and press conferences in about a dozen locations would have been much larger if the AFL-CIO, major veterans' organizations, or any big-name politicians had bothered to endorse these or show up. Few regarded privatization as a major threat at the time.

A Renewed Assault

Trump's second-term assault on every public service provided by federal workers—along with their jobs and bargaining rights—was a big wake-up call for some of those MIA five years before. On the anniversary of D-Day in 2025, thousands of demonstrators gathered on the Mall in Washington, DC, under the Unite for Veterans/Unite for America banner. The event was sponsored by the Union Veterans Council of the national AFL-CIO and the Chamberlain Network, a nonprofit that hoped the event and others like it around the country would "encourage the administration to make the right decisions for veterans."

Veterans, including some belonging to AFGE, NNU, National Federation of Federal Employees, and other unions, heard speeches from past or present service members in Congress like Sen. Tammy Duckworth (D-IL) and former Republican House member Adam Kinzinger from Illinois, who became a major critic of Trump during Trump's first term. Cecil Roberts, the Vietnam vet who went on to become president of the UMWA also spoke.

Many more protesters participated in 225 simultaneous actions in other locations around the country, including in vet-heavy red states like Alaska, Alabama, Florida, Georgia, North Carolina, Idaho, Kansas, and Kentucky. Some "watch parties," organized for real-time viewing of the DC event, were held in local union halls to highlight the labor-vet overlap. The grassroots political organization Indivisible was a local partner as well.

The livestream from DC was greatly enlivened by the Dropkick Murphys, the Celtic punk rockers from Boston that Union Veterans Council director William Attig had regularly listened to while on active duty as an eighteen-year-old marine. This prolabor band got wild applause after performing a new release well suited to the occasion. Its chorus, belted out by lead singer Ken Casey, asked: "Who'll stand with us? / Don't tell us everything is fine / Who'll stand with us? / Because this treatment is a crime."

Everything Is Fine?

In the run-up to the event on the anniversary of D-Day, Trump's new

VA secretary, Doug Collins—like Robert Wilkie before him—had been assuring vets and their organizations that everything was going to be fine, despite his planned elimination of more than eighty thousand VA jobs by the end of the year.

One speaker who challenged Collins directly was forty-three-year-old Matt Stevenson, a primary care physician at the VA Medical Center in Palo Alto. Making it clear he was speaking in a personal capacity, Stevenson lauded the VA as "a mission-driven, patient-centered, cost-effective, integrated American health care system ... which delivers higher-quality care at lower cost than any other system in the country."

But then he ticked off all the "worrisome signs of a renewed attempt to dismantle and privatize the VA." According to Stevenson, the DOGE-led assault on his employer had left VA staff members feeling "disparaged, bullied and intimidated." He argued that "those who would take this public treasure—built over generations, by many hands, working long nights in dark hospitals—and sell it off in the name of choice or modernization or efficiency or political gain" could be stopped if VA defenders came together "around a shared vision."

A few months later, Stevenson enlisted 170 coworkers to join him in signing a letter to Collins and Congress—some publicly and others anonymously—warning them that if VA facilities were closed, vets around the country would be "forced into costlier, often overburdened community health systems ill-equipped to meet their specialized needs."[1]

Caregivers Quitting

One of the things that inspired some veterans to attend events was learning that their doctors, nurses, or therapists were quitting due to deteriorating workplace conditions under Collins. David Magnus, a navy veteran from Pittsburgh, told the *Guardian* that he had traveled to DC because his trusted provider revealed her decision to leave the VHA during a recent mental health appointment. Similar stories were shared on the other side of the country, outside the Veterans Memorial Building in San Rafael, California. Katie Weber-Linhart, a disabled army veteran, lamented the recent resignation of a popular therapist who treated many vets at an outpatient clinic in Ukiah, in rural Mendocino County.

Weber-Linhar now helps a retired VHA physician hold a weekly protest, attended by patients, family members, and local union members, at a VA outpatient clinic in Santa Rosa, in Sonoma County. She and others definitely ignored any messaging from inside the Beltway about how Unite for Veterans was not supposed to be "an anti-Trump event or a partisan protest."

Handmade placards in San Raphael included one dissing DOGE as a bunch of "Douchebag Oligarchs Grabbing Everything" and others identifying the sign holder as a "Veteran Against Trump" and critic of "Trump's America" because of its "Cages for Kids, Cuts for Vets." Ernie Bergman, a cancer survivor and seventy-seven-year-old leader of Vietnam Veterans of America in Marin County, blasted "this current government" for trying to take money away from medical research and innovative treatment that saved his life.

VSOs Were MIA

Iraq combat veteran Kristofer Goldsmith, a former staffer for the Vietnam Veterans of America turned podcaster and founder of Task Force Butler, a "veteran-led nonprofit dedicated to upholding democratic values and countering the rise of authoritarianism," said he was thrilled that so many D-Day event participants were not the usual suspects. He told us: "I had people come up into me who had flown to DC from every part of the country who had never been at a protest before but who wanted to be part of something historic."

Goldsmith was not happy that some major inside-the-Beltway players were missing—namely, representatives of the "big six" veteran service organizations (VSOs). Just a few months earlier, he had been much encouraged when the national commander of the Veterans of Foreign Wars (VFW) urged his 1.4 million members to "march forth" to Capitol Hill and "stop the bleeding" at the VA. As a life member of the VFW but a past critic of overly cautious and conservative VSO behavior, Goldsmith viewed this development as "nothing short of extraordinary."

On the day of the event, however, the VFW, American Legion, and other major VSOs did not endorse the rally or turn out for it. According to Goldsmith, there were VSO headquarters staff members present "in a personal capacity," but there was no official representation from the "big six." In his view, "[If the big VSOs] were making enough noise and standing up to the cuts in a way that reflects the urgency of the moment, they would have been on the stage with us."

Will Attig, the Union Veterans Council leader and a key rally organizer who served in both Iraq and Afghanistan before joining a plumbers and pipefitters local in Illinois, said that rally organizers had worked with the VSOs "behind the scenes." The result was a "very exciting event that shows what can happen when veterans come together around their issues," locally and nationally.

James Jones, a Gulf War veteran from Boone, North Carolina, traveled to DC because he wanted legislators to understand how important the VA has been to veterans like himself. "I lost friends during the Gulf War, and I've dealt with health issues because of exposure to ... you name it," Jones said, "airborne toxins, oil well fire smoke, burn pits, depleted uranium residue. I've been a VA patient since 1993, and the VA has been beneficial to me because they understand PTSD, military trauma, and everything else."

Jones now works for the National Park Service, belongs to AFGE, and has been an outspoken member of the Labor Notes–assisted Federal Unionists Network. He's urging all his friends who are vets, his fellow VA patients, and other federal workers to start "going to rallies, and join these groups that are really fighting back. The government needs to keep the promise it made to veterans. We served our country, and now they're breaking their promise to take care of us. We can't accept that."

PART V

WHY THE VA IS WORTH SAVING

In part 3 of this book, readers learned that promises made in Washington, DC, to provide high-quality care for hundreds of thousands of new VA patients—who suffered from burn pit exposure during post-9/11 wars in the Middle East—won't be fulfilled if there is further bipartisan complicity with VA privatization.

As noted in part 4, the Capitol Hill push for VA outsourcing has a lot in common with business-backed efforts to privatize the US Postal Service. If the latter efforts succeed, there will be a similarly adverse impact on an equivalent number of vets who found good union jobs serving their communities as mail sorters, deliverers, and postal clerks.

A much bigger objective for corporate America (and its friends in both major parties) is further privatization of the national health insurance that has covered all senior citizens in the United States since 1965. This bipartisan betrayal of an overlapping slice of the US population three times larger than former service members has little popular support. It can be thwarted—but only if major unions, veterans' organizations, the single-payer movement, and their smaller number of political allies on Capitol Hill start connecting the dots.

Right-wing ideologues, reliably serving their paymasters in the billionaire class, will always peddle the illusion that a Medicare Advantage plan or a patient referral outside the VA is a far better deal than public provision in its original form—particularly if the latter has already been undermined by incremental privatization. The reality on the ground, as reported here, is actually quite different.

20

Parallel Privatization Threats

When powerful private interests obtain new profit-making opportunities feeding off public programs, it becomes very hard to reverse the process.[1] The parallel struggles over corporate profiteering that have undermined federally funded healthcare for sixty-two million seniors and nine million military veterans illustrate the political challenges involved—for labor, healthcare reformers, and the broader left. At stake in both anti-privatization fights is the future of existing single-payer systems as a working model for future tax-supported medical coverage for all Americans.

If the ongoing assault on traditional Medicare and the public healthcare system operated by the Department of Veterans Affairs is successful, "Medicare for All" will become much harder to achieve, if not impossible. And our best example of real "socialized medicine" in the United States, the VA, will be defunded, discredited, and dismantled as well.

Corporate Democrats and conservative Republicans in Congress and policymakers in the Bush, Obama, Trump, Biden, and now second Trump administrations have brought these political threats to the tipping point. To make matters worse, some of the advocacy organizations ostensibly devoted to the best interests of constituencies adversely affected by privatization are now embracing the trend instead of mobilizing against it.

Among those letting their members down are some major public sector unions, retiree organizations, and VSOs like the American Legion and Veterans of Foreign Wars, which in the past have been stronger defenders of the VA.

For single-payer activists in the labor movement, this feels like déjà vu. Past disagreements between unions, over the desirability of replacing job-based medical coverage for active workers with national health insurance, now take the form of internal disputes between some unions and their own retirees over whether the latter should be herded into private insurer-run Medicare Advantage plans, rather than the more cost-effective traditional Medicare coverage they prefer.

Organized labor's mistaken embrace of Medicare Advantage plans has helped the healthcare industry convince millions of consumers that they will save money and get additional benefits if they switch to them.

Creating Market Competition?

Creating "market competition" for Medicare patients or those getting direct care at the VA has been a corporate-backed, bipartisan project that got its greatest boost under the presidencies of George W. Bush and Donald Trump. When Democrats like Barack Obama or Joe Biden seek the White House, they may criticize the policies of their Republican predecessors or rivals, but once elected they don't diverge much from them.

For example, during a 2008 presidential debate, Obama sharply disagreed with Sen. John McCain over the merits of the "Medicare Modernization Act of 2003." McCain strongly applauded this Bush initiative; his Democratic Party opponent denounced partial privatization as a costly and wasteful scheme, not beneficial to taxpayers or Medicare recipients. But once in office, Obama forgot about his debate pledge to end Medicare Advantage. He focused instead on getting the Affordable Care Act (ACA) passed, albeit without any "public option" that would have created unwanted competition for the private insurers benefiting from the ACA's expansion of federally subsidized healthcare coverage.

By the end of Obama's eight years in the White House, Medicare Advantage plans had greater market share than ever before. New Trump administration appointees then gave them a further boost. "Despite having overhead costs almost seven times that of traditional Medicare (13.7 percent versus two percent), Medicare Advantage plans have grown rapidly," *The Nation* reported in 2019. "They now cover more than one-third of Medicare beneficiaries, up from thirteen percent in 2005."

When Joe Biden got elected in 2020, he stayed on the same path as the first Trump administration. The Centers for Medicare and Medicaid Services (CMS) continued to facilitate the movement of millions of Medicare beneficiaries "into mostly commercial, for-profit plans, called Direct Contracting Entities (DCE)," that would "further waste taxpayer money" and "fully privatize Medicare," according to Physicians for a National Health Program (PNHP).

Like Obama before him, Biden failed to reestablish the primacy of Medicare in its original form. Instead, he replaced Trump's DCE scheme with what PNHP called "a nearly identical program, called ACO REACH." Influenced by an industry-backed lobbying and advertising blitz, Biden opted for a three-year phase of minor Medicare Advantage reforms, which failed to "stop price gouging by insurance companies," according to House Progressive Caucus leader Pramila Jayapal (D-OR).

"It's now clear," Jayapal said, "that Medicare Advantage is simply a profiteering venture that hurts patient care. Without a complete overhaul, it will be impossible to stop bad actors. These plans have spent years scamming seniors and overcharging the government to pad their own profits." But, by the time Biden left office, nearly thirty-one million Americans—about half of all Medicare recipients—were covered by MA plans.

When Trump returned to power in January 2025, he put Dr. Mehmet Oz, the former TV doctor and failed Republican Senate candidate in Pennsylvania, in charge of the CMS. Oz strongly favors Medicare Advantage (MA) over traditional Medicare; soon after he was confirmed by the Senate, CMS authorized a $25 billion increase in 2026 federal spending on MA plans, which two years earlier already cost more than $83 billion annually. From 2007 to 2023, privatized Medicare coverage has cost $600 billion, and it is on track to require $1 trillion in spending over the next decade.

Soon after his confirmation, Oz launched what the *New York Times* described as a "pilot program that may pave the way for traditional Medicare to adopt some of the most unpopular practices of private insurers," offering MA coverage. In six states, seniors who have not switched to MA plans will be forced to get more prior authorization for various treatments—which will require a review of their medical records by private companies using artificial intelligence!

As the *Times* noted, "the A.I. companies selected to oversee the program would have a strong financial incentive to deny claims" because CMS "plans to pay them a share of the savings generated from rejections." According to one former senior CMS official, "we are taking the most unpopular part of Medicare Advantage and applying it to traditional Medicare."

A Bipartisan Project

Incremental privatization of the VA has been implemented in much the same fashion during an overlapping twenty-year time frame. John McCain and Mitt Romney, the Republican candidates defeated by Obama in 2012, both favored a Cato Institute plan to replace VA-delivered care with vouchers that veterans could take to any private doctor or hospital, who would then get Medicare-style reimbursement from the government.

In pursuit of this goal, McCain insisted that any big Obama administration increase in funding and staffing for VA direct care be accompanied by an experiment in outsourcing treatment in places where VA wait times for appointments were too long. (The VA had always referred patients outside its own system, based on medical need, when in-house care was not available.)

The resulting compromise with McCain in 2014—brokered with then Veterans' Affairs Committee chair Bernie Sanders—resulted in passage of the Veterans Choice Act, which did provide much-needed funding for VA's national network of 171 medical centers and 1,112 outpatient sites. But the Choice Act also opened the door for diverting billions of dollars from the VA's direct care budget to pay private doctors and for-profit hospitals to treat veterans at greater cost and often with less effectiveness.

When Choice Act provisions related to outsourcing were due to expire, there was no Democrat in the White House, and the Senate Veterans' Affairs Committee was chaired by Jon Tester (D-MT), who was not a strong VA defender like Sanders.

Impact of the VA MISSION Act

Tester worked with Republican allies and fellow corporate Democrats to hand Donald Trump one of his biggest bipartisan victories—the VA MISSION Act of 2018. In the House, only seventy Democrats, including later vice presidential candidate Tim Walz, voted against it. In the Senate, only four members joined Sanders in opposition. The Senator from Vermont warned that the MISSION Act would lead to "the draining, year after year, of much-needed resources from the VA," setting the stage for hospital closings and disruption of a highly integrated system of coordinated care.

In June 2022, VA secretary Denis McDonough, a former Obama White House chief of staff, confirmed that outsourcing was now costing his agency more than $30 billion a year, nearly one-third of the VA's entire direct care budget. Its growth rate—a 7 percent increase over the previous fiscal year—was not sustainable. It would soon result in nearly half of all veterans' care being delivered outside their own system, a tipping point, according to McDonough, that would seriously "harm the VA's training, research, and emergency preparedness missions."

Nevertheless, McDonough continued to insist, in the face of all available evidence, that the nation's largest public healthcare system and its outside contractors were engaged in a "healthy competition to be the best, most accessible, highest quality option" for patients. Throughout his four years in office, he never used his administrative rulemaking authority to revise the Trump-era patient referral rules, promulgated under his Republican predecessor, that opened the floodgates for outsourcing.

Medicare Disadvantage Plans

Healthcare researchers in labor and the single-payer movement have understandably paid more attention to the adverse impact of privatizing a program covering a much larger patient population. As more seniors ended up in what critics dubbed "Medicare Disadvantage" plans, their downside became the subject of much investigative reporting in outlets like *The Lever.*

In his series of articles there, former Communications Workers of America researcher Matthew Cunningham-Cook reminded readers that the Medicare system was set up to make set payments directly to healthcare providers. It "was founded on the principle that seniors should get the care they need without an insurer middleman." In contrast, MA plans utilize "provider networks that force patients to choose health care providers selected by the insurance company, or else they face potentially enormous financial penalties."

As Cunningham-Cook documented, through profiles of individual patients these "private insurers have an inherent incentive to deny care. The less medical attention they provide beneficiaries, the more government money they can pocket as profits."

As a cost control measure, MA plans require preauthorization for many services. A February 2023 study by the Kaiser Family Foundation found that two million prior authorization requests had been denied by such plans in 2021, more than triple the denials just two years earlier. A report by the Department of Health and Human Services' own inspector general found that MA plans had wrongly denied 1.5 million payment claims—18 percent of the total claims—in a single year, 2019.

Traditional Medicare only covers about 80 percent of care costs. So nearly all Medicare patients purchase "Medigap" coverage—or have such supplementary coverage on a group basis, often as union retirees. As Cunningham-Cook reports, due to a loophole in federal law, Medigap plan providers in most states "are allowed to reject patients or discriminate against them by charging them far higher premiums based on preexisting conditions after they have elected for a Medicare Advantage plan.... So once a patient enters the Medicare Advantage system, they typically cannot afford to leave."

MA providers have gained market share because their plans supposedly offer more choice—in the form of additional benefits like dental check-ups or gym memberships. In reality, as one healthcare economist told the *New York Times* in 2023, "Medicare Advantage ... really takes away choice."

VA Coverage Is Not Insurance

The VA system—before the Choice and MISSION Acts—was a true outlier in US healthcare, providing high-quality care to a patient population predominantly poor and working-class. Like caregivers employed by the National Health Service in Britain, VA doctors, nurses, therapists, and other professional and nonprofessional staff are salaried and mission-driven. They don't work for investor-owned hospital chains or medical practices that get reimbursed by private insurers, Medicare, or Medicaid on a "fee-for-service" basis, which often leads to fragmented and uncoordinated care.

Biden administration reports to Congress confirmed what many independent studies have long documented: "VA direct care has been consistently shown to outperform most private sector hospitals in core measures of inpatient quality of care." According to Biden's VA secretary, veterans "trust the VA to provide equal or better care than the community" and "find accessing direct care easier than accessing community care." Yet, according to McDonough, some patients steered outside the VA by MISSION Act–mandated outsourcing "are driving [farther] or waiting longer for that care than they would if the VA provided that care.... Veterans are also experiencing fragmentation of care, duplicative testing, and unnecessary and improper billing from community providers."

Worst of all, incremental privatization has forced VA staffers who want to be caregivers into new and unwanted roles as managers of 1.7 million outside vendors. These non-VA providers are eager to be paid promptly but slow to provide documentation of their services or share patient information necessary for proper coordination and integration of outside and inside care.

Same Private Firms Profiting

Some VA contractors have definitely engaged in fraudulent billing practices, according to the agency's Office of the Inspector General (OIG). In 2020, the VA was billed for nearly $80 million in medical services that were never actually provided or whose cost was inflated through the fraudulent billing practice known as "upcoding."

The VA has also paid billions to two private insurance companies, TriWest and Optum, the latter a subsidiary of UnitedHealth Group, to serve as third-party administrators of its MISSION Act–mandated network of outside providers. When TriWest and another private insurer, Health Net, served as the third-party administrators for the predecessor program created by the Choice Act, the OIG found that the two companies were responsible for improper billing of their own.

Health Net, owned by a Medicare Advantage plan provider called Centene, had to repay the federal government nearly $100 million. TriWest had to return nearly $180 million because of its overcharging, yet that didn't stop Trump appointees, then Biden's, and now Trump's again, from continuing to use the firm as an outsourcing network administrator.

Medicare Advantage plans engage in similar billing fraud and financial abuse on a much larger scale. Their backers include firms like UnitedHealth, an insurer worth $450 billion, which is already feeding at the VA privatization trough. UnitedHealth made more than $14 billion in profits in 2022, while the other three-largest for-profit Medicare Advantage insurers earned an additional $10 billion. (Among the large stock-holdings Dr. Oz agreed to sell in order to become director of CMS under Trump II was $600,000 worth of UnitedHealth shares.)

According to a Kaiser Family Foundation study, these firms generate twice as much gross profit from their Advantage plan business as from their sale of other types of insurance. In 2022, Humana generated more than 80 percent of its revenue from five million Medicare Advantage customers. Yet, as the *Times* reported: "Eight of the ten biggest Medicare Advantage insurers—representing more than two-thirds of the market—have submitted inflated bills, according to federal audits. And four of the five largest players—UnitedHealth, Humana, Elevance Health, and Kaiser Permanente—have faced federal lawsuits alleging that efforts to overdiagnose their customers crossed the line into fraud."

In 2020, this "upcoding" drained $12 billion from the Medicare trust fund. According to PNHP's analysis of 2022 spending on Medicare Advantage plans, overbilling now costs US taxpayers between $88 billion and $140 billion each year. Even the sum at the low end of that estimate is large enough to cover the one-year cost of adding dental, hearing, and vision benefits to traditional Medicare as a benefit improvement for all Americans over sixty-five.

Meanwhile, since many of the nine million veterans receiving VA care are old enough to be Medicare-eligible, MA plan providers like those listed above benefit from what one *Health Affairs* study called "substantial, duplicative wasteful spending" by the federal government. This occurs when veterans who primarily rely on the VA for their care enroll in MA plans, as more are being encouraged to do. Their private insurers then collect full capitated payments, regardless of whether or not these new enrollees actually use any Medicare-covered services. This kind of billing cost the CMS an estimated $1.3 billion in 2020—and it will be more in the future if this rip-off is not ended.

Given the political spending of big healthcare insurers, it's no surprise that Medicare Advantage has a big bipartisan fan club in Congress. During the Biden administration, 80 percent of all House members signed a letter putting the White House on notice that they were "ready to protect the program from policies that would undermine it"—despite little action by Biden to better regulate MA plans.

Labor and Consumer Group Complicity

Shockingly, the industry's bamboozling of seniors and raids on the US Treasury have been aided and abetted by consumer and labor groups that partner with Medicare Advantage plan providers and share in their profits.

The biggest offender is the AARP (formerly known as the American

Association of Retired Persons), which claims to have thirty-eight million dues-paying members. In 2021, as a result of its lucrative partnerships with UnitedHealth and other for-profit firms, the AARP collected $814 million in "royalties"—an amount twice its dues revenue that year. Even the national AFL-CIO began advertising its own "Medicare Advantage group plans ... available exclusively to retired union members" via the "comprehensive coverage" provided by Anthem, a giant private insurer. Like the AARP, the Alliance for Retired Americans, a much smaller retiree group linked to the AFL-CIO, scrupulously avoided any public criticism of MA plans.

Among national veterans' organizations, a similar betrayal of the interests of members dependent on VA care has occurred over the past decade, as some of these groups have become more dependent on corporate largesse. Veteran service organizations—including the American Legion, Veterans of Foreign Wars, AMVETS, and Iraq and Afghanistan Veterans of America (IAVA)—welcomed the Choice Act of 2014. Four years later, despite mounting evidence that outsourcing was undermining the VA, they backed the even more pro-privatization MISSION Act of 2018.

Under the Biden and second Trump administrations, both the Legion and VFW have continued to support Republican-backed bills that would force the VA to divert an even bigger share of its $128 billion annual healthcare budget from direct care to Medicare-style reimbursement of private sector doctors and hospitals. Officially, of course, neither old-line VSO favors privatization. In fact, one of them, the Legion, commissioned one of us (Suzanne) to coauthor a 2017 report called "VA Health Care: A System Worth Saving," which is still available on the national organization's website.

As we documented in *Our Veterans*, the creeping "corporatization of veterans affairs" was best personified by IAVA. In its early years, the group supplemented its limited income from membership dues with donations from wealthy Wall Street types and firms like TriWest and Cerner Corporation, the recipient of a VA-related non-bid contract worth $16 billion. Another IAVA benefactor was Cigna, the giant private insurer whose foundation received one of the IAVA annual Corporate Leadership Awards. Other past IAVA donors include the Pharmaceutical Research and Manufacturers of America and several of its affiliated biotechnology firms.

Not to be outdone by IAVA, AMVETS has partnered with Humana, the nation's third-largest for-profit insurer. Both Cigna and Humana have been implicated in Medicare Advantage abuses.

A Sell-Out of Single Payer

The AFL-CIO's embrace of Medicare Advantage has aroused the ire of longtime single-payer activists and a growing number of central labor bodies. Ed Grystar, a former labor council president in western Pennsylvania and healthcare union contract negotiator, is one of many "Medicare for All" advocates who have been forced to wage a defensive fight on behalf of Medicare, as championed by the AFL-CIO in the mid 1960s. Says Grystar: "Even as labor negotiations continue to be inhibited by rising healthcare costs, labor refuses to expose the corruption and waste within the ongoing privatization of Medicare, harming its members, reducing union credibility, and contributing to the downward spiral of health benefits for all." That's why, he reports, state and local labor federations in New York, Vermont, Maine, Washington, Kentucky, Texas, and California have passed resolutions or supported petitions opposing the privatization of Medicare coverage.

Unfortunately, even AFGE—the largest federal employee union and most active campaigner against VA privatization—bought into the AFL-CIO's promotion of a "Member Benefit Medicare Advantage" plan. This contradictory union stance greatly angered Robert Bonner and Colleen Evans, two retired VA nurses and former AFGE local presidents in Pittsburgh. In an open letter to AFGE president Everett Kelley and other national executive board members, they urged the union to stop promoting Medicare Advantage plan enrollment. "The waste, fraud, and corruption of the insurance industry are well documented," Bonner and Evans wrote. "These are the same forces seeking privatization of the VA and not an entity we should embrace. As a public employee union, we should consistently defend and promote the growth of the public sector." They received no response from AFGE headquarters.

The Labor Campaign for Single Payer (LCSP) has sounded the alarm as well and urged its affiliates to remind AFL-CIO president Liz Schuler and President Biden that "Medicare provides bedrock coverage for retired and disabled union members and serves as a template for fulfilling labor's historic commitment to making healthcare a right for everyone." But as Mark Dudzic, a former OCAW activist and LCSP cofounder, warns, "allowing insurance companies and hedge fund managers to be the gatekeepers for retiree healthcare is a recipe for disaster."

In April 2025, the LCSP issued an invaluable guide titled *Medicare Advantage: What Union Leaders Need to Know*. It warned union members that "even the best union-negotiated MA plans" are still based on a "business model that requires limiting access to care—through utilization of networks and prior authorization—to make a profit."[2]

Rank-and-File Pushback

Some smaller unions have been heeded the LCSP's advice, while other much bigger labor organizations have not, much to the anger and frustration of their retired members. A new direct affiliate of the national AFL-CIO—the Vermont State Employees Association (VSEA)—waged a model campaign in 2023 against Republican governor Phil Scott's unilateral attempt to steer ten thousand retired state workers into MA plans. Scott claimed that Vermont taxpayers and retired state government workers would together save $9 million a year, while keeping the same level of coverage and paying smaller Medigap policy premiums.

By educating and mobilizing active and retired members, and enlisting support from a Democratic-controlled state legislature, the VSEA succeeded in blocking Scott's move. "We want to maintain collective bargaining [over this issue] and not privatize this benefit to enrich an industry that is renowned for denying healthcare services to people when they need them the most," said VSEA executive director Steve Howard.

In New York City, when public sector union leaders began parroting a Republican governor's claims about Medicare Advantage, Marianne Pizzitola, a former New York Fire Department emergency medical services staffer, helped organize Public Service Retirees. Its supporters include retired members of AFSCME District Council 37, the United Federation of Teachers, and other municipal unions willing to give up what *Labor Notes* called "the best retiree health coverage in the country."

Their cross-union formation has waged a four-year fight to keep 250,000 pensioners out of a for-profit Medicare Advantage plan run by Aetna. In the course of this ongoing struggle, hundreds of retirees have filed lawsuits, marched and protested, made creative use of social media, enlisted City Council allies, and targeted scandal-scarred New York City mayor Eric Adams, a major promoter of Medicare Advantage.

Even after Adams won a state higher court decision giving him the green light to proceed with that switch, he suddenly announced—during his doomed 2025 reelection campaign—that he had found "other ways" to address skyrocketing retiree healthcare costs. In November 2025, voters replaced Adams with Zohran Mamdani, a state senator and Democratic Socialists of America member who pledged to "reject Medicare Advantage" and work with labor opponents of "for-profit healthcare."

A Not-So-Hidden Agenda

Medicare and the VA healthcare system have been partially privatized under the guise of saving money and giving seniors and military veterans more "choice"—a cruel illusion for VA patients explored further in the next chapter. The corporate interests and right-wing politicians that favor privatization of both have a not-so-hidden agenda, which is to undermine both of these tax-supported programs. By disrupting the federal government's ability to provide direct care to nine million vets or public insurance coverage for sixty-two million Americans in a cost-effective manner, they hope to discredit "government-run healthcare" in any form.

As Paul Sullivan, a Gulf War combat veteran and former deputy secretary of the California Department of Veterans Affairs, points out, "The forces against quality healthcare for all Americans know that a fully funded and staffed VA would set a shining example for the national healthcare they bitterly oppose." Likewise, a well-run Medicare program—not yet saddled with unnecessary costs and tainted by private insurer involvement—was long our best advertisement for "Medicare for All."

Defenders of the VA and traditional Medicare now face an even bigger fight to prevent either form of single-payer healthcare from suffering further—and possibly fatal—damage during the second Trump administration.

21

The Illusion of Choice

At his confirmation hearing in January 2025, Secretary of Veterans Affairs Doug Collins, a former Republican congressman from Georgia, assured the Senate Committee on Veterans' Affairs that he would protect the specialized, high-quality medical care available in the nation's largest and only truly integrated public healthcare system.[1] But Collins, a chaplain in the Air Force Reserve, also explained that President Trump wanted to make it "easier for veterans to get their health care when and where it's most convenient for them," by giving them greater choice between in-house and outsourced care. Republicans in Congress similarly assert that veterans can easily find faster and even better treatment outside the VA.

These claims assume that the nation's non-VA hospitals, primary care providers, specialty physicians, and mental health therapists—currently handling a patient load of 330 million other Americans—are ready and able to treat 9 million veterans as well.

A survey of the healthcare landscape in all fifty states confirms that it is not the case, particularly in the rural (and remote rural) areas where about one-quarter of all veterans reside and where 2.8 million are currently enrolled in the VA. Data on the current availability of primary and specialty care, mental health treatment, and acute care hospital capacity reveal how badly the United States is failing to meet the basic medical and mental health needs of nonveterans. Hundreds of hospitals in rural counties and underserved areas have curtailed critical services or closed entirely, and thousands of counties are experiencing significant health provider shortages, according to federal data.

These preexisting conditions will only get worse as President Trump's "One Big, Beautiful Bill" is implemented. Passed narrowly by Congress in July 2025, this legislation will result in a trillion dollars' worth of reduced spending on Medicaid and Affordable Care Act coverage. An estimated seventeen million people may lose their health insurance as a result. States will have less money to help fund their Medicaid programs; hospitals will see a big spike in uncompensated care costs. All of this will lead to additional hospital closures and more shortages of healthcare personnel.

Says one former VA official: "Imagining that you can send even more vets into a private health system reeling from—and contracting because of—federal funding cuts is nothing short of cruel and delusional."

Coordinated Care at Risk

Such ideological delusion takes many forms in Trump-era policy-making in Washington, DC. In the field of veterans' healthcare, its casualties will be vets like seventy-five-year-old Will Smith (a pseudonym for reasons of medical privacy). Smith fought in the Vietnam War and got his care at a West Coast VA medical center.

Because of his combat experience, Smith struggled with PTSD after leaving the military. Thanks to VHA therapists and many years of peer group support, he no longer abuses alcohol or prescription drugs. Like other Vietnam vets exposed to Agent Orange, he has diabetes, which has led to chronic heart problems and kidney disease. Because of the heavy backpacks he carried "in country," he also suffers from osteoarthritis in his hips and knees, severely limiting his mobility. To get around, he depends on an electric wheelchair provided by the VA. He takes eighteen different drugs (all delivered free of charge) to help control multiple "comorbidities."

Smith's primary care physician (who chose to remain anonymous) is responsible for coordinating with numerous specialty providers at the large VA medical center where Smith gets his care. The PCP consults regularly with Smith's cardiologist, pulmonologist, nephrologist, and everyone else dealing with his physical and mental health problems, which have included suicidal ideation.

A Team Approach

Smith's Patient Aligned Care Team includes a medical resident who is training at the VA, like tens of thousands around the country. An RN, a licensed vocational nurse, and a medical service assistant—all of whom have known Smith for years—help make sure that he schedules and shows up for his appointments. A clinical pharmacist monitors Smith's use of medications to ensure that he's taking his pills correctly: some with food, some in the morning, and not at night.

Smith's doctor schedules sixty-minute, in-person visits with Smith every three months and a telehealth appointment every six weeks. In between these consultations, Smith's weight and blood pressure are checked daily through a VA telemonitoring service, which sends alerts to his care team if worrisome changes are detected. There is no patient fee for this service. If Smith needs equipment essential to facilitate his care, like a laptop, iPad, or smartphone, the VA also provides it, free of charge.

The VA's integrated health service provides Smith with acupuncture and chiropractic sessions to help him manage chronic pain. When able, Smith tries to attend a chair yoga class, one of many such offerings that include popular mindfulness meditation sessions.

In terms of his complex care needs, Smith is not an outlier at the VA. As a 2016 RAND study reported, the agency cares for "a sicker population with more chronic conditions, such as cancer, diabetes, and chronic obstructive pulmonary disease, than the population treated by civilian providers."

Veterans who rely on the VA for healthcare are also more economically disadvantaged than most other patients in the United States, with the exception of Medicaid recipients. They tend to have less formal education and lower household incomes. According to VA data, about 50 percent of veterans have a personal annual income of $50,000 or less; less than 5 percent, mainly former officers, have an annual income of $200,000 or more.

Whether they live in urban or rural America, veterans steered away from the VA through expanded outsourcing will become "customers" of a private healthcare industry that operates quite unlike the VA and with corresponding inferior results.

Medical Deserts

As the Commonwealth Fund points out, the United States has one of the industrialized world's highest suicide rates and the highest rate of avoidable mortality, as well as fewer hospital beds, physician visits, and even practicing doctors than other equivalent countries have.

Although access to primary care is widely recognized as central to "health equity and care access," more than 89 percent of counties in the

United States are officially designated primary care Health Professional Shortage Areas. About eighty million Americans, nearly one-quarter of the total population, live in areas without enough primary care providers.

As a result, residents of almost all rural counties face a significantly higher risk of poor health, with those who live in Alabama, Georgia, Mississippi, New Mexico, and Texas at greater risk. Rural America contains about 25 percent of the veteran population.

The numbers are staggering. Arizona will face a shortage of 8,280 physicians by 2030, according to the Cicero Institute; Texas will need 20,420 more physicians by that year. Many of Louisiana's parishes have only one or two full-time primary care physicians, and nearly half of Kentucky's primary care physicians work in just two of its 120 counties. Fifty-two of Montana's fifty-six counties have serious shortages of primary care providers; every county in Idaho, South Dakota, and Wyoming has severe shortages of mental health providers. In rural areas of Colorado east of Denver, there is only one primary care physician for every 5,636 residents.

Despite such well-documented staffing shortages, promoters of privatization always insist—with little available evidence—that the VA still has longer wait times than private sector care providers. Of course, we know what VA wait times are, because the agency actually calculates and publicly posts them.

The Wait Time Problem

Equivalent information about private sector wait times is much less accessible because there are no reporting requirements. One private consultant, AMN Healthcare (formerly Merritt Hawkins), collects wait time data for six medical specialties—cardiology, family practice, orthopedic surgery, obstetrics/gynecology, dermatology, and gastroenterology—in fifteen major metropolitan areas.

The scope of its surveys is both limited and not very reassuring. AMN's 2025 survey found that, since 2022, the average wait time for physician appointments increased by 19 percent, with the average time for an appointment at thirty-one days. The average wait for an appointment with a family practice physician is 23.5 days, with a high of 207; for a cardiologist, the wait was on average 32.7 days, with a high of 175 days. A woman spent on average of 41.8 days, or a high of

231 days, waiting for an ob/gyn appointment. Someone worried about a suspicious blotch on their face could wait up to 291 days to have a dermatologist tell them whether it was malignant.

Experts expect these personnel shortages and wait times to worsen in the next decade, due to an aging physician workforce. Doctors aged sixty-five or older make up 20 percent of the clinician workforce, and those between ages fifty-five and sixty-four are 22 percent. A significant number of physicians will thus be retiring soon.

Unless current trends change, the Association of American Medical Colleges reports that by 2036 the United States will face a shortage of between 20,200 and 40,400 primary care physicians, between 10,100 and 19,900 physicians for surgical specialties, and potentially 5,500 physicians for medical specialties. A 2020 study by other researchers predicts that the United States will have nearly 140,000 fewer doctors than it needs by 2030.

Mental Health Care Shortages

The national picture in mental health isn't much better, and that does not bode well for the private treatment of more than 40 percent of VA patients who have mental health conditions.

In the United States, 123 million people, over one-third of the population, live in a Mental Health Professional Shortage Area. In rural counties, 81 percent do not have a single psychiatric nurse practitioner, and 65 percent do not have a single psychiatrist. This may help explain why the suicide rate in rural communities is between 18.3 and 20.5 per hundred thousand residents, about 50 percent higher than the rate in urban areas.

Americans with low incomes—and not coincidentally more mental health and substance abuse problems than those in the general population—have even more trouble finding needed care. According to a report from the Medicaid and CHIP Payment and Access Commission, 50 percent of Medicaid enrollees with a serious mental illness are unable to access care because only about one-third of psychiatrists accept new Medicaid patients.

Even in those urban areas better stocked with licensed mental health professionals, six of ten psychologists may not accept new patients, and one-third of psychologists and 45 percent of psychiatrists may not accept insurance of any kind. This means that even patients with good insurance may be unable to arrange treatment unless they pay out of pocket for it.

The cost of mental health evaluations and treatment varies widely—from $65 to as much as $250 per session—depending on the place of service delivery. In the Bay Area, therapists charge between $235 and $500 for a single one-hour session of cognitive behavioral therapy (CBT), a gold-standard evidence-based treatment that is widely used at the VA to treat PTSD, insomnia, and many other afflictions. Few of these providers accept health insurance for CBT treatment.

A veteran seeking inpatient psychiatric care outside the VA will encounter the same shortage of beds as other patients and their families. According to a recent American Psychiatric Association report, the number of beds available for acutely ill patients has declined significantly in the past sixty years. As a result, patients experiencing a severe mental health crisis who end up in a hospital emergency room can languish there on a gurney, sometimes for several days, while waiting admission to a psych ward. Others end up warehoused in jail or living untreated on the streets.

Rural Hospital Closings

Even before the Trump-imposed Medicaid cuts of 2025, hospitals in rural America were in dire financial straits. The Center for Healthcare Quality and Payment Reform (CHQPR) notes that in the last decade over one hundred rural hospitals have closed. Since 2005, Texas has lost twenty-five rural hospitals, the most in the nation, and Tennessee has lost fifteen.

The CHQPR report estimates that more than seven hundred rural hospitals, one-third of all rural hospitals in the United States, are at risk of closing. In Arkansas (64 percent), Hawaii (62 percent), Vermont (62 percent), Alabama (60 percent), Oklahoma (60 percent), New York (58 percent), Texas (56 percent), and Mississippi (54 percent), at least half of all rural hospitals are at risk. Over 90 percent of rural hospitals in Florida report operating losses, as do 83 percent of rural hospitals in Wyoming.

Rural hospitals that have yet to close are cutting back services. According to Chartis, the healthcare research group, "293 rural hospitals stopped offering OB services between 2011 and 2023, while 424 ceased chemotherapy services between 2014 and 2023." In July 2025,

Becker's Hospital Review noted that eighteen hospitals and emergency departments had closed in that year alone. Hospitals and emergency departments in Alabama, Pennsylvania, Texas, Ohio, Missouri, Maine, New York, Florida, Oklahoma, and Washington, D.C., were shuttered.

The National Rural Health Association (NRHA) estimates that rural hospitals will lose almost $70 billion over the next ten years due to Medicaid spending reductions. Experts predict that a new $50 billion rural hospital fund—created by Congress to soften the impact of those cuts—will be inadequate to avert the spate of hospital closings predicted by the NRHA. A small hospital in Curtis, Nebraska (population nine hundred) became the first scheduled to close, due to anticipated loss of Medicaid revenue.

Healthcare Freedom?

One would think that even members of Congress who favor VA privatization and voted for the VA MISSION Act to get it, would be troubled by a Chartis warning that "rural hospital closures and declining access to community care could potentially hinder the intended benefits of the Act." (The ones who are concerned have come up with a not-very-helpful solution—namely, proposed legislation that would steer more VA-purchased care toward rural hospitals and clinics to shore up their finances.)

Mike Bost (R-IL), the MAGA republican who chairs the House Veterans' Affairs Committee, regularly blasts the VA for allegedly trapping its nine million patients in a "bureaucracy" that "poses a greater danger to their health than the illnesses they seek treatment for." So he and his GOP colleagues in the House and Senate have introduced bills that would open the floodgates of outsourcing even further.

In 2025, senators Marsha Blackburn (R-TN), Tim Sheehy (R-MT), Roger Wicker (R-MS), and Tommy Tuberville (R-AL) sponsored the Veterans Health Care Freedom Act, to "provide veterans with greater autonomy to access the care they need." This would, by statute, further loosen the patient referral guidelines that Doug Collins introduced earlier in his tenure as VA secretary, which made the rules never revised by his Biden-appointed predecessor even more outsourcing-friendly. VA patients would be allowed to make appointments with private sector providers without any prior consultation with, or authorization from, their in-house caregivers.

If enough corporate Democrats help pass legislation based on the conservative fantasy of healthcare freedom—which some have done in the past—they won't be getting many thank-you letters from veterans like Will Smith. While the GOP continues to tell vets they can have their cake and eat it too, cannibalizing the VA's direct care budget to spend billions on non-VA providers will eventually lead to the closing of underused VA facilities. Rather than having more healthcare options, VA patients will end up with fewer choices, and those outside the VA will often be more illusory than real.

PART VI

OFFICER CLASS ENEMIES

The Republicans have been far more successful than Democrats electing veterans to Congress. But not all former officers with right-wing politics are successful as political candidates when they return to their home state or parachute into someone else's. After failed bids for the Senate, two of the three Trump allies profiled here—Daniel Gade and Pete Hegseth—did become state or federal government appointees, with widely varying degrees of influence over military or veterans' affairs.

Doug Collins, who joined the second Trump administration along with Hegseth, was elected to the US House four times but lost a Republican senatorial primary in Georgia when he tried to move up in 2000. This made him available to become secretary of veterans affairs, four years later—with many of his former colleagues on Capitol Hill, in both parties, supporting his nomination.

Throughout their professional careers, Gade, Hegseth, and Collins have all used their past service, decorations, and/or current reservist rank to further a conservative agenda that is not in the best interests of the 90 percent of veterans who are former enlisted people (or surviving Vietnam-era draftees).

At the Pentagon, Hegseth, the former Fox News commentator and Koch brothers–backed leader of Concerned Veterans for America, was put in charge of the largest workforce and biggest budget in the federal government. At the VA, Collins took command of the agency with the second-largest workforce and third-largest budget. During year one of Trump II, both became key field generals in the MAGA offensive against an overly "woke" military and a veterans' healthcare system already weakened by incremental privatization.

22

The Entitlement Reformers

The assault on federal jobs, programs, and services—launched by Elon Musk's Department of Government Efficiency, with Donald Trump's blessing—was the latest escalation in a forty-five-year-old Republican drive to downsize the welfare state.

Until recently, conservative ideologues like the Koch brothers and their allies in Congress have not taken aim at the VA-run Veterans Benefits Administration (VBA), because it has long been a sacred cow for politicians of all stripes. Who, after all, wants to run for reelection after messing with the disability pay of combat veterans and other former service members with injuries and illnesses acquired while in uniform, at home or abroad.

Nearly seven million Americans currently receive payments for service-related physical or mental health conditions that left them partially or totally impaired; among them are 1.3 million men and women who served in Iraq and Afghanistan. Their total compensation, plus pensions, costs US taxpayers more than $193 billion per year.

The now-infamous Project 2025 report from the Heritage Foundation and the publication of a book that got less notice both suggest that the ceasefire over veterans' benefits has ended inside the Beltway.[1] Project 2025 recommendations related to veterans' healthcare and benefits were crafted by two Trump advisors during his first term—retired marine lieutenant colonel Brooks Tucker and former air force captain Darin Selnick. (The latter had an abortive tour of duty at the Pentagon early in Trump's second term; for more on that, see the next chapter.)

Daniel Gade, a retired US Army lieutenant colonel who became Virginia's commissioner for veterans services, teamed up with an ex–*Wall Street Journal* reporter, Daniel Huang, to promote "entitlement reform" of the same sort in their 2022 book *Wounding Warriors: How Bad Policy Is Making Veterans Sicker and Poorer.*

As our Veterans Healthcare Policy Institute coworkers Jasper Craven and Russell Lemle have reported, "Project 2025 calls for a review of the VA Schedule for Rating Disabilities to 'target significant cost savings from revising disability rating awards for future claimants.' Not only would these changes result in less money in the pockets of disabled veterans, but for those failing to meet the new standards, their eligibility for VA healthcare would disappear."[2]

Officer-class critics of the VA like Tucker and Selnick also want the Trump administration to limit its direct care to "service-connected conditions"—medical or mental health problems that were acquired or exacerbated by military service. Under the current system, as Craven and Lemle explain: "Once veterans prove they have a service-related condition, they can receive care for that problem as well as any other conditions that they may develop. For example, a veteran whose leg was amputated in the military would not only have lifetime care for that, but also for high blood pressure or cancer that they developed, later on, in civilian life."

This is a major and very positive difference between the VA as a federal workers' compensation system for former military personnel and state workers' comp programs for anyone injured on the job elsewhere in the public or private sector. Many American workers are familiar with the shortcomings of the latter systems. In most states, benefit levels are too low. Employers fight workers' claims. Rehabilitation services are fragmented and managed by private insurers. Workers only get treatment for the specific work-related illness or injury they filed a claim over.

Meanwhile, if unable to return to their old workplace, they eventually lose whatever job-based health insurance they had for themselves and their families and end up on Medicaid, if they can qualify based on low income. Or they must purchase private coverage subsidized under the Affordable Care Act. So even some successful workers' comp claimants can end up in personal bankruptcy due to unpaid bills for care not paid for by their former employer's workers' comp insurer.

If the Trump administration moves in the direction recommended by Tucker and Selnick, millions of veterans with wide-ranging medical needs would be engaged in a similar scramble for healthcare coverage.

Those without job-based coverage would be forced to purchase, at their own expense, private insurance or fall back on a Medicaid program facing massive funding cuts thanks to Republican passage of Trump's "Big, Beautiful Bill" in 2025. (Such consequences were, of course, little noted by reporters and editors of the Jeff Bezos–owned *Washington Post* when they produced a series of investigative reports in the fall of 2025, claiming that "disability claims fraud" was widespread at the VA, not well policed by the agency, and in urgent need of "reform" by Congress and the Trump administration.)

A "Disability-Industrial Complex"?

In their book, Gade and Huang critique what they call a "disability-industrial complex." They argue that monthly checks from the VBA foster a costly and unhealthy culture of dependence among veterans and should be sharply restricted, not expanded.

In *Wounding Warriors*, the authors further contend that VA disability ratings have been "misapplied to mental health disorders like PTSD, which have been repeatedly demonstrated to improve with effective therapies." In their view, such ratings are "an appropriate designation" only "for veterans with disabilities that are truly static and unlikely to improve—amputations, spinal cord injuries, etc." The "only veterans for whom employment is not a reasonable option are those few whose brain injuries are truly devastating and impossible to overcome." As for the rest, including those who may be suicidal, "we pay veterans to be sick and then we wonder why we have so many sick veterans."

Gade himself earned two Purple Hearts, a Bronze Star, and the Legion of Merit during twenty years of service, which included combat duty in Iraq. In 2004, he was so severely wounded that he spent a year in a military hospital recovering and lost his right leg. According to Gade, "while [his] new, serious disability was life-changing, he decided to thrive."[3] While still in the military, he earned both a master's and a doctorate in public administration and spent six years on the faculty at West Point before retiring in 2017. He then became a professor at American University's School of Public Affairs in Washington, DC.

In *Wounding Warriors*, Gade displays little sympathy for poor and working-class soldiers who didn't get the taxpayer-funded educational or job opportunities he enjoyed as an officer and who subsequently faced a harder transition to civilian life. According to Gade, too many veterans who lack a "truly static" disability liked his own amputation "are diverted from paths of self-sufficiency and shuffled down paths of dependency and dysfunction."[4]

Dirty Loafers?

Such officer-class criticism of less-fortunate comrades echoes from the past two centuries. As Richard Severo and Lewis Milford note in their book *The Wages of War*, hundreds of thousands of demobilized Union soldiers had great difficulty supporting themselves and their families after the Civil War. Only the severely disabled were eligible for care in a few newly created soldiers' homes. Nevertheless, the *Army and Navy Journal* advised veterans to avoid becoming "dirty loafers" if they wanted to succeed in civilian life. Those who developed "new muscular habits," rather than succumbing to personal despair and reliance on charity, would eventually find jobs and housing; those who sought any special help would end up fatally dependent on it.

In 1890, members of Union veterans' organization the Grand Army of the Republic were finally awarded pensions not tied to death or disability resulting from active duty. But this legislative victory was not universally applauded. *The Nation* bemoaned, "The ex-union soldier is ... a helpless and greedy sort of person, who says that he is not able to support himself and whines that other people ought to do it for him."

Of course, back then there was hardly any social safety net for poor or disabled persons, other than private charity or local "poorhouses." Throughout the twentieth century, as the United States finally developed a modern welfare state (meager though it was) that better protected its most vulnerable citizens, conservatives seized on any instance of fraud or abuse, real or imagined, that might discredit public assistance and trigger calls for benefit cuts.

By the 1970s, no domestic bogeyman was more popular on the right than the proverbial "welfare queen." Echoing welfare fraud exposés in the mass media, California governor Ronald Reagan made tall tales about such grifters a staple of his presidential campaigning in the 1970s. During one oft-repeated speech, he claimed that a single female defrauder—never identified by name or race, of course—was raking in $150,000 worth of Social Security, Medicaid, food stamps, and welfare benefits every year, creating an enduring myth that has been weaponized by the right and even some austerity-minded Democrats ever since. (According to Reagan, this welfare queen was also collecting veteran benefits on "four nonexisting deceased husbands.")

During Gade's 2020 campaign for the US Senate, he favored privatization of Social Security and opposed universal health coverage, free higher education modeled on the GI Bill, and student loan forgiveness (as "an immoral transfer of risk"). His Reagan-like stance against handouts to the undeserving poor drew 44 percent of the vote in Virginia.

A New Mission

After his failed Senate bid, Gade formed the New Mission PAC to support other Republicans who want to "better serve our nation's veterans." In Georgia, his PAC did 2020 election turnout among veterans for Senators Kelly Loeffler and David Perdue, who ended up being defeated by Democrats Raphael Warnock and Jon Ossoff, respectively. Gade's PAC targeted Warnock and Ossoff because both are allegedly part of a "political left ... deeply invested in the VA's system of 'enlistment-to-grave' care as a prototype for single-payer healthcare."

The coauthors of *Wounding Warriors* criticize all the major veteran service organizations because they are similarly invested in single-payer care (albeit, in most cases, for their members and other veterans only). The VSOs function much like associations of injured workers and unions have throughout US labor history. At the local level, they help individuals pursue claims for compensation and healthcare, while seeking legislative changes benefiting larger classes of veterans like victims of Agent Orange during the Vietnam War or post-9/11 veterans exposed to toxic burn pits. Gade and Huang argue that this membership service and related lobbying make the American Legion, Veterans of Foreign Wars, AMVETS, and others into "enablers" of a "victim mentality" among former military personnel.

Longtime veterans' advocates like Steve Robertson and Paul Sullivan reject this characterization of their work. Both have dedicated their post-military careers to defending publicly funded healthcare and benefits for veterans, and they strongly oppose slashing VA budgets on the grounds that beneficiaries of its programs are "undeserving."

Robertson is an air force veteran and a forty-year member of the American Legion who once served as its national legislative director. During Bernie Sanders's tenure as chair of the Senate Veterans' Affairs Committee, he was the committee's staff director. He remains active in American Legion Post 290 in Stafford, Virginia, where he serves as benefits officer.

Not Defenders of Fraud or Abuse

Robertson supports efforts by the VA's inspector general to deal with any benefit fraud or abuse. But, in his experience, the VSOs don't help vets get benefits they don't deserve; they help them get benefits they have definitely earned, the hard way.

Paul Sullivan served as an army cavalry scout in the 1991 Gulf War and now belongs to the Legion, VFW, and Disabled American Veterans. As past executive director and then national vice chair of Veterans for Common Sense (VCS), he was a key advocate for former soldiers exposed to toxins in Middle Eastern war zones over three decades.

Between 1990 and 1991, an estimated 697,000 service members developed what is known as Gulf War Illness or Gulf War Syndrome after being exposed to widely used pesticides or releases of the nerve agent sarin—or both. As described in one VA advisory committee report, "This complex of multiple concurrent symptoms typically includes persistent memory and concentration problems, chronic headaches, widespread pain, gastrointestinal problems, and other chronic abnormalities not explained by well-established diagnoses." According to the report's authors, "No effective treatments have been identified for Gulf War illness[,] and studies indicate that few veterans have recovered over time."[5]

Such research findings do not impress the authors of *Wounding Warriors*. Their fundamental thesis is that veterans without visible proof of the costs of war shouldn't be adding to them by filing claims for physical or mental disabilities. Air Force Reserve colonel Robert Wilkie—the right-wing Republican who served as VA secretary during Trump's first term—has joined Gade's call for benefit cuts from his own perch at the Heritage Foundation.

At a Veterans Day appearance with Gade in November 2021, Wilkie similarly claimed that the VA was overly "focused on getting veterans checks and not getting them well and getting them back into society." Like Gade—who was about to become Virginia governor Glenn Youngkin's commissioner for veterans' services—Wilkie accused veteran service organizations of encouraging their members "to play disability"—with the result being that too many noncombat veterans are getting undeserved compensation.[6] (Of course, the former VA secretary's criticism of the VSOs might have had something to do with their call for his resignation in late 2020, shortly before he and Trump left office.)[7]

With or without their own wounds of war, members of the officer class—like Tucker, Selnick, Wilkie, and Gade—tend to fare better in civilian life than enlisted personnel do. One reason for that is the well-known "revolving door" that leads them from DOD employment to other federal agencies, like the VA, then to DC think tanks, talking head jobs at Fox News, campus sinecures, and, last but not least, the private sector.

As the Project on Government Oversight (POGO), a nonpartisan research group, found in 2018, hundreds of former high-ranking Pentagon staffers have landed lucrative jobs with DOD contractors, with nearly a quarter becoming employees of Lockheed Martin, Boeing, Raytheon, General Dynamics, or Northrop Grumman.[8] In these new positions, POGO found, they use relationships with former colleagues to help conflate "what is in the best financial interests of defense contractors—excessively large Pentagon budgets, endless wars, and overpriced weapons systems—with what is in the best interest of military effectiveness and protecting citizens."

After serving in the Virginia state government for two years, Gade (along with a group of fellow investors) became the owner and new CEO of a company called Interfuze, a DOD contractor for three decades. Its services include "[firing] range management, weapons test and operations and assisting ... clients with large-scale infrastructure programs which improve warfighter readiness to make our world a safer place."[9]

23

The Princeton Tory

Speaking of making the world a safer place (not), let us now turn to the illustrious career of a better-known officer-class enemy, one with a long history of directing friendly fire at veterans less fortunate than himself.

In the first year of the second Trump administration, there was no more commanding figure (in his own mind) than former Fox News host Pete Hegseth, a devoted Christian nationalist with a distinct lack of Christian charity. Hegseth started out as secretary of defense but with much media fanfare soon became "secretary of war." What was behind that rebranding? It was all part of the administration's "dewoking" of the Pentagon. As Hegseth explained at the White House in September 2025, "We're going on the offensive, not just on defense. Maximum lethality, not tepid legality. Violent effect, not politically correct. We're going to raise up warriors, not just defenders."

Hegseth's campaign to increase warfighter readiness—and ditch dreaded "diversity"—racked up casualties very quickly. Women and Black men who gained top military leadership roles under Biden were replaced, with few thank-yous for their service. Hegseth had to soft-pedal his views on military sexual assault and the role of women in the military to win Senate confirmation. But once that was done, he soon announced an overhaul of procedures used to investigate allegations of officer misconduct of the sort uncovered in the Vanessa Guillén case. No longer would "complainers, ideologues, and poor performers" (or Fort Hood murder victims?) end up "in the driver's seat." Under Hegseth's leadership, there would be "no more frivolous complaints, no more anonymous complaints, no more repeat complaints, no more smearing reputations, no more endless waiting, no more legal limbo, no more sidetracking careers, no more walking on eggshells!"[1]

The career prospects of younger female officers, even if they refrain from filing any sexual harassment complaints, did not look bright. These officers were probably not at the top of any promotion lists approved by Hegseth, who said that having women "in combat roles hasn't made us more effective, hasn't made us more lethal ... [and] has made fighting more complicated."[2]

Another new Hegseth rule: "No more beardos." Any male soldiers who "don't want to shave and look professional" would have to find "a new position or profession." This decree threatened the active-duty status and military careers of hundreds of Sikhs, previously given permission to wear a beard and turban while in uniform, as an accommodation to religious beliefs and martial traditions, valued worldwide for three centuries.[3]

Next up for being purged entirely were the forty-four hundred transgender men and women in the military (0.2 percent of the active-duty total). According to a Pentagon memo issued in February 2025, their medical diagnosis of gender dysphoria was incompatible with further service—despite the fact that some of those "dudes in dresses," as Hegseth called them, earned more decorations and higher rank than he did.[4] Simply discharging them was not good enough for air force brass eager to win the boss's approval. The *New York Times* reported:

> At least a dozen transgender men and women serving in the Air Force who had applied for early retirement to avoid being kicked out of the service for their gender identity have had their retirement approval rescinded by the service. The airmen, all of whom have served fifteen to eighteen years, must now choose between a voluntary separation package or involuntary separation that is typically reserved for cases of misconduct and comes with few, if any, benefits. Either course of action will result in a substantial loss of financial, medical and other benefits worth hundreds of thousands of dollars to each of them.[5]

Around the same time, the family of a deceased air force vet named Ashli Babbitt learned that she could have a funeral with full military honors, plus the Trump administration was paying them $5 million to settle a wrongful death case, filed after she was fatally shot during the January 6, 2021, Capitol break-in. (At the moment of her martyrdom, Babbitt was wearing a Trump flag on her back like a cape).[6]

January 6 Turning Point?

January 2021 was a turning point for Hegseth too. In his 2024 book *The War on Warriors*, he recalls joining "the Army to fight extremists in 2001" and then adds: "Twenty years later, that same Army labeled me one."[7] That did not happen because Hegseth switched sides and became an Islamic fundamentalist. Instead, right before he was scheduled to provide security at Joe Biden's inauguration, as a member of a Army National Guard unit, another soldier flagged him as an "insider threat" due to his tattoos.

As our colleague Jasper Craven reported in *Politico*, that suspicious inking included "a large Jerusalem cross associated with the Christian right and another that reads 'Deus Vult' or 'God wills it'—a motto from the Crusades that has been adopted by white supremacists and was seen at their march in Charlottesville, Virginia, in 2017."[8]

A veteran of past deployments to Middle East, where he earned two Bronze Stars, Hegseth resigned from the military with the rank of major shortly after his canceled call-up to defend Capitol Hill. "The military I loved, I fought for, I revered ... spit me out," he claims in his book (although he faced no disciplinary action over his tattoos).

Hegseth first embraced the military and rejected political correctness during his tour of duty in the Ivy League. He was a ROTC cadet at Princeton when the 9/11 attacks occurred. In a letter to the official student newspaper, the *Princetonian*, he praised the Bush administration for "making certain we identify the correct perpetrators before responding in an appropriate and effective manner"—not the way many people still think of the open-ended, $8 trillion dollar "Global War on Terror" that ensued.[9]

Offended by campus antiwar activism and the "gospel of moral relativism" preached in the Princeton chapel, Hegseth started writing for the *Princeton Tory*, a conservative student magazine whose alumni include Republican senator Ted Cruz.

A Failed Political Candidate

After graduating with an officer's commission, Hegseth spent eleven months at the Guantánamo Bay detention center with his Army National Guard unit and later spent a year in Iraq and a shorter period in Afghanistan. In 2007, Hegseth moved into leadership roles in Vets for Freedom (VFF), which backed John McCain's campaign for the presidency the following year. As the chair of VFF, Hegseth blasted Barack Obama for supporting "a dangerous policy of irreversible withdrawal" that he said would deprive the United States of "military victory" in Iraq.[10]

In 2012, Hegseth became a "service candidate" himself but failed to get the Minnesota Republican Party nomination to run for the US Senate. Like Daniel Gade, he then formed a PAC to support like-minded candidates, but in this case about a third of the money raised ended up going to his friends and family.[11]

Hegseth then landed a life-changing job with the Koch brothers–funded Concerned Veterans for America (CVA), whose only redeeming feature has been its anti-interventionist stance on foreign policy questions. During his stints with VFF and CVA, Hegseth first applauded and then criticized the wars in Iraq and Afghanistan, a flip-flop characteristic of his entire career.[12] A fellow Iraq War veteran named Jon Soltz, cofounder of VoteVets, once told the *New York Times*: "I have been debating Pete Hegseth for years, and I can't tell you what he stands for other than himself and his own ambition."

CVA was an astroturf newcomer in the field of veterans' affairs and an outlier in favoring VA privatization.[13] Traditional VSOs like the American Legion or Veterans of Foreign Wars may be stodgy, bureaucratic, and conservative. But they do have actual members who pay dues (as opposed to relying on wealthy donors) and elect their own leaders, just like trade unionists do. They have local chapters and national conventions. They have roots in the community and provide valuable services to individual veterans who need help filing disability claims for service-related conditions, which qualifies them for VA care.

Foe of Government Healthcare

With few actual dues-payers, no VSO-style membership service programs, and a political agenda shaped by libertarian billionaires, CVA has advocated for few, if any, bills that actually benefited the nation's veterans. Instead, during the Obama era, the media-savvy group became a battering ram against taxpayer-funded healthcare in any form, a longtime bête noire of the Kochs.

Hegseth became CVA's most visible and effective mouthpiece in a wide-ranging campaign to discredit VA care and the Affordable Care Act.[14] In 2013, CVA ran video ads warning, in Hegseth's words, that all

Americans would soon "face long wait times, endless bureaucracy, and poor service" if Congress expanded healthcare access by subsidizing private insurance coverage. The result, he claimed, would be billions of dollars wasted on "a nationalized health care plan that [would] bring the same bureaucratic dysfunction to the larger U.S. healthcare market"—as if the VA were a model for "Obamacare," which it certainly wasn't.

A year later, this propaganda offensive, closely coordinated with right-wing Republicans on Capitol Hill, claimed the scalp of retired four-star general Eric Shinseki, the Vietnam veteran who was Barack Obama's first VA secretary. Shinseki became the fall guy for a localized scandal involving misconduct by a few VA hospital managers in Phoenix. Their doctoring of data on medical appointment wait times—to earn bonus payments—led to CVA-amplified false claims that forty Phoenix area vets had died due to delayed care. The result was mainstream media-packed journalism at its worst and then political pressure for more outsourcing of VA care despite its higher quality, lower cost, and greater accessibility than private alternatives.

On Capitol Hill, bipartisan majorities passed the VA Choice Act of 2014 and, four years later, the VA MISSION Act. Both opened the floodgates for increasingly costly and disastrous privatization of the nation's most extensive public healthcare system. CVA helped engineer the passage of each measure. After stepping down as CEO of CVA (amid complaints about his personal misconduct and mishandling of money), Hegseth became a Fox News commentator and influential adviser to President Trump on veterans' affairs. Other CVA alums, like navy veteran Darin Selnick, served in official positions at the White House or VA headquarters between 2017 and 2021.[15]

A White House Advisor

Neither Hegseth nor Selnick liked Trump's first VA secretary, who had served in Barack Obama's administration and dragged his feet on privatization. As a result, Dr. David Shulkin, an experienced hospital system administrator in the private and public sectors, was sacked by Trump in 2018. In Shulkin's memoir, *It Shouldn't Be This Hard to Serve Your Country*, he blames his firing on Hegseth, who "never worked at the VA, knew nothing about managing a healthcare system, and had little understanding of the clinical and financial impact of the policies he was advocating."[16]

During the Biden years, Hegseth's place in the conservative media spotlight paid more handsome rewards than his stint at the *Princeton Tory*. As a *Fox and Friends* talking head, paid speaker, and best-selling author, he became a multimillionaire (despite two messy and costly divorces).[17] Like other former officers, his past and future benefit packages in the private sector leave him with little need for the VA, federally subsidized insurance coverage obtained through the ACA, or, when he retires, Medicare, either in traditional form or via a Medicare Advantage plan.

As secretary of war (as of November 2025 the department he headed was still legally the Department of Defense), Hegseth was paid a mere $250,000 a year. Lucrative "revolving door" opportunities in the future will quickly make up for that temporary pay cut when he transitions back to the private sector. Given Hegseth's past political aspirations, outsized ego, and high-profile cabinet position, he could be a competitor for Trump's crown in 2028, if fellow vet JD Vance doesn't gain the inside track by replacing the president before then due to the latter's death or disability.

Even in the case of old comrades—like his fellow campaigners for VA privatization at Concerned Veterans for America—Hegseth's personal loyalty has its limits, as demonstrated by the fate of Iraq War vet Dan Caldwell, who served briefly as his senior advisor at the Pentagon, and Darin Selnick, who was his first deputy chief of staff. In a *New York Times* op-ed piece, both conservative veterans made a very timely appeal for more Pentagon spending to replace moldy housing, crumbling healthcare, and inadequate schools for active-duty service members and their families on military bases. Caldwell and Selnick pointed out that "the lobbying power" of weapons manufacturers in search of new Pentagon contracts "far outmatches those speaking up for military personnel," as they were doing. As a result, past administrations had failed to spend a sufficient fraction of a soon-to-be-trillion-dollar annual DOD budget on better living and working conditions for rank-and-file soldiers and their dependents.[18]

By the end of 2025, Caldwell and Selnick were no longer working in top jobs at the Pentagon. Both were suspended under murky circumstances, involving accusations of leaking to the press. But Secretary Hegseth soon weighed in, very clearly, on the question of "quality of life" improvements on military bases. He decided that the schedule for reducing chemical contamination at 140 US military sites around the country should be slower, rather than faster, despite the many PACT Act claims already generated by toxic exposure there. The *New York Times* reported: "The Pentagon's new timeline would delay cleanup by nearly a decade in some cases but vary by site." This represents "a significant revision from the Pentagon's earlier cleanup timetable, released in December 2024, in the final days of the Biden administration.... The delays come as the National Defense Authorization Act for 2026 also seeks to significantly cut funding for the cleanup of toxic sites."[19]

So, for the foreseeable future, old moldy housing might be the least-problematic health hazard facing working-class recruits to the military, thanks to the officer-class indifference of the Princeton man running the Pentagon today.

24

An Air Force Chaplain from Georgia

In early 2025, Pete Hegseth's Senate confirmation as secretary of the Department of Defense was a squeaker. He needed the tie-breaking vice presidential vote of former marine JD Vance.

In contrast, Trump's pick for secretary of the Veterans Affairs Department—former Georgia congressman Doug Collins—had considerable bipartisan support. Twenty-two Senate Democrats voted for him, along with Sen. Bernie Sanders (I-VT), who did manage to question him more effectively than any other member of the Senate Veterans' Affairs Committee (SVAC) but then joined a nearly unanimous SVAC majority favoring his nomination. How could these putative defenders of the VA—and Sanders has been a real one for years—fall for the southern charm of an Air Force Reserve chaplain who would soon become a worse VA secretary than Robert Wilkie, the right-wing Republican who replaced David Shulkin after Hegseth and Selnick got him sacked during Trump's first term?

It helped that Collins has always been more lawyerly and clean-living (and less tattooed) than the hard-drinking, skirt-chasing, twice-divorced former ROTC cadet from Princeton. Collins's confirmation hearing was a master class in a nominee dissembling, not remembering, and not being very specific, while at the same time feeling the warm glow of being back on Capitol Hill, among former Republican colleagues eager to facilitate his cabinet appointment.

When asked about Project 2025 recommendations on the VA, Collins, like Trump, claimed that he had not read the Heritage Foundation report. (One GOP senator asked him to "pinky swear" that he was a foe of privatization, which he did.) Collins even soft-soaped his long history of opposition to reproductive rights by saying he would just follow the law in that area, instead of rescinding a Biden administration rule that authorized the VA to provide abortion counseling and, in some cases, the procedure itself to female veterans.[1]

Working Together with Labor?

Few other nominees to Trump's cabinet mentioned their past union membership, but Collins did. He told the SVAC that he belonged to the United Food and Commercial Workers while working for five years at a Georgia grocery store chain. To further reassure Democrats on the committee, he told them: "I believe that the employees of the VA, whether they're union or not, are very valuable and I respect that . . . I get the issue."

At another point in his confirmation hearing, Collins pledged to "be the biggest cheerleader for every VA employee out there who is getting up every morning, doing it right [and] making sure we are taking care of our veterans." And during questioning about White House plans to end remote work arrangements throughout the federal government, Collins acknowledged that "a large portion of the VA workforce is unionized and they're in contracts," so "we're going to have to work together to get people back to work."

Six months later, there was little evidence of Collins and VA union members working together on anything. Instead, the new VA secretary became an eager implementer of Trump's unlawful cancellation of collective bargaining rights for almost all VA employees—on the grounds that they do "national security work." Collins ordered the dismissal of twenty-four hundred VA probationary employees, including some who had worked at the agency for years and had just been promoted to a new job. He dutifully developed a DOGE-driven plan to cut more than eighty thousand jobs by the end of 2025.[2] He canceled hundreds of contracts with university researchers whose work directly supports patient care.[3] He ended remote work arrangements and ordered mental health care providers to report back to facilities not properly set up for telehealth work. In August 2025, Collins introduced a new policy that would, as the *Intercept* reported, "severely narrow access to abortion—eliminating exceptions for health, rape, and incest, and only allowing the procedure in situations deemed to threaten the life of the mother. The rule would also ban any counseling for abortion through the VA.[4]

DOGE-Driven Chaos

Collins's chaotic first six months in office resulted in widespread workplace disruption, much uncertainty for thousands of career employees at the VA, plummeting morale, and mounting protests by veterans and their families who had not participated in such events before.[5]

After voting to confirm Collins, Sen. Richard Blumenthal (D-CT), a Vietnam-era veteran whose son uses the VA in Connecticut, denounced the Collins-Musk "plans to slash and trash the VA" and declared that "nine million veterans are watching you give them the middle finger and we're not going to stand for it!"

Blumenthal proved to be a better confirmation hearing questioner when Collins's senior advisor—Maj. Gen. John Bartrum, an air force veteran—was nominated by the White House in the summer of 2025 to become undersecretary for health at the VA. Yet Bartrum's eventual confirmation made him the first VA healthcare system leader in thirty-five years who was not a physician. As one worried headquarters official told the *American Prospect*, this unusual choice clearly puts "political and economic concerns above the health interests of VA patients, which, in turn, puts them at risk."[6]

Under questioning by Blumenthal, Bartrum acknowledged his role in decisions made by Collins to reduce staffing and pull the plug on VA research projects. A *ProPublica* investigation found: "Among those canceled contracts was one to maintain a gene sequencing device used to develop better cancer treatments. Another was for blood sample analysis in support of a VA research project. Another was to provide additional tools to measure and improve the care nurses provide."[7] One former coworker told the *Prospect*, in Bartrum's defense, "He wants to cut, but do it more effectively and efficiently. John's not like DOGE."

Meanwhile, Collins announced that eighty-three thousand jobs—15 percent of his agency's workforce—would be eliminated. After a huge outcry from veterans, their organizations, and congressional Democrats, Collins announced that his head count reduction target was only thirty thousand. These cuts would come not from a reduction in force (R.I.F.) but "normal attrition" or the lure of early retirement or severance payments. "A departmentwide RIF is off the table," Collins declared. "As a result of our efforts, VA is headed in the right direction—both in terms of staff levels and customer service."[8]

In December of 2025, Collins announced staffing caps that could eliminate as many as thirty-seven thousand unfilled positions from the VA organizational chart. He also unveiled a controversial plan to reorganize VA healthcare delivery by consolidating what are called Veterans Integrated Service Networks. Under the guise of reducing bureaucracy, Collins is trying to reduce the number of skilled administrators in the system and enhance the role of political appointees, with far less healthcare expertise. "Things have been very challenging," one mental health leader told us. "But this is really going to impact patient care."

Unhappy Customers

Nothing about Collins's first year on the job was reassuring to former service members with a strong personal or professional connection to the VA—as patients, former VA officials, or leaders of groups fighting to save it. Some of the VA secretary's most outspoken critics were female veterans like Kyleanne Hunter, who flew a Cobra attack helicopter on dangerous missions in Iraq and Afghanistan; Arlys Herem, a nurse who served in Vietnam; former marine Joanna Sweatt; and Kayla Williams, an army veteran of the Iraq War and author of two books about her experience in the military.[9]

Unlike the more cautious and conservative American Legion and Veterans of Foreign Wars, the Iraq and Afghanistan Veterans of America (IAVA)—under Hunter's leadership—has backed VA staff members who risked their jobs and has signed a letter to Collins and Congress protesting his staffing cuts and other policy changes.[10] According to Hunter, "Women veterans need a strong and highly functioning VA because we have unique needs, not only when compared to those of male veterans but also to women who are civilian patients. Anyone who takes care of women veterans needs to understand the jobs women had in the military and the injuries and exposures they may have sustained and how that impacts their health."

Women are the fastest-growing part of the veteran population—about 10 percent—and now comprise about 18 percent of all active-duty military personnel.[11] About 30 percent of all new VA patients are female, and six hundred thousand use VA services of one sort or another. As one study found, former service members more likely to use VA are "Black, younger, female, unmarried, with less education and lower household incomes" and who "served longer in the military and in combat."[12]

When Disabled American Veterans surveyed female vets in 2018, the group found that 60 percent felt their military service had been injurious to their mental or physical health. The suicide rate among female vets is 2.5 times higher than among women in the general population and is increasing faster than the rate of male vet suicides. Women with PTSD also have higher-risk pregnancies; higher risk of suicidality, cancers, and arthritis; and are "more likely to die of all-cause mortality than their civilian counterparts."

Research That Saves Lives

The VA has created the Women Veterans Health Strategic Healthcare Group (now Office of Women's Health), a Women Veterans Call Center, and the Center for Women Veterans to make its services more welcoming to women and to educate staff and other patients about their needs.[13] The VA also conducts a National Survey of Women Veterans and includes them in its Million Veterans Program, which has amassed the largest genetic data bank in the world to study how genes impact health.

In 2024, the VA Office of Research and Development established the Women's Health Research Integration Workgroup to facilitate studies involving female vets and better coordinate with any Pentagon research work related to specific military occupational specialties. Such interagency cooperation has led to legislation like the ACES (Aviator Cancer Examination Study) Act, which directed the VA to study cancer rates among pilots and air crews.[14]

Like her fellow aviators, Kyleanne Hunter was a member of this high-risk group. During a routine screening at the VA, she learned that, without having any symptoms, she had developed uveal melanoma. This rare cancer (5 percent of all melanomas) is not visible to patients or easily detected without a dilated eye exam involving special equipment.[15] If ocular melanoma is not detected and treated early, it can become very aggressive, leading to vision loss and blindness. If it metastasizes to other parts of the body, patients have a very high mortality rate. (One study showed that patients with late-stage disease had a 15 percent, five-year survival rate.)[16] "I was fortunate to be in the VA, where I was actively screened for this particular cancer," Hunter told us. "I shudder to think what would have happened to me if I had no contact with this kind of specialized care."

Female-Friendly Care

Prior to the Trump administration, every major VA medical center had essential reproductive health services, including abortion counseling and abortion services, which, in the event of an emergency, can preserve a woman's fertility and be lifesaving. If the VA lacked the personnel or equipment to do mammograms or deliver babies, patients were properly referred to private sector providers at the VA's expense.

Female patients who prefer less interaction with men can access some clinics at stand-alone sites. Other women can receive care in clinics located in separate areas inside a VA medical center. Any designated VA provider who is male—and treats women—must undergo specialized training in women's healthcare issues.

Arlys Herem, a Veterans for Peace member who has used the Minneapolis VA healthcare system for years, has personally experienced the gender-sensitive, teamwork approach of VA staff in a positive way. When she complained of "particular muscular problems," she was initially sent to a male physical therapist. "When he couldn't help me," Herem says, "he sent me to a female PT who specialized in pelvic floor [physical therapy] and pelvic muscle problems. I didn't even know such a thing exist[ed], but it really helped."

Joanna Sweatt, national organizing director for Common Defense and a coordinator of its "VA Not for Sale" campaign, has had similar experiences.[17] Sweatt uses the VA for all her healthcare needs, including treatment for the military sexual trauma (MST) she experienced in the marines and for her premenopausal symptoms, which she attributes to having kids at an early age. Based on her own experience, she has defended abortion access for women in the military and veterans, speaking out in media interviews, newspaper opinion pieces, and other forums.[18]

According to Sweatt, the VA Phoenix Health Care System, where she gets her care, has made great progress, but it is at great risk under Secretary Collins. "If you can believe it, we used to be sent to a gloomy basement space, and now we have a beautiful women's clinic. It's amazing how much the VA has invested in women's healthcare in the last decade."

Cultural Competency?

Gains made by women veterans and their advocacy organizations are threatened in multiple ways. VA research contracts have been cancelled, VA teaching hospital relationships with medical and nursing schools have been disrupted. The VA is referring an ever-increasing number of patients to private sector contractors with insufficient "cultural competency" and far less clinical experience dealing with service-related conditions, if they recognize them at all.

Former VA psychologist Russell Lemle points out, "The MISSION Act of 2018 required the VA to develop competency standards for non-VA providers offering care to veterans with MST and other conditions for which the VA has special expertise. The VA developed a thirty-minute core training in MST. But, during Trump's first term, this was waived as a mandatory requirement." As a result, less than 1 percent of outside therapists providing mental health care to VA patients have taken the training, according to a recently issued GAO report.[19] "It would only take thirty minutes of their time," Lemle says, "and they still wouldn't do it."

What difference does this make for individual patients referred outside the VA, whether they want to be or not? Kayla Williams is one female patient who has long appreciated the "camaraderie" factor at the VA. For her, being in a therapy group made up of other women veterans "was profoundly valuable and validating. To realize how shared some of those experiences are, it was like ... oh, there's not something uniquely wrong with me."

But this Iraq combat veteran also knows the agency well from bottom to top because she has served at VA headquarters in Washington as director of its Center for Women Veterans and, then during the Biden administration, as assistant secretary of public and intergovernmental affairs. She has also been a researcher at the Center for New American Security and the RAND Corporation and has written frequently about the importance of stable, reliable, trusted, and experienced VA caregiving.

In 2023, Williams discovered that her own therapist was leaving the VA for another job. She switched to a women veteran's therapy group for MST that was run virtually, but two years later its facilitator decided to leave in the wake of Secretary Collins's mass firings of all probationary employees and directive to many such tele-health providers that they report for duty again at a VA facility. (As Collins's chief spokesman Peter Kasperowicz explained, "the VA is no longer a place where employees can phone it in from home.").[20]

Williams's therapist, like many others, did not want to come back to work in an open cubicle in a crowded office. In that unprofessional setting, the therapist explained, patient confidentiality would depend on her wearing noise-canceling headphones and nobody walking behind her and looking at her screen. "I don't blame her for choosing not to stay," Williams told us.

Williams then got a referral to a mental health professional who has signed up to be part of the VA's MISSION Act–mandated "community care" network. At her first appointment she was asked, "What brings you here?" Williams replied that she was "dealing with this and that and MST." The therapist looked at her quizzically and asked, "What's MST?" Williams was stunned. One out of three women veterans have experienced some form of sexual trauma—due to harassment or assault while in the military.[21] Every VA mental health provider is required to take a basic MST training, and some specialize in treating it.

"I couldn't believe it," Williams said. "This immediately destroyed any trust I could have had in the provider. I mean, you're taking referrals from the VA to care for veterans, and you don't even bother to have the minimum amount of clinical or cultural competency. You're essentially asking your patient to train you." Williams decided that, even if her next appointment at the VA took longer to arrange, thanks to chaotic conditions and high staff turnover at her past employer, it would be worth the wait.

PART VII

A COMMON DEFENSE AGAINST THE RIGHT

In this concluding section of the book we examine the challenges facing individuals and groups trying to thwart the right-wing drift in US politics before it becomes an even more dominant current. Readers will find profiles in courage and perfidy in the chapters below: vets in politics, federal worker resistance to union busting, and anti-Trump organizing by former soldiers opposed to war, militarism, and the dismantling of federal programs serving poor and working-class people.

25

Can "Service Candidates" Save the Republic?

In a memoir about his post-9/11 military service in Iraq, one disillusioned former army officer denounced the entire "generation of politicians currently in power" who have "failed America's veterans—and the American people."

Criticizing the shortcomings of both major parties, Paul Rieckhoff—who now directs the Independent Veterans of America—argued that "only veterans have the credibility to reach across party lines and represent everyone."

Unlike ordinary civilians, they "have been trained and hardened in the most extreme conditions and possess a unique set of skills that make them exceptional political candidates." According to Rieckhoff, if more veterans ran for public office, they could "lay the groundwork for a populist political movement that challenges the status quo" in Washington.

Since this optimistic prediction two decades ago, both major parties have doubled down on their recruitment, training, and funding of so-called service candidates. But few of the former military officers and NCOs, foreign service personnel, or national security agency staffers, elected as Republicans or Democrats, have posed any populist threat to the status quo.

Their "reaching across party lines" has mainly been in the service of causes like VA privatization, crypto deregulation, or increased Pentagon budgets, including more than $20 billion for military aid to Israel during its assault on Gaza.

A MAGA Majority

On Capitol Hill, right-wing Republicans who served in the military far outnumber moderate Democrats who did. The GOP's vet caucus in

Congress earned MAGA laurels in 2024 for leading the Trump-Vance campaign attack on vice-presidential candidate Tim Walz, a former House colleague, twenty-four-year member of the Minnesota National Guard and rare pro-labor service candidate.

Then Ohio senator JD Vance—a former public affairs officer for the marines who spent six months in Iraq in a non-combat role—accused his rival for the vice presidency of "stolen valor."[1] This allegedly took the form of Walz misspeaking (in a 2018 appeal for gun control) about the need to curb domestic use of "weapons that I carried in war."

As Walz quickly explained, he had handled lots of guns but never in a combat zone; when he deployed abroad in 2003, it was only to support other troops being sent to Afghanistan. Nevertheless, Vance's assault on Walz was joined by fifty other veterans serving in Congress.[2]

In an open letter, they denounced Walz for leaving the Minnesota Guard in May 2005—before a deployment order was issued to his unit in August that year—so he could run for Congress the following year. According to Representative Brian Mast, the Florida Republican who chaired Veterans and Military Families for Trump in 2024, Walz was guilty of "abandoning the men and women under his leadership" and making "blatant misrepresentations."

Many of these same Capitol Hill critics, like Mast, were among the thirty-five veterans who refused to certify the 2020 presidential election results based on the far more blatant misrepresentation that the vote was "stolen."[3]

The Democratic Vet Minority

Looking and sounding better than this type of "service candidate" is a low bar in the Trump-Vance era. But the dominant influence of big money in politics tends to reinforce bipartisanship of the worst sort on Capitol Hill, as illustrated by the recent career trajectory of Ruben Gallego, an Iraq War vet from a working-class Latino background in Arizona.

As a House member, the Harvard-educated Gallego was a defender of the VA and signed an "End the Forever War" pledge, which was backed by Bernie Sanders and Elizabeth Warren and circulated by Common Defense, the progressive vets' group that helped him get elected.

When the former marine geared up for his ultimately successful bid for a Senate seat in 2024, he let his membership in the House

Progressive Caucus lapse (claiming that its dues had become too high!). After that drop out, his votes on anything related to US support for Israel's war on Gaza got progressively worse.

Gallego ended up winning his Senate race with the help of wealthy backers seeking less regulation of crypto currency; their "independent expenditures" on him exceeded $10 million. Total crypto industry spending on him, now Michigan Senator Elissa Slotkin, and other candidates involved in tight 2024 races was $130 million.

That investment paid off in mid-2025. Gallego and Slotkin joined sixteen other Senate Democrats in voting for the Guiding and Establishing National Innovation for U.S. Stablecoins (GENIUS) Act. As Massachusetts senator Elizabeth Warren warned, this legislation provides inadequate protections for consumers and the banking system, while allowing tech companies to issue their own private currencies and "take control over the money supply." Warren called it "a superhighway for Donald Trump's corruption" that increases the risk of another speculator-driven disaster on the scale of the 2007–8 financial crisis."[4]

Capturing the Flag?

Shortly after this Republican legislative triumph, eighteen Democrats in the US House formed a new Veterans Caucus. Co-chaired by Representatives Ted Lieu, Pat Ryan, and Chris Deluzio. the DVC is trying to create "a pipeline for the next generation of veteran and national-security-expert elected leaders" like Gallego and Slotkin.

Its favored Democratic candidates—largely former officers—will get much financial help from the wealthy donors behind VoteVets. This Democratic Party-aligned Super PAC showered $30 million on 2024 candidates, including Slotkin.

The new Michigan senator first entered politics, as a successful candidate for the House in 2018, after three tours of duty in Iraq as a CIA analyst. Slotkin then served as a top-level Pentagon official, whose responsibilities included "ensuring Israel's qualitative military edge." She has been the lucky beneficiary of more than $650,000 in campaign spending by the American Israel Public Affairs Committee-PAC.

In an interview with *Politico* about 2026 mid-term election strategy, the usually hawkish Slotkin discouraged other candidates from attacking the "oligarchy" because this won't help their party ditch its reputation for being "weak and woke." Instead she urged Dems to get some "goddamn Alpha energy" and "fucking retake the flag."[5]

The DVC has helpfully sounded the alarm about MAGA threats like President Trump's "politicization" of the military and unlawful multi-state deployment of the National Guard for domestic policing purposes. According to Deluzio, a former navy officer, it's a very "powerful thing for us to organize, as Democratic veterans, on some of those issues where we can't reach compromise, and nor should we. We should fight for our values where we can."

Yet, not long afterwards, most Democratic vets in the House folded, rather than fight, when pressed by Republicans to vote for a resolution honoring "a fierce defender of the American founding and its timeless principles of life, liberty, limited government, and individual responsibility."[6] The recipient of this praise was none other than a recently deceased nonveteran from Arizona named Charlie Kirk, a man lauded by eighty-five other House Democrats, in the same resolution, as a model citizen who engaged in "respectful, civil discourse" and "worked tirelessly to promote unity."

Only three DVC members voted against this tribute because of Kirk's actual record as a racist, misogynist, homophobic, immigrant-bashing denier of 2020 presidential election results. (A few other DVCers voted "present" or abstained.)

Refusing Unlawful Orders

Deluzio, Slotkin, and four other Capitol Hill colleagues displayed more "Alpha energy"—and political courage—when they posted a timely November 2025 video message reminding active-duty military personnel and National Guard members that they are obligated to refuse illegal orders. This elicited a furious series of social media post by President Trump denouncing their 'SEDITIOUS BEHAVIOR" as a crime "punishable by death." His suggested method: "HANG THEM!"

Eager to please, as always, Secretary Pete Hegseth announced that one of offenders—Arizona senator Mark Kelly, a former astronaut who flew thirty-nine combat missions as a navy pilot—would be investigated by his department based on the "serious allegations of misconduct" coming from the White House. FBI agents were dispatched to interview the House members, whose shorter-term military service or non-vet status (like Slotkin), put them beyond Hegseth's "jurisdiction."

The defense secretary claimed that the "despicable, reckless, and false" video made by the "Seditious Six" encouraged active duty troops to "ignore the orders of their commanders." To punish Kelly, Hegseth issued "a formal letter of censure" that was placed in his personnel file. He also sought to reduce Kelly's rank and retirement pay via a rarely used process that involved recalling him to active duty and then applying further military discipline. As Kelly's legal challenge noted, such action had been taken in the past only to address serious criminal misbehavior by retired service members. But Hegseth was trying to sanction a US senator and Armed Services Committee member for speaking out in an official capacity on a public policy issue. (In late January 2026, Kelly and his five colleagues also dodged a DOJ attempt to indict them when a federal grand jury in DC rejected the claim that their expression of dissent was a criminal act.)

Among the fellow veterans rushing to Kelly's defense were members of Common Defense. In solidarity, they began posting video statements designed to "inspire younger service members, support veterans in Congress facing intimidation and help counter misinformation among our troops about their duty to uphold the Constitution over unlawful orders."

Paycheck Populism

Progressive, pro-labor vets running for House or Senate seats in 2026—Richard Ojeda in North Carolina, Zach Shrewsbury in West Virginia, Nathan Sage in Iowa, and Graham Platner in Maine—echoed these sentiments. Win or lose, in their respective primary or general election campaigns, they were doing their patriotic duty, as civilians, by challenging some of Trump's most eager enablers on Capitol Hill.

All of these service candidates embraced a brand of "paycheck populism" first road-tested by navy and National Guard veteran Dan Osborn. To the shock and awe of many, Osborn's labor-backed independent campaign for the Senate in 2024—which bypassed Nebraska's Democratic primary—garnered 47 percent of the vote in a state that Kamala Harris lost by 59 to 39 percent.

Osborn became a public figure by leading a successful eleven-week strike by five hundred fellow workers at a Kellogg's cereal factory in Omaha. Before working in that plant for eighteen years and becoming local union president, he dropped out of college and joined the military.

When Kellogg's fired him after the strike, he became a working member of Steamfitters Local 644 and began repairing boiler systems.

Osborn's challenge to Republican Deb Fischer, a corporate-funded, two-term Trump-loving incumbent, was initially given little chance of success—even without a Democratic Party vote-splitter on the ballot in that 2024 race. His blue-collar agenda highlighted the need for labor law reform, minimum wage increases, paid family leave, stronger rail safety enforcement, and consumer protection measures.

Osborn blasted both major parties for being "bought and paid for by corporations and billionaires." But mainly he called attention to the gross underrepresentation of workers in a congressional "country club full of Ivy League graduates, former business execs, and trust fund babies." To address that problem, Osborn helped create a Working Class Heroes Fund to recruit, train, and support more blue-collar candidates for public office.

When Osborn announced his second run for the Senate—as an independent—the state Democratic Party indicated it would, again, bow out of the race. Osborn's new sparring partner is "Wall Street Pete" Ricketts, an ultra-rich Republican who voted for the "One Big, Beautiful Bill" in 2025 that cut his own taxes while taking billions "away from social services and healthcare for hard working people" dependent on Medicaid in Nebraska.

Will Trump voter remorse over this and other betrayals be enough to put Osborn over the top in 2026? "They were sold a bill of goods that if you work hard in this country, your government is going to be there, to have a level playing field for you to get ahead," Osborn told the *New York Times*. "But now we're seeing tax cuts for the billionaires at the expense of workers, people that are struggling to get by.... I love the ideas America is supposed to stand for. Right now, I feel like that is under threat from corporations and billionaires carving it up for themselves."[7]

26

Federal Workers Find Their Voice

During the first few months of 2025, life and work in federal office buildings in Washington, DC, were interrupted by a new lunchtime routine. It developed in response to the myriad depredations of the Department of Government Efficiency (DOGE), which briefly operated under the direction of one of those billionaires good at buying elections.

Paid staffers from national union headquarters and the AFL-CIO would arrive outside an agency headquarters with neatly printed signs and approved messages. Worried civil servants would join them at noon, to mill about, share the latest alarming rumors, and brandish their placards. Union PR people would buttonhole the press and hand out media advisories. Often, the big news of the day involved yet another lawsuit being filed against DOGE—to fight mass dismissals, agency defunding, or reorganizations.

Top union officials and their putative friends on Capitol Hill would show up like clockwork to deliver rally rhetoric or leave statements of support in their wake. In some cases, these were Senate Democrats, like Richard Blumenthal, who had recently voted to confirm an agency head, like Doug Collins at the VA, who then did DOGE's dirty work in the same federal department that was the protest site of the day.[1]

During this unsettling period inside the Beltway, everyone seemed most comfortable training their fire on the evil genius of Elon Musk. Not busy enough running Tesla, Starlink, SpaceX, and X, the world's wealthiest (or second-wealthiest) guy took three months out of his busy schedule to blow up as much of the federal government as he could, with a volunteer army of Silicon Valley underlings. Musk soon left town, but DOGE—and the Project 2025 blueprint for dismantling the "regulatory state"—remained a major influence on a longer-lasting crew of Republican appointees. Before leaving office, Trump hopes to expand their ranks from four thousand to fifty thousand by stripping that many jobs of civil service protections and turning them into "at-will" positions.

No United Front?

Despite representing hundreds of thousands of workers suddenly under attack, AFL-CIO unions long accustomed to dealing with federal employers who behaved differently were slow to develop a coordinated response or take the fight against Musk, DOGE, and Trump to cities and states across the country where most federal workers live.[2]

Why was that? As forty-year-old Mark Smith, a Canadian-born VA occupational therapist, politely explained at the time, his own union, the National Federation of Federal Employees (NFFE), and others like it are "a bit siloed."[3] Instead of looking for ways to unite all workers in the federal sector, their top officials and staff like to promote their own organizational brand. They cultivate separate connections to politicians and agency managers and focus on their different local or national bargaining units, which often lack strong locals and high levels of voluntary dues-paying membership. To save money—in the face of cascading legal threats—some national unions did agree to share the mounting cost of DOGE-related litigation and cooperate on courtroom strategy.

Like Smith in California, Colin Smalley (an Army Corps of Engineers geologist who leads International Federation of Professional and Technical Engineers [IFPTE] Local 777 in Chicago) and Chris Dols (then president of IFPTE Local 98 in New York City) decided this limited form of cooperation was not good enough to meet the challenges of the moment.[4] Those organizational threats would soon include an unprecedented White House attempt to end collective bargaining with NFFE, the American Federation of Government Employees, National Nurses United, the Service Employees International Union, and other labor organizations.

Fortunately, founders of the Federal Unionists Network (FUN) had been in contact with each other, via a WhatsApp chat, prior to the Labor Notes conference in Chicago in April 2024 and stayed in close touch after their face-to-face meetings there.[5] In Chicago, they also compared notes with foreign trade unionists who, as Smalley recalls, were already dealing with "autocratic and, at times, even fascist regimes, which exploit public employees as scapegoats."

With little national union headquarters encouragement and few resources, Smith, the new president of NFFE Local 1 in San Francisco, and other FUN activists called for a nationwide "day of action" on February 19, 2025.[6] In an email blast issued in the name of the "nurses, scientists, park rangers, protectors of our country, researchers, and attorneys who serve our communities every day," they urged workers around the country to plan local events to protest federal funding freezes, the threatened elimination of three hundred thousand jobs, and the disruption of vital services and their further privatization by Trump. "If we speak out together," FUN declared, "we can make it clear to the public why Trump's attack on our jobs is designed to make all of our lives worse."

A Rank-and-File Initiative

Federal workers, along with labor and community allies, responded to FUN's appeal in thirty-five cities, including New York City, where one thousand protesters gathered in Lower Manhattan's Foley Square to hear speakers like longtime VA defender, Alexandria Ocasio-Cortez.

In San Francisco, outside an already much-picketed Tesla dealer at the corner of Van Ness and O'Farrell, a crowd of three hundred assembled, including members of Smith's own local at the city's VA Medical Center. They were joined by staffers of the Environmental Protection Agency, the Consumer Financial Protection Board (CFPB), the Park Service, Army Corps of Engineers, National Labor Relations Board, the General Services and Social Security Administration, and the US Departments of Education and Housing and Urban Development.

CFPB attorney Hai Binh Nguyen was one of many participants eager to tell the press about their commitment to serving the public. "I think it's really rare," she said, "that we get to be in a place that has a really amazing mission, which is to make the market fair and protect everyday consumers." She and her coworkers were there to protest a stop-work order issued by the Trump administration, which, in her office, immediately disrupted pending investigations of consumer fraud.[7]

Members of the FUN-organized crowd chanted and cheered, while hoisting banners and hand-lettered signs: One placard read: "Federal

Workers: Here to Serve, Not Afraid and Not Leaving," which pretty well summed up the sentiment of the group. In his remarks, the rally organizer reminded everyone of who does the real work of the federal government. "I've never seen a billionaire carry the mail," Mark Smith said. "I've never seen a billionaire put out a forest fire. I've never seen a billionaire make sure people get their Social Security checks on time. I've never seen a billionaire answer a phone call from a suicidal veteran on the VA crisis line."

Belated Backing

On the eve of FUN's after-work events and coordinated workplace solidarity activities, the DC-based headquarters of NFFE, the National Treasury Employees Union, and the International Federation of Professional and Technical Engineers (IFPTE) endorsed the "Day of Action." The American Federation of Government Employees, the largest federal worker union, and National Nurses United, which represents fifteen thousand VA nurses, did not.

Yet, less than a month later, the national presidents of AFGE, NFFE, and IFPTE, along with AFL-CIO president Liz Shuler, were all eager participants in a live-streamed, FUN-sponsored event, "Save Our Services," that drew more than twenty thousand views. In a nod to FUN's catalytic role as a cross-union formation favoring direct action, Shuler assured her listeners, "We're filing the lawsuits, yes, we're fighting back in Congress, but most importantly, we're mobilizing in the streets." In April and June 2025, FUN activists around the country formed highly visible contingents in the much bigger and broader "Hands Off" and "No Kings Day" demonstrations, organized by labor allies, that drew millions of supporters.

The AFL-CIO began recruiting and training one thousand lawyers in forty-two states to serve as a Federal Workers Legal Defense Network.[8] These volunteers will provide legal advice and support for individual employees who face adverse action by their agencies but still retain civil service rights and protections. AFGE became more proactive in signing up new members and briefly reached a new all-time high membership of 321,000. Such recruitment efforts were succeeding, the union said, because more workers want "to have a voice at work and fight efforts to undermine the federal government and democracy."[9]

All federal worker unions have long operated on the "open shop" basis mandated by federal law. But now workers who sign up to become members must pay their dues via alternative methods like AFGE and NNU's "E-dues" collection systems, because payroll deduction of dues was discontinued by the Trump administration.[10] In the wake of the president's illegal repudiation of labor agreements covering nearly one million workers in August 2025, unions without much recent history of membership mobilization had to adapt to challenging new conditions, including not being able to provide day-to-day representation in their usual fashion. Six months later, according to Smith, some NFFE members were "dropping off in their dues without collective bargaining rights."

Labor historian and Georgetown University professor Joe McCartin observed, "The sudden conversion of federal workers to what is effectively at will status and the simultaneous termination of their bargaining rights puts them in the same position as the vast majority of private sector workers who lack union representation." On the positive side, McCartin speculated that Trump could be "reawakening a long dormant tradition of collective action among otherwise seemingly docile federal workers."[11]

FUN led the way in warning that the system of labor-management relations familiar to today's federal workers was reverting, for the time being, to its condition before 1962. That's when the Kennedy administration first granted collective bargaining rights, albeit with more limited scope than in the private sector, to head off growing unrest among federal workers. As McCartin notes, from 1956 to 1981 they staged more than one hundred illegal work strikes of varying durations, culminating in the PATCO walkout referenced earlier, which did not have a favorable outcome.

Acting Like a Union

To navigate this challenging new terrain, FUN organizers became active in the legislative/political campaign to restore bargaining rights, while continuing to "educate workers about their remaining legal protections." On the first front, FUN helped stage a January 2026 rally on Capitol Hill, with participation from most federal unions, to push for Congressional passage of the Protect America's Workforce Act. (Even twenty House Republicans backed this proposed restoration of collective bargaining in the federal sector, which did not have sufficient support in the Senate.)

Federal workers, like Sam Forstag, a NFFE local officer and Montana "smoke-jumper," are mounting electoral challenges to anti-union incumbents in Washington. With backing from Bernie Sanders and his national union, Forstag joined a 2026 primary race to determine which local Democrat should run against right-wing congressman Ryan Zinke. The latter failed to meet with Forest Service workers concerned about DOGE-driven cuts that adversely affected wilderness fire-fighting capacity in Zinke's own district.

To coach federal workers on how they can come together and "act like a union" in their workplaces even without formal bargaining, FUN used a guide prepared by Colin Smalley and distributed by the Emergency Workplace Organizing Committee.

FUN's recommended responses to abuses of management authority include: "Speak out: get creative with whistleblowing. A well-scripted 'march on the boss' or a petition are great ways to take collective action that's protected by the Whistleblower Protection Act, so long as they disclose any violation of law, regulation, rule, or policy, or an abuse of authority."[12]

In a related Zoom tutorial, "How to Be a Union No Matter What the Boss Says," Jason Freeman, a campaign coordinator for SEIU, encouraged participants to use "administrative grievance procedures," which remain in effect even though management can now ignore an agency's negotiated grievance process (while Trump's contract cancellation is being litigated). The bottom line, Chris Dols told the group: "Everybody needs to become an organizer now.... If you're a federal employee and you don't know who your union is, get involved with the FUN; we'll help you figure it out. If you don't have a union, we'll help you learn how to organize one."

FUN has recruited a network of experienced organizing "mentors" and continues to benefit from its connection to Labor Notes. With an activist core of nine hundred workers, a growing network of "regional hubs," and thousands more who support its activities, FUN has raised enough money to hire several full-time organizers. They include its new codirectors, Dols and Alissa Tafti, who led AFGE Local 2211 when she was a government economist.

"One of the FUN's earliest and most powerful principles is voice,"

Tafti says. "For decades, federal workers have been expected to remain invisible—diligent but silent. But we took an oath to serve and protect the Constitution and that means protecting and serving our communities. When institutions are gutted, programs shuttered, and colleagues fired *en masse*, silence is no longer an option."[13]

27

Progressive Vets Versus Trump and Vance

Former marine Alexander McCoy describes Common Defense, the group he cofounded in 2016, as a "progressive, working class, membership organization of veterans, building a base of tens of thousands of volunteers engaged in grassroots lobbying of elected representatives and policy makers to win a more just democracy."

Throughout much of a decade—spanning three presidential election cycles—Common Defense has been countering the siren call of the MAGA movement among post-9/11 vets who returned from their deployments in Iraq or Afghanistan angry, disillusioned, or embittered about what they experienced there.

Through issue-oriented and electoral campaigns, Common Defense (CD) activists have tried to convince other former soldiers that their interests, as citizens and workers, are not well served by conservative Republicans or corporate Democrats in Washington. With few exceptions, member of Congress voted to spend trillions of dollars on regime change wars in the Middle East that lasted for two decades. Then, by even bigger bipartisan majorities, Congress provided $22 billion to the state of Israel to help finance its military assault on several million civilians trapped in Gaza.[1]

For all its ten-year history, CD has found itself engaging with the rise, fall, and rise again of Donald Trump. As we write this in 2025, that roller coaster ride for its own members and the millions of other Americans is not over. CD's growth and experience illustrates how fellow participants in "the resistance" can partner productively with unions, adapt to changing circumstances by focusing on new issues and causes, and be a welcoming and supportive place for people not always as comfortable in other progressive spaces.

"What drives so many veterans into action is not only the injustice faced by immigrants and protesters, but also the larger threat to democracy rooted in government brutality and militarization," explains Jose Vasquez, an army veteran who serves as Common Defense's national executive director. "The disturbing escalation in arrests and violence signals that the basic freedoms we once swore to protect are under attack."

Using Veterans as Props

Common Defense grew out of grassroots organizing against Trump's first bid for the presidency in 2016. Cofounders of the group met during vet-organized demos over the Republican candidate's failure to donate money to veterans' charities after promising to do so during a campaign event in Iowa.

One of those protesters was McCoy, who joined the marines because, for him, like many others, it was "the family business," and he "didn't have a ton of good prospects other than the military." A self-described navy brat, he moved all over the world during his dad's twenty-four-year career as a naval officer. Alex became a Barack Obama admirer while still in boot camp and then served six years, primarily as an embassy guard. In 2016, McCoy and a group of like-minded vets "felt really strongly that Trump was constantly using veterans as props while running a campaign that was so founded in hate and division."

Nevertheless, as they discovered that election season, Trump tapped into a vein of veteran discontent, despite his own lack of military service and what for any other candidate might have been a series of fatal political gaffes. Among them was calling Sen. John McCain, America's most famous prisoner of war, a "loser" for being captured in Vietnam, dissing a family who lost a son in Iraq, and dismissing sexual assault as a threat to women in the military.

In contrast, Hillary Clinton, as New York's junior senator, had been very attentive to the needs of National Guard members and reservists seeking greater access to health benefits. During her 2016 presidential run, she released a comprehensive white paper on veterans' affairs. Trump's campaign statement on the same subject was less than one page long. Clinton won endorsements from 110 former military leaders, which demonstrated much broader officer class support than Trump's shorter list of far-right military retirees.

An "Antiwar" Candidate?

Unfortunately, the Clinton campaign did not regard veterans—who vote in disproportionate numbers and represent about 13 percent of the nation's active electorate—as a constituency worth cultivating. Her phone bankers failed to collect information about past military service that could have been used to make targeted follow-up calls. Instead of veteran-focused messaging, her campaign employed generic "get out the vote" scripts. And Clinton, unlike Trump, was not a campaign critic of the forever wars in Iraq and Afghanistan, which she, as senator and secretary of state, had enthusiastically supported.

The Republican Party ground campaign behind Trump easily out-organized the Democrats among veterans and military families. With a multimillion-dollar budget, the party-backed group known as GOPVets was tasked with boosting vet voter turnout, which ended up being an estimated 2.8 million greater in 2016 than four years earlier. GOPVets deployed fifty former members of the military to work as full-time organizers and set up task forces in swing states with large veteran populations, including North Carolina, Florida, New Hampshire, Ohio, and Pennsylvania. Hundreds of volunteers were trained on veterans' issues and then knocked on more than a million doors.

With Pete Hegseth no longer at the helm, Concerned Veterans for America used its ample funding from the Koch brothers to knock on 250,000 more doors in 2016. Pro-Trump mailers were not just mailed out, they were handed out, face-to-face with voters, by veterans who volunteered to do so at American Legion posts, NASCAR races, and Blue Angel air shows.

On Election Day in 2016, Trump lost the popular vote by more than three million. Unfortunately, veterans played a key role in his electoral college edge over Clinton. Nationwide, 60 percent of all veterans cast their ballots for a wealthy recipient of five draft deferments, based on his pledge to boost active-duty soldiers' pay, "make America great again," and improve veterans' healthcare. Among former military personnel, Trump beat Clinton by a twenty-six-point margin nationwide, a bigger percentage of the vet vote than John McCain's share when he ran against Barack Obama in 2008.

A later analysis of 2016 voting data conducted by University of Minnesota professor Francis Shen and Cornell University's Douglas Kriner found exceptionally high support for Trump in blue-collar communities that had suffered some of the highest post-9/11 combat casualty rates. Their findings suggested that this voter turnout was crucial to Trump's narrow defeat of Clinton in three decisive swing states: Pennsylvania, Michigan, and Wisconsin.

An Impeachment Campaign

Once in office, Trump did finally put the United States on a negotiation path out of Afghanistan. (That turned into a hurried final withdrawal, under Biden, in the wake of an unanticipated puppet government collapse.) Otherwise, US military and foreign policy changed very little. Trump packed his administration with former generals who earned their stars in the nation's costly "forever wars." He proposed ever-larger Pentagon budgets and new weapons programs. When confronted with COVID-19, Trump declared himself to be a "wartime president." But that troubled public health battle, the pandemic's disastrous economic impact, and the White House response to nationwide protests against police brutality raised the 2020 presidential hopes of more than a dozen Democrats who believed they would have more battleground state appeal than Hillary Clinton.

During Trump's first term, Common Defense tried to give him a push out the door, in various ways, including building up a network of twenty thousand supporters who called for his impeachment. In one of the group's first nonelectoral campaigns, Common Defense members made repeated overtures to members of Congress, on Capitol Hill and in their home districts, seeking their public support for bringing the wars in Iraq and Afghanistan to a "responsible and expedient" conclusion.

A Pew Poll conducted in the fall of 2019 showed that Trump remained popular among veterans, even as his ratings began to sink among other constituencies. US military intervention in the Middle East—which Trump criticized as a candidate in 2016 and again at West Point the following year—was now viewed unfavorably by a majority of the vets surveyed. In an attempt to help Trump win a second term, the Republican Party once again targeted veterans as a key voting bloc. During the 2019–20 Democratic presidential primary process, before it was cut short by the pandemic, Common Defense made a dual endorsement of Sens. Bernie Sanders and Elizabeth Warren. Both had helped round up other congressional signers of its pledge to end wars in the Middle East.

A Second Choice Against Trump

When Joe Biden emerged as the party nominee, Common Defense activists tried to prevent the GOP from out-organizing the Democratic Party among veterans and military families. By the summer of 2020, with the presidential election still three months away, these efforts seemed to be paying off. Not only was Trump faring poorly in presidential preference polls conducted among all likely voters, his stock was also dropping among those who had helped him gain office in 2016. About half of all active-duty military personnel surveyed by the *Military Times* had developed an unfavorable view of the president, opposed to just 37 percent when he was first elected. Among officers, his disapproval rating was even higher.

As Election Day neared, the Biden campaign was clearly making inroads among post-9/11 veterans who were younger, female, and nonwhite, while ex-soldiers who were older white males living in longtime Republican strongholds remained a harder bloc to crack. With a pandemic still raging, the economy cratering, and millions of workers, including veterans, finding their jobs, unions, or healthcare at risk, there were many reasons for voters who served in the military to choose a new commander in chief.

People of color on active duty, even some officers among them, expressed public disapproval of Trump's threatened use of the military against Black Lives Matter protesters in the summer of 2020. Others were turned off by his insistence that military bases named after Confederate generals should be keep their names.

In November 2020, Trump's share of the vet vote fell to 54 percent versus Biden's 44 percent—a ten-point swing from four years prior, according to *New York Times* exit polls. Common Defense political director Naveed Shah, an Iraq War veteran, noted later, "While Biden won more than 81 million votes across the country, the real margin came down to tenths of a percent in a few swing states thanks [to] veterans and military families and overseas voters."

In the spring of 2024 Shah warned that a Biden-Trump rematch would be "the most consequential election in our lifetime." Because "veterans and military families [would] again play a pivotal role in key states and districts," it was "up to the Democrats not to squander that opportunity" to keep them in their camp.[2] In the game-changing June 2024 presidential debate between a still incoherent Trump and a shockingly catatonic Biden, there were squandered opportunities galore. The rhetorical fog that enveloped their brief exchange about veterans was probably the least of them. Trump claimed that his policy of giving VA patients greater "choice" of healthcare providers won him "the highest approval rating" among veterans, while Biden had "the worst" because he "reversed all these great things we did."

President Biden, of course, did not reverse course on VA privatization, although he should have. In his retort, Biden was at least able to point out that "veterans are a hell of a lot better off since I passed the PACT Act ... which [Republicans] opposed." According to Biden, "one million of them now have insurance, and their families have it"—which was untrue. Unlike Medicare, Medicaid, or federally subsidized Affordable Care Act coverage, the VA only serves veterans, via direct care. The agency only became a major insurer, to its own detriment, when VA privatization took root under Obama, expanded under Trump, and continued unchecked under Biden.

In his jumbled exchange with Trump, the soon-to-be lame duck Democratic president did recall his late son Beau's own burn pit exposure, during a year spent in Iraq. And the fact that one motivating factor for his administration "doing more for veterans than ever before in our history" was a Delaware National Guard member in his own family "coming back with stage four glioblastoma."

In September 2024 sequel to that debate, Vice President Kamala Harris took on Trump for the first and only time. With so many other urgent matters to discuss, the VA didn't come up at all nor did it during that season's vice presidential candidate debate. That was more surprising and unfortunate for the Democrats because both national parties nominated a military veteran as vice president. In that secondary contest, only one of the former noncommissioned officers (NCO) on the ballot was progressive and prolabor.

Former NCOs Square Off

Sixty-year-old Tim Walz, the former high school teacher and football coach who served more than two decades in the National Guard, looked a lot less like your average Common Defense member than forty-year-old JD Vance, an ex-marine corporal from the same post-9/11 veteran cohort. But the governor of Minnesota picked to run with Harris—with much applause from Common Defense—couldn't have been more different than his fellow Midwesterner who went to Yale Law School, where he met libertarian billionaire Peter Thiel, who ushered him into the world of venture capitalism. With $15 million in personal "independent spending," Vance's friend, mentor, and post–law school employer then helped him become a US senator from Ohio. By this time, thanks to his hookup with Thiel, Vance and his wife owned three homes, and their net worth was in the $5–11 million range.[3] Like his fellow Ivy Leaguer Pete Hegseth, Vance had little need for VA care, a small monthly disability check, or any other costly "entitlement" making him "dependent" on such handouts.

Lacking wealthy benefactors, Tim Walz got his start in electoral politics as "a Kerry man"—not the Irish immigrant sort but rather the kind of volunteer canvasser in 2004 who hoped to replace a warmongering George Bush with a Vietnam vet from Massachusetts. Walz had used his own GI Bill benefits to attend state colleges, getting bachelor's and master's degrees, so he could become not a multimillionaire but instead unionized public-school teacher. He was encouraged to run for office by Wellstone Action, a group named after the progressive senator from Minnesota who died in a 2002 plane crash.[4]

After winning the first of six congressional races, Walz joined the House Committee on Veterans' Affairs, a low-status assignment. There he became an effective advocate for fellow veterans with service-related conditions. His own hearing loss resulted from repeated exposure to artillery blasts during twenty-four years of National Guard training exercises.[5] He also cosponsored a bill focused on suicide prevention services; it was named after a marine veteran who killed himself in 2011 after long struggles with PTSD and depression.

In 2018, Walz joined just sixty-nine other House Democrats in opposing the VA MISSION Act, one of Trump's proudest legislative achievements and the basis for his 2024 campaign pledge to make VA "patient choice" more widely available. Walz warned, prophetically, that MISSION Act outsourcing would force the VA to "cannibalize itself" by diverting billions of dollars from direct care delivery to reimbursement of private sector providers.[6] This incremental defunding of VHA hospitals and clinics would leave them in a "can't-function situation."

Walz's service in Congress before becoming governor is fondly recalled by AFGE members in Minnesota. During Walz's first House race, he reached out to fellow union member Jane Nygaard to find out more about AFGE issues at the VA. After Walz got elected, she discovered that "he's not someone who just says something to make you happy, he actually takes action." In Nygaard's case, this took the form of his office getting the Federal Mediation and Conciliation Service (FMCS) involved in trying to improve labor relations at her VA facility.

As a 2024 presidential candidate, Trump pledged to "take action" also—but not to help anyone in AFGE. Instead, he promised, loudly and publicly, to "fire every corrupt VA bureaucrat who Joe Biden outrageously refused to remove from the job." (After his reelection, he even began to dismantle the FMCS—a tiny agency he couldn't have found on an organizational chart without Project 2025 help).

A Peter Thiel Protégé

For his 2024 presidential campaign, Trump was quite savvy to beef up his MAGA tag team with Vance, who added youth, past military service, and a brand of faux populist politics of his own, first on display in his best-selling memoir *Hillbilly Elegy*. That conservative tract blamed the welfare state for the personal struggles and family dysfunction of his own relatives and their blue-collar neighbors, rather any larger economic forces like the decline of the steel industry and its good-paying union jobs with benefits.

In his nomination acceptance speech at the Republican National Convention in Milwaukee, Vance referred to his working-class roots in a once prosperous, now economically depressed Middletown, Ohio, "a place cast aside and forgotten by America's ruling class in Washington." He recalled, "I was a senior in high school when Joe Biden supported the disastrous invasion of Iraq.... And at each step of the way, in small towns like mine in Ohio, or next door in Pennsylvania or Michigan, in other states across our country, jobs were sent overseas, and our children were sent to war."

After the chant "Joe must go!" died down, Vance's claim to be a friend of labor got an unfortunate boost that same week from International Brotherhood of Teamsters president Sean O'Brien in his RNC speech. O'Brien's own 2021 election was hailed at the time by admirers in both Teamsters for a Democratic Union and Labor Notes as a new day for the union. In the area of politics, this turned out to be not the case. In his speech to the delegates, O'Brien rattled a few with his anticorporate, pro-union rhetoric. But he also lavished praise on Vance as part of "a growing group" of Republicans "who truly care about working people" as demonstrated by their willingness "to sit down and consider points of view that aren't funded by big money think tanks."

On the 2024 campaign trail thereafter, Trump and Vance were a one-two punch on VA-related issues. Whether they had read Project 2025 or not (and Vance most certainly had), the "big money think tank" known as the Heritage Foundation provided their talking points. At a national convention of the National Guard Association of the United States, where he was warmly received, Trump again accused the Biden-Harris administration of gutting his many "VA reforms" related to "choice" and "accountability." He hailed VA outsourcing as a great system of "rapid service," in which patients "go to an outside doctor ... get themselves fixed up, and we pay the bill."

At an invitation-only event at a VFW hall in western Pennsylvania, Vance referenced the very real healthcare access problems of "our veterans living in rural areas." But according to the senator, the VA, there and everywhere, is so slow-moving and uncaring that "veterans spend three hours on the phone trying to get an appointment," and you even "have people commit suicide, because they're waiting twenty-eight days to get an appointment with a doctor." The solution, he insisted, was to "give people more choice" and "save money in the process."

According to Vance, Tim Walz's past opposition to "bipartisan legislation that expanded veterans' access to quality care and cut needless red tape" was just more proof that he was "not the kind of leader veterans need in Washington."

Like Walz and Vance themselves, the 2024 major party platforms on veterans' issues were a study in contrasts. The GOP had a plan to "take care of our veterans," and it was described in forty-eight words. Its main thrust was immigrant bashing, promising elimination of all the "luxury housing and taxpayer benefits" made available to border-crossers so "those savings can be used to shelter and treat homeless Veterans."

The equivalent Democratic Party statement covered homelessness and suicide, PACT Act implementation, improving mental health programs, new services for female veterans, support for family members caring for VA patients, and strengthening the VA "by fully funding inpatient and outpatient care and long-term care, and by upgrading medical facility infrastructure." The Democrats also reminded voters that, as president the first time, Trump "pushed to cut funding for veterans' benefits"—which will definitely be a Trump priority again, at some point.

Despite these substantive differences, exit polling by CNN confirmed that vet voters broke for Trump by a 65 to 34 percent margin in the 2024 presidential election—a statistical replay of Trump's performance versus Clinton eight years before. In anticipation of the possibility that—for the third time in twenty-four years—the electoral college would decide the outcome, not the popular vote, Tim Walz briefly used his campaign for the vice presidency to tell voters: "The Electoral College needs to go. We need a national popular vote."

As governor of Minnesota, Walz had the year before signed, after the necessary state legislative approval, "the National Popular Vote Interstate Compact [NPVIC], an agreement in which each state would allocate all its electoral votes to whoever wins the popular vote for president, regardless of how individual states voted."

The idea of abolishing the Electoral College—or, more feasibly, bypassing it via the NPVIC—was too radical an idea for Joe Biden's vice president. The Harris campaign quickly disavowed her running mate's advocacy for this key political reform.

Déjà Vu All Over Again

Before and after his one and only popular vote victory, Trump reverted to the same anti-intervention head feints that helped him beat a hawkish candidate like Clinton in 2016. "I'm not going to start a war," he told cheering crowd of supporters on election night in 2024. "I'm going to stop the wars."

In usual Trump fashion, this pronouncement was "fake news" for Palestinians in Gaza (before and after any truce there), other civilians near US military targets in Yemen, Iran, and Venezuela, and 360 million Americans who now find themselves living in a country with a "Department of War" conducting military "training exercises" in major cities.

As those urban war zones proliferated, no one was better suited to challenging militarized policing and brutal ICE roundups than activists from Common Defense, Veterans for Peace, and About Face. Their heroic response, in the fall of 2025, was well reported in the *Guardian* by former Iraq War correspondent Aaron Glantz. His 2008 book *Winter Soldier: Iraq and Afghanistan: Eyewitness Accounts of the Occupations* described the initial wave of dissent among post-9/11 veterans, and his later one, *The War Comes Home*, chronicled the difficult personal transitions, from military to civilian life, that many soldiers had to navigate during that period.

In Glantz's national survey of recent protest activity by veterans, he uncovered profiles in courage like John Spitzberg, a disabled eighty-seven-year-old veteran of the army, air force, and Air National Guard. A member of Veterans for Peace who uses a walker, Spitzberg left his assisted living facility in Florida and traveled to Washington, DC, where he was arrested on the eve of President Trump's June 14 military parade.

Adding Insult to Injury

Five months later, Trump's deployment of federal agents and out-of-state National Guard members to Chicago turned that city into a cauldron of resistance. Among those arrested at an ICE detention center in Broadview, just west of Chicago, was Common Defense member Dana Briggs, a seventy-year-old air force vet charged with felony assault on a federal officer after he was pushed to the ground by one. According to Demi Palecek—a National Guard member running for the Illinois legislature—the confrontation could have been worse.

Palecek pointed out, "[The way ICE agents] handle weapons is reckless and dangerous.... Their fingers on the trigger of real M16s, pointing M9s directly at people.... With this level of escalation and incompetence, people will die." This criticism was echoed by John Cerrone, a thirty-five-year-old former marine arrested at Broadview the day before Briggs. "Their conduct was completely unprofessional in my experience in combat infantry," Cerrone told Glantz. "Even in Afghanistan, we had very clear rules of engagement. The conduct of these agents was such that if it occurred in Afghanistan, they would be removed from the front line. They would be court-martialed."

Another protest site was the parking lot of the Edward Hines Jr. VA Hospital in Chicago. It was occupied by ICE agents and used as a staging ground for their raids. According to About Face member Aaron Hughes, this resulted in some "veterans staying away and not getting healthcare or coming in carrying their passports," because they feared ethnic profiling outside the facility. When Hughes, a former Illinois guardsman and Iraq War veteran, organized anti-ICE picketing, he gained the support of Tammy Duckworth, the disabled army veteran who serves as US senator from Illinois.

Duckworth slammed VA headquarters for surrendering resources "in support of reckless, paramilitary activities that do *nothing* to enhance Veteran care—and even worse, are actively harming Veterans and U.S. servicemembers by rounding up ... patriotic Americans, along with their family members, and deporting them with little or no due process out of the country they were willing to risk their lives to defend."

In his response to that statement (and Glantz's reporting on it), VA press secretary Peter Kasperowicz (of "far left canard" fame) denied there had been any "impact on veteran care or facility access." Furthermore, Secretary Collins was "proud to support VA's federal partners in the fight against illegal immigration."

"It's Getting Real"

JD Vance, a better-known MAGA critic of immigration, was outraged by the actions of his fellow vets from the Midwest and the press coverage they attracted. In an interview about whether President Trump would sidestep mounting federal court challenges to his federalization of state National Guard units for domestic law enforcement, the legal scholar from Yale explained: "The problem here is not the Insurrection Act of 1807 or whether we actually invoke it or not. The problem is the fact that the entire media in this country, cheered on by a few far-left lunatics, have made it OK to tee off on American law enforcement. We cannot accept that." (In December 2025, by a six-to-three vote, even the Trump-friendly US Supreme Court could not accept the administration's rationale for deploying the National Guard in a state over the objections of its governor, a decision which led to withdrawal of Guard units sent to Chicago, Los Angeles, and Portland.)

Trump's return to the White House created many other threats for Common Defense to mobilize against—like VA privatization and Medicaid cuts that will adversely affect millions of working-class people, including members of veterans' families not eligible for VA care. The group increased its national staff hiring, recruitment of volunteers, and local chapter building, particularly in red states. Its causes now ranged from reproductive rights to voting rights, from defending immigrants to saving the environment, and, as always, trying to help elect fellow veterans committed to peace and new priorities.

On one nationwide organizing call to promote its "VA Not for Sale Campaign," more than 350 supporters of Common Defense heard an update from executive director Jose Vasquez. Many were surprised to see the fifty-year-old VA patient appear on their Zoom screen lying in bed and dressed in a hospital gown. "I am coming to you live from the Manhattan VA," Vasquez explained. "I've just had surgery for pancreatic cancer, and the idea that the Trump administration would want to cut eighty-three thousand positions and fire that many people from VA facilities is ludicrous. The VA just saved my life."

"It's getting real," Vasquez warned. "They're coming after our veterans' benefits, but we're not going down without a fight." That message was echoed by other vets on the call. They pledged to bombard politicians and the press with their stories of life-changing experiences with VA programs and services. Among those waging the fight that way—by penning op-ed pieces and letters to the editor for local news outlets—was Perry O'Brien, Jose's coworker at Common Defense and an Afghan war vet who lives in Camden, Maine.

O'Brien warned readers of the *Bangor Daily News* that further privatization of the VA by the Trump administration would "result in more Maine veterans finding themselves in the same long lines and 'medical deserts' as their friends, neighbors, and nonveteran relatives, while the first health choice of most veterans—the VA—is dismantled."

The name that Common Defense founders chose nearly a decade ago had considerable resonance back then, amid the first round of resistance to Trumpism and the challenge of uniting disparate forces to counter its spread. As Veterans Day 2025 approached, Common Defense and its growing roster of organizational allies like FUN were planning events that were, to paraphrase Mother Jones, more about "fighting for the living" than commemorating the dead.

Mounting the broadest possible challenge to the current MAGA embrace of war, austerity, and authoritarianism was not just another "single-issue" campaign. Nor did it, in the run-up to the midterm elections of 2026, have any short-term electoral goal more ambitious than helping to "flip the House" for damage control until 2028, while preventing any GOP vote-tampering designed to thwart that midterm election outcome. If and when US political conditions change for the better—permitting more organizing on the offense, rather than just for defensive purposes—the "militant minority" that Common Defense represents will be more battle-tested than ever before and able to resume its long march with others in labor and on the left toward a more just and peaceful society.

Epilogue

A Shutdown, Shootings, and a General Strike

On Veterans Day, 2025, it was not just military veterans who were feeling betrayed by policymakers in Washington. Millions of Americans whose lives were negatively impacted by the longest-ever federal government shutdown had just learned that some Senate Democrats had broken ranks with their own party to join hands with Republicans to end a budgetary dispute over extending federal subsidies for Affordable Care Act coverage.

For forty-three days, the Democratic minority in the Senate had held out for a deal that would keep healthcare a little more affordable for millions of ACA beneficiaries, by shielding them from big upcoming price hikes. This laudable goal—made complicated by the costly and byzantine structure of private insurance subsidies under the ACA—required much financial sacrifice by federal workers and other citizens, including veterans, who depend on various forms of federal assistance.

About 780,000 federal employees had to work without pay; another 670,000 were furloughed entirely. Among the former service members in the first category were many Federal Aviation Administration workers, whose job conditions and staffing levels steadily worsened. By late October, 2025, their union, the National Air Traffic Controllers Association, reported that hundreds of its members had been forced to take "second jobs driving for Uber and Lyft, delivering food or working in food stores," before or after their control tower shifts.

Food costs increased for the 1.2 million veterans living in households whose low income qualified them (and 41 million other Americans) for Supplemental Nutrition Assistance Program (SNAP) benefits. Also going without food stamps during the shutdown were the families of an estimated twenty thousand active-duty service members who depend on SNAP. Furloughed Park Service worker James Jones, the army vet who became active in FUN, reported that his Republican neighbors in North Carolina were telling him, "I didn't vote for this."

Healthcare delivery, for Jones and nine million other vets, did continue during the shutdown. But the plight of thirty-seven thousand VA staffers not involved in direct care, who were furloughed or working without pay, suddenly became a matter of great concern to Secretary Doug Collins. "The Democrats' government shutdown is limiting services for Veterans and making life miserable for VA employees," he declared. "It's time for Democrats to stop using the suffering of Americans as political leverage to give free health care to illegal immigrants."

Per usual, Collins was displaying his penchant for press release fibs—in this case about both ACA federal marketplace coverage and expanded Medicaid eligibility, neither of which extends to undocumented immigrants. The VA secretary's statement blaming Senate Democrats for the shutdown came right on the heels of AFGE president Everett Kelley's call for Congress to pass a spending bill without any agreement on future ACA funding.

Seeing headlines like "Top Federal Workers' Union Breaks with Democrats Over the Shutdown" riled rank-and-file members of AFGE, other federal workers in FUN, and even military vets in the Senate backed by Kelley's union in the past, like Arizona senators Mark Kelley and Ruben Gallego. Gallego asserted, "We also need to be looking out for the 24 million Americans, including the nearly 500,000 Arizonians, who will see their premiums double or lose health care coverage altogether if we don't address ACA subsidies."

That view was echoed in a September 29, 2025, open letter, titled "No Bad Budget in Our Name," issued by FUN and twenty-five sponsoring local unions. The signers implored Democratic leaders in Congress to continue "fighting against the centralization of executive power and for the long-term survival of critical federal services, even if that means allowing the government to temporarily shut down."

In AFGE, several hundred of its local officers, shop stewards, and retirees circulated a petition sharply critical of Kelley's call for "an unconditional end to the shutdown that ignores the voices of AFGE's membership and the historic opportunity that we have to press Congress to protect the interests of working people." Among the signers was FUN member Mae apGovannon, a VA claims processor in Portland, Oregon, and local union steward whose past work as chair of AFGE Pride has received national recognition by the AFL-CIO.

As apGovannon told the media: "I was shocked when I read President Kelley's statement. We were helping each other hold on without pay as long as we could.... We saw the shutdown as a way of highlighting that we all stand together until we win, or we suffer together. Now, it's like our continued sacrifice was ignored—and those of us who aren't billionaires were sold out again." (Two days before the shutdown ended, according to the *New York Times*, Kelley lashed out at FUN in an AFL-CIO executive council meeting, suggesting that the group's continued support for the Democratic filibuster was undermining AFGE. Apparently, not all the assembled national union presidents agreed with Kelley, although none are fond of internal dissidents.)

In response, such internal critics started organizing under the banner of "AFGE Reformers" and joined FUN's "Nationwide Week of Service and Action" in late November. FUN leaders acknowledged that the congressional deal did provide "temporary protections against illegal RIFs [reductions in force] through January 30, 2026, and reversed mass firings that occurred during the shutdown." It also ended uncertainty about the Trump administration providing back pay for federal workers impacted by the shutdown, as required by existing law.

Nevertheless, according to AFGE steward Paul Osadebe, a FUN steering committee member, the shutdown settlement did "nothing to prevent the ongoing destruction of public services and jobs." So, buoyed by the popular response to their shutdown food pantries, social mixers, and other forms of solidarity and mutual aid, FUN volunteers planned to organize further town hall meetings, local relief projects, public demonstrations, and accountability sessions with elected officials.

On Veterans Day, President Trump traveled to Arlington Cemetery to proclaim his satisfaction with how the shutdown ended. During a wreath-laying ceremony at the Tomb of the Unknown Soldier, he called it a "very big victory" for himself and his party. He praised the recent performance of vets in his cabinet like Doug Collins, JD Vance, and Pete Hegseth, and he lauded several combat veterans in the audience for their past service in Vietnam, Afghanistan, and Syria.

In his usual factually challenged fashion, Trump also reprised his 2024 presidential campaign trail bashing of the VA. He bragged again:

"We fired thousands of people who didn't take care of our great veterans. They were sadists. They were sick people. They were thieves. They were everything you want to name.... But we got rid of them, permanently. We replaced them with people who love our veterans."

At very different events from coast to coast, members of Common Defense, About Face, VFP, and other anti-Trump groups came together over that same Veterans Day weekend. Hundreds of participants renewed their commitment to saving the VA, resisting attacks on immigrants and federal workers, opposing domestic military deployments to suppress dissent, and US intervention abroad. Last but not least, they also resolved to survive—through more sacrifice and struggle—another 1,165 days under a federal government once again open for business but still headed by Donald Trump and JD Vance.

The first few months of 2026 provided little relief for beleaguered federal workers, their embattled unions, and allies in progressive vet groups. The Trump-Vance administration's use of military force, off the coast of Venezuela, culminated in a "Special Operators" raid on the presidential palace in Caracas. Navy SEAL Eddie Gallagher, long retired in Florida, was not involved in that mission, but his former Fox News defender, Pete Hegseth, certainly was. Under Hegseth's direction, Venezuelan president Nicolás Maduro and his wife were captured by US troops and transported to New York City to face drug smuggling charges. After the fact, some Democrats in Congress tried, unsuccessfully, to contest Trump's latest intervention in the internal affairs of another country.

Not content with bombing Iranian nuclear facilities as part of one-two punch, landed with Prime Minister Netanyahu of Israel in June of 2025, President Trump kept US sabers rattling in the Middle East. Early in the New Year, he threatened to deploy the forty thousand US troops stationed the region in a renewed assault on a deeply unpopular Iranian regime, already facing massive popular protests by its own citizens. Their latest attempt at "regime change" from below was brutally suppressed and would, of course benefit little from a renewed US assault on their theocratic rulers, by Israel's best friend in America, Donald Trump.

In January, the brave citizens of Minneapolis and St. Paul resisted, in similar but more successful fashion, a brutal ICE-led assault on their state's undocumented workers (estimated to be no more than eighty thousand). One resulting fatality was Renee Good, a gay mother of three murdered in her car, with her wife at her side.

Not surprisingly—given ICE recruitment of so many ex-soldiers, cops, and correction officers—her killer was a former Indiana National Guard member who served as "a machine gunner on a gun truck" in Iraq. Jonathan Rose joined ICE in 2015 and became a member of its "special response team" and the FBI's Joint Terrorism Task Force. According to the White House, he was simply "acting according to his training" and any claims to the contrary were "propaganda" and "garbage."

Shortly thereafter, the Trump administration inadvertently delivered on the president's Veterans Day pledge to get rid of some VA workers "permanently." On January 24, 2026, Border Patrol agents fatally shot RN Alex Pretti ten times in the back—a particularly brutal way of reducing the head count at the Minneapolis VA Medical Center. The thirty-seven-year old AFGE member was off duty at the time. He was peacefully filming their activity, when he came to aid of a female protester who had just been pepper-sprayed. She was his last patient.

The White House used the fact that Pretti was legally carrying—but not brandishing—a concealed weapon to smear him as a "domestic terrorist" who planned to "murder federal agents." That pretext for his summary execution—after he had been disarmed and restrained—unraveled pretty quickly. It became yet another "tipping point" in the ongoing popular struggle to restrain (and eventually abolish) ICE. And even gun owner groups, which backed Trump in the past, went ballistic when leading figures in his administration implied that Pretti had misused his Second Amendment rights.

VA Secretary Doug Collins hewed closely to the MAGA party line, as it wavered back and forth. In a social media post, he sent his "condolences to the Pretti family." But who, he asked, was really to blame for "chaos and death in American cities?" In the Twin Cities, Collins argued, "such tragedies" were actually the result of Democrats (like fellow veteran Gov. Tim Walz) failing to cooperate with Homeland Security's deportation of "dangerous criminals."

For friends, family, or coworkers of a highly regarded, but now dead VA caregiver, this was not a great display of the pastoral manner that Collins claimed to have developed, in the past, while ministering to families of deceased post-9/11 service members. But, even on a bad day, the Southern Baptist running the VA ranks higher on the empathy scale than the ex-Marine (now a Catholic convert) serving as Trump's vice president. During media questioning about his social media smear of Pretti as "someone who showed up with ill intent at an ICE protest," JD Vance was asked if he planned to apologize to Pretti's family. "For what?" he asked.

While these two veterans displayed their usual degree of complicity with the latest outrage unleashed by their commander in chief, other past or present federal workers with military experience reacted with courage, compassion, and renewed commitment to sparing others from the fate of Alex Pretti. Arlys Herem, the Collins critic who served in Vietnam as an army nurse and now tries to "Save Our VA" as a VFP member, found her fellow RN's death to be "just devastating." After suffering from anaphylactic shock, Herem once spent four days in the Intensive Care Unit (ICU) in the VA hospital where Alex worked at the time of his death.

"I don't know if Alex Pretti was one of my nurses," she told us. "But I can tell you that they were super knowledgeable and competent. ICU staff deal with every organ system in a patient's body. It's such complex work, managing medications, complex technology, and then dealing with patients' families." What Harem does know for sure "is that Alex Pretti died doing nursing work. His last words on this earth were uttered to an injured woman: 'Are you OK?'"

In Washington, DC, AFGE President Everett Kelley called for an independent investigation into the killing of "a fallen brother from AFGE Local 3669," the "patriotic IUC nurse" who had "devoted his life to serving America's veterans." Kelley also demanded the resignation of Homeland Security Secretary Kristi Noem, who was sacked soon thereafter. According to the AFGE president, Noem's masked and heavily armed underlings in Minneapolis put "lives at risk"—as she had done previously, with nationwide impact, via her "sustained attacks" on AFGE members providing airport security at the Transportation Safety Agency and disaster relief at the Federal Emergency Management Agency.

Left unmentioned was how Kelley planned to deal, then or later, with his National Border Patrol Council, a pro-Trump AFGE affiliate which some AFGE rank-and-filers want kicked out of the union. "We can't have it both ways," said Chicago VA social worker Aimee Potter.

"We can't advocate for our communities and for 'ICE Out' and, at the same time, be connected to an organization that is terrorizing our members and our communities."

AFGE's organizational rival as a representative of VA nurses—National Nurses United—responded to Pretti's killing by demanding "the immediate abolition of ICE" as a "violent, racist, and lawless agency that poses a dire public health threat." They then organized a "Week of Action in Honor of Alex Pretti" that was not limited to other federal workers. Instead, the union tried to engage two hundred thousand unionized nurses nationwide—including those in our hometown, Richmond, California, where Kaiser RN's reminded their bosses that if "you take on one of us, you take on all of us."

AFGE headquarters did issue a headquarters call for a national "Day of Remembrance" for Alex Pretti on February 1, 2026. This led to two dozen local vigils, including one at VA headquarters in Washington, DC, where Secretary Collins was not at work because it was a Sunday. AFGE President Kelley flew all the way to Minneapolis to personally address VA workers on their day off. Always batting cleanup for—and going deeper than—the national union officialdom, FUN distributed what it called a "Justice for Alex Toolkit." This workplace solidary guide included "a sample meeting agenda and facilitation guide to bring co-workers together to plan vigils and other actions." Its emphasis, per usual, was not just on displays of grief and anger, but longer term organizing to build power in federal workplaces stripped, temporarily, of union contracts.

Responses by any single union paled in comparison to the massive "Day of Action with no work, no school, and no shopping," organized by the broader Twin Cities labor movement on Friday, January 23, 2026. In a twenty-first-century echo of the Minneapolis general strike of 1934, a crowd estimated to be one hundred thousand marched and rallied in subzero temperatures, while tens of thousands of others stayed home from work and hundreds of businesses, small and large, closed for the day in solidarity.

CWA Local 7250 president Kieran Knutson, who rallied rank-and-filers against National Guard use of the St. Paul labor center for local policing purposes in 2021, now had much more company. Responding to the general strike call were Minnesota Nurses Association members again, along with thousands of others represented by UNITE-HERE,

AFSCME, SEIU, the UE, ATU, OPEIU, IATSE, Twin City teacher unions, and the Centro de Trabajadores Unidos en la Lucha (CTUL), a workers' center. By coming together in such dramatic, cohesive fashion, these labor organizations and their community allies created a template for similar action by state and local labor coalitions elsewhere, during the final three years of the Trump-Vance regime.

In a post–January 2026 report from the front lines, Knutson noted, "We're still learning to use muscles that the labor movement has not used for generations—and we are finding our power against a vicious enemy—but we cannot let up. We cannot accept cosmetic changes. The politicians will not save us—it is up to us!" That was good advice not only for fellow union members and military veterans but everyone else in the US fending off the further assaults on democracy and human rights that lie ahead.

Appendix

Resources

Veterans' organizations

About Face
aboutfaceveterans.org

Black Veterans Project
blackveteransproject.org

Common Defense
commondefense.us

Courage to Resist
couragetoresist.org

Iraq and Afghanistan Veterans of America (IAVA)
iava.org

Swords to Plowshares
swords-to-plowshares.org

Veterans for Common Sense
veteransforcommonsense.org

Veterans for Peace/Save Our VA (SOVA) campaign
veteransforpeace.org

Veterans Studies Association
veteranology.org

Vietnam Veterans Against the War
vvaw.org

Vietnam Veterans of America
vva.org

VoteVets
votevets.org

Trade Union Networks

AFL-CIO Veterans Council
unionveterans.org

American Federation of Government Employees
afge.org

Federal Unionist Network
federalunionists.net

National Federation of Federal Employees
nffe.org

National Nurses United
nationalnursesunited.org

Labor Campaign for Single Payer
laborforsinglepayer.org

Labor Notes
labornotes.org

Strategic Organizing Center
thesoc.org

Research and Advocacy Groups

Veterans Healthcare Policy Institute
veteranspolicy.org

Costs of War project
watson.brown.edu/costsofwar

Eisenhower Media Network
eisenhowermedianetwork.org

Quincy Institute
quincyinst.org

Up in Arms
upinarms.life

Win Without War
winwithoutwar.org

Notes

Introduction "People Are Waking Up"

1 Shawn Hubler, Anna Griffin, and Eric Schmitt, "Judge Blocks National Guard Deployment in Oregon as Trump Expands His Targets," *New York Times*, October 5, 2025.

2 Miriam Jordan, "He Raised Three Marines. His Wife Is American. The U.S. Wants to Deport Him," *New York Times*, September 17, 2025.

3 Greg Jaffe, "This Program Rescued Army Recruiting," *New York Times*, October 4, 2025.

4 Alexandra Yoon-Hendricks, "Disabled U.S. Army Veteran in 'Limbo' at Tacoma ICE Detention Center," *Seattle Times*, September 9, 2025.

5 Karissa Braxton, "Mayor Harrell Statement on the Detainment of Muhammad Zahid Chaudhry," https://harrell.seattle.gov/2025/08/28/mayor-harrell-statement-on-the-detainment-of-muhammad-zahid-chaudhry/, August 28, 2025.

6 Joe Sommerlad, "Irish Grandmother and Green Card Holder Held by ICE over $25 Bad Check," *Independent*, September 10, 2025.

7 Micah L. Sifry, "A Different Kind of Anti-Trump Resistance," *New York Times*, April 5, 2025.

8 Steve Early and Suzanne Gordon, "There Should Be No Path Forward to Privatizing Veterans Affairs," *Common Dreams*, July 12, 2022.

9 Bonnie Castillo, "A Movement as Fierce as Our Veterans," National Nurses United, July 9, 2025, nalnursesunited.org.

10 "San Diego Nurses and Veterans to Rally Against VA Staffing Cuts," National Nurses United, April 14, 2025, nalnursesunited.org.

11 "As Musk Slashes Federal Gov't and Fires Thousands, Workers, Trump Appointees, Judges and Media Push Back," *Democracy Now*, February 25, 2025, democracynow.org.

12 Kassandra Frederique, "Trump's Funding Cuts Jeopardize Fentanyl Overdose Prevention and Recovery," International Drug Policy Consortium, March 12, 2025, idpc.net.

13 Aimee Potter, "Saving the VA: A Social Worker's Perspective," *The Veteran*, Spring 2025, vvaw.org.

14 Potter, "Saving the VA."

15 Brian Todd, "VA Move to Pay Nearly $2 Billion for Private Health Providers Inflames Partisan Debate over 'Privatizing' Veterans' Care," CNN, August 28, 2025.

16 Sarah Lazare, "What It Means When Federal Union Contracts Disappear," *American Prospect*, September 3, 2025, prospect.org.
17 "GOP Town Hall Gets Heated over Firings of Federal Workers," posted February 25, 2025, by More Perfect Union, YouTube, 2 min., 58 sec., youtube.com/watch?v=pLEMe8EJAOc.
18 Jason Alatidd and Jack Harvel, "What Roger Marshall Said After Contentious Town Hall Meeting in Western Kansas," *Topeka Capital Journal*, March 3, 2025.
19 Robert Jimison, "Republicans Face Angry Voters at Town Halls, Hinting at Broader Backlash," *New York Times*, February 23, 2025.
20 Katie Edmondson, "Republican House Members Told to Stop Holding In-Person Town Halls," *New York Times*, March 4, 2025.
21 Katie Edmondson and Karl Hulse, "Health Care Politics Bolster Democrats in Shutdown Fight," *New York Times*, October 7, 2025.
22 Tony Romm, "Mass Layoffs Trump Is Threatening in Shutdown Fight May Be Illegal," *New York Times*, October 7, 2025.
23 Meg Lebowitz, "C-SPAN Caller Confronts House Speaker Mike Johnson About Shutdown Effects: 'My Kids Could Die,'" NBC News, October 9, 2025.
24 Author interview with Richard Ojeda.
25 Author interview with Richard Ojeda.
26 Nathaniel Rakich, "Everything Is Partisan and Correlated and Boring," *FiveThirtyEight*, November 20, 2018, fivethirtyeight.com.
27 Quotations in this and following paragraph: Steve Early and Suzanne Gordon, "With 'Better Alpha Energy': Can a Squad of Progressive Vets Storm Capitol Hill in 2026?," Stansbury Forum, October 31, 2025, stansburyforum.com.

1 ROTC Redux

1 Quoted in Steve Early, "The Rise, Fall, and Rise Again of School-Based Military Training," review of *Breaking the War Habit*, *New Politics*, October 20, 2023, newpol.org.
2 Seth Kershner, Scott Harding, and Charles Howlett, *Breaking the War Habit: The Debate Over Militarism in American Education* (University of Georgia Press, 2023).
3 Kershner, Harding, and Howlett, *Breaking the War Habit*, 17.
4 Kershner, Harding, and Howlett, *Breaking the War Habit*, 40.
5 Kershner, Harding, and Howlett, *Breaking the War Habit*, 78.
6 Kershner, Harding, and Howlett, *Breaking the War Habit*, 81.
7 Mike Baker, Nicholas Bogel, and Ilana Marcus, "Sexual Abuse of Teens in the Military J.R.O.T.C. Program," *New York Times*, July 9, 2022.
8 Baker, Bogel, and Marcus, "Sexual Abuse of Teens."
9 Ellen Mitchell, "Congress Reviews Sexual Assault Allegations in Junior ROTC Program," *The Hill*, August 16, 2022.
10 David Philipps, "With Few Able and Willing, U.S. Military Can't Find Recruits," *New York Times*, July 14, 2022.
11 Philipps, "With Few Able and Willing," 119.
12 Philipps, "With Few Able and Willing," 114.
13 Philipps, "With Few Able and Willing," 39.

2 I Am Vanessa Guillén

1 This chapter was first published, in different form, in the *Hollywood Progressive*, December 1, 2022, hollywoodprogressive.com.

2 Ellen Mitchell, "Gillibrand Slams Committee Leadership, Pentagon for Military Justice Reform Cuts," *The Hill*, December 8, 2021.

3 The Friends of Eddie Gallagher

1 First published, in different form, as "A Very Special Operator: The Eddie Gallagher Story," *CounterPunch*, November 4, 2021, www.counterpunch.org.

4 Trading One Uniform for Another

1 First published, in different form, as "Trading One Uniform for Another," in the *LA Progressive*, June 20, 2020; and "Tangled Up in Blue: Lessons from Police Reform," *Beyond Chron*, March 23, 2021, beyondchron.org.

2 John T. Bennett, "Trump Visits Police, Troops in D.C.," *Roll Call*, August 26, 2025, rollcall.com.

5 Prisoners After War

1 First published, in different form, as "Trading One Uniform for Another: The Military to Prison Pipeline," *The Veteran*, Spring 2025, vvaw.org.

2 "Freedom's Price, Democracy's Debt: Reflections from a Memorial Day Service Inside Stateville Prison," *Chicago Votes*, November 11, 2024, chicagovotes.com.

6 A Gangster for Capitalism

1 First published, in different form, as Steve Early, "A Memorial Day Salute to a Repentant Ex-Marine," *Popular Resistance*, May 26, 2022, popularresistance.org.

2 Selam Gebrekidan, Matt Apuzzo, Catherine Porter, and Constant Meheut, "Invade Haiti, Wall Street Urged. The U.S. Obliged," *New York Times*, May 20, 2022.

7 Pathways to Dissent

1 First published, in different form, as "Three New Books by Former Soldiers That the U.S. Military Does Not Want You to Read," *Jacobin*, February 5, 2022.

8 A Working-Class Veteran for Peace

1 First published, in different form, as "Patriotic Dissent: How a Working-Class Solider Turned Against Forever Wars," *Portside*, July 21, 2020, portside.org.

9 Leaving the Soldier Box

1 First published, in different form, as "A UK War Resister Reflects on Troubled State of 'Veteranhood,'" Stansbury Forum, April 24, 2022, stansburyforum.com.

III Wounds of War (Introduction)

1 Eyal Press, *Dirty Work: Essential Jobs and the Hidden Toll of Inequality in America* (Macmillan + ORM, 2021).

2 Heather Linebaugh, "I Worked on the US Drone Program. The Public Should Know What Really Goes On," *Common Dreams*, December 29, 2023, commondreams.org.

3 Ken Olsen, "The Casualties of K2," *American Legion*, March 2021.

4 Todd South, "Veteran, Gitmo Whistleblower Investigates Burn Pits and Their Victims in New Book," *Military Times*, June 3, 2019.

10 The PACT Act and Its Problems

1 First published, in different form, as "PACT Act Problems," in *The Progressive*, April 6, 2023.
2 Tara Coop, "DoD: At Least 126 Bases Report Water Contaminants Linked to Cancer, Birth Defects," *Military Times*, April 26, 2018.
3 Kayla Williams, "Health Issues Facing Women Veterans," in *Invisible Veterans: What Happens When Military Women Become Civilians Again*, ed. Kate Hendricks Thomas and Kyleanne Hunter (Praeger, 2019).
4 Carla Soenko, "Jon Stewart Calls Out GOP 'Cruelty' After Vote Against Veterans' PACT Act," *Newsweek*, July 28, 2022.
5 Rebecca Kheel, "Making Sure Vets Get PACT Act Benefits Is New House Veterans Affairs Chairman's Top Priority," Military.com, January 31, 2023.
6 *Disadvantaging the VA: How VA Staff View Agency Privatization and Other Detrimental Policies* (Veterans Healthcare Policy Institute, 2023).
7 "VA Disability Exams: Better Planning Needed as Use of Contracted Examiners Continues to Grow," US Government Accountability Office, March 23, 2021.
8 Suzanne Gordon, "Trump's VA Legacy: Human Capital Mismanagement," *American Prospect*, January 19, 2022.
9 "VA PACT Act Performance Dashboard," Department of Veteran Affairs, September 19, 2025.
10 Peter Montague, "Trump Is Breaking the Promise Our Nation Made to Military Veterans," *Common Dreams*, August 24, 2025, commondreams.org.
11 "Hirono, Colleagues Demand Complete and Updated List of Cancelled VA Contracts," Mazie Hirono's official website, May 20, 2025, hirono.senate.gov.
12 Full-Year Continuing Appropriations and Extensions Act, H.R. 1968, 119th Cong. (2025).

11 Invisible Storm

1 Helene Cooper, "Reported Sexual Assaults in Military Rose 13% in 2021, Officials Say," *New York Times*, August 31, 2022.

12 Suicide by Rental Truck

1 Bill Hutchinson, "Marine Awarded Purple Heart Charged in Deadly North Carolina Waterfront Bar Shooting," ABC News, September 29, 2025.

14 A Real Culture of Solidarity

1 Kevin Vigilante et al., "Camaraderie Among US Veterans and Their Preferences for Health Care Systems and Practitioners," *JAMA Network Open* 8, no. 4 (April 15, 2025).

15 When Soldiers Become Workers

1 Steve Early, "What Today's Labor Reformers Can Learn from a Rank-and-File Coal Miners' Victory 50 Years Ago," *In These Times*, December 14, 2022.
2 Steve Early, "Reviving the Strike in the Shadow of PATCO," *Monthly Review*, March 2012.

3 Joseph A. McCartin, *Collision Course: Ronald Reagan, the Air Traffic Controllers, and the Strike That Changed America* (Oxford University Press, 2011), 278–79.

4 Steve Early and Suzanne Gordon, "A Common Defense: Mobilizing Veterans in Labor to Beat Trump and the GOP," *Labor Notes*, November 2, 2020.

5 "CWA Veteran Delivers Powerful Speech at No Kings Rally," Communication Workers of America, July 10, 2025, cwa-union.org.

6 Claire Savage, "More Black and Latina Women Are Leading Unions—and Transforming How They Work," AP News, October 6, 2024, apnews.com.

7 Ted Goldberg, "Union Says Chevron Fired Several Richmond Refinery Workers Who Went on Strike," KQED, February 5, 2023, kqed.org.

16 The GI Bill, Then and Now

1 Les Leopold, *The Man Who Hated Work and Loved Labor: The Life and Times of Tony Mazzocchi* (Chelsea Green, 2007), 483–84.

2 "Biden Backs Free College," *New York Times*, March 15, 2020.

3 Jasper Craven, "Scrutiny of Colleges That Get Billions in GI Bill Money Remains Mired in Bureaucracy," *Hechinger Report*, March 30, 2020, hechingerreport.org.

4 Carrie Wofford and James Schmeling, "Betsy DeVos vs. Student Veterans," *New York Times*, February 18, 2019.

5 "Consumer Financial Protection Bureau Takes Action Against Bridgepoint Education, Inc. for Illegal Student Lending Practices," Consumer Financial Protection Bureau, September 12, 2016, consumerfinance.gov.

6 Natalie Gross, "Vet Groups Are Blasting Trump's Education Secretary. Here's Why," *Military Times*, February 19, 2019.

7 Erica L. Green, "Over Veterans' Protests, Trump Vetoes Measure to Block Student Loan Rules," *New York Times*, May 29, 2020.

8 *VA's Oversight of State Approving Agency Program Monitoring for Post 9/11 GI Bill Students* (US Department of Veterans Affairs, Office of Inspector General, 2018).

17 Can the National Guard Be Organized?

1 First published, in different form, as "How Border Deployment Led to Union Organizing in Texas," *Convergence*, April 28, 2022.

2 Ken Klippenstein, "Exclusive: Operation Excalibur in Los Angeles Was Show of Force," *Substack*, July 7, 2025, kenklippenstein.com.

3 Rory Fanning, "ICE Is Functioning like an Occupying Army. I Know Because I Served in One," *Counterpunch*, November 14, 2025, www.counterpunch.org.

4 Chris Hippensteel, "Trump Is Expanding the National Guard's Role. Some Former Generals Worry," *New York Times*, September 21, 2025.

5 Joel Geier, "The Soldier's Revolt," *Against the Current*, September/October 2025.

6 Adam Cahn, "Texas State Professor Calls for Overthrow of US Government," *Texas Scorecard*, September 10, 2025, texasscorecard.com.

18 Defending, Not Defunding, Public Service Jobs

1 First published, in different form, as "Support Veterans by Defending, Not Defunding, Public Sector Jobs and the Post Office and the VA," *Labor Notes*, November 8, 2022.

2 Jake Bittle, "The US Postmaster Appointed Under Trump Is Still Raising Alarm—but Can He Be Stopped?," *Guardian*, December 16, 2021.

3 Hansi Lo Wang, "David Steiner of FedEx Is Tapped to Be the U.S. Postal Service's New Leader," NPR, May 9, 2025, npr.org.

4 Esther Fung, "Six Facts About David Steiner, the New U.S. Postmaster General," *Wall Street Journal*, May 9, 2025.

19 Labor and Vets, Unite and Fight

1 Aaron Glantz, "VA Doctors Warn Cuts, Privatization Threaten Veterans' Healthcare," *Guardian*, September 24, 2025.

20 Parallel Privatization Threats

1 First published, in different form, as "Parallel Fights Against Privatization," *Against the Current*, November/December 2023.

2 Labor Campaign for Single Payer, laborforsinglepayer.org/resources.

21 The Illusion of Choice

1 First published, in different form, as "Veterans Healthcare Choice: The False Promise of Privatization," *American Prospect*, August 2025. Material in this chapter is also drawn from the introduction of a much longer Veterans Healthcare Policy Institute report, *Veterans Healthcare Choice: Myth or Reality?*

22 The Entitlement Reformers

1 "The 'Mandate for Leadership' Series," Heritage Foundation, mandateforleadership.org.

2 Russell B. Lemle and Jasper Craven, "Opinion: Project 2025 Would Slash Veterans' Hard-Earned Benefits," *Task and Purpose*, July 21, 2024, taskandpurpose.com.

3 Adrienne Mayfield, "Candidate Profile: Daniel Gade (VA Senate)," WJHL-TV, September 30, 2020, wjhl.com.

4 Daniel Gade, "Veterans Need Help Becoming Civilians Again," *Wall Street Journal*, November 11, 2021.

5 Research Advisory Committee on Gulf War Veterans' Illnesses, *Gulf War Illness and the Health of Gulf War Veterans: Research Update and Recommendations, 2009–2013* (Government Printing Office, 2014).

6 Suzanne Gordon and Steve Early, "A VA Critic Becomes Virginia's New Veterans Affairs Chief," *Washington Monthly*, February 10, 2022, washingtonmonthly.com.

7 Leo Shane III, "Big Six Veterans Groups Ask Trump to Fire VA Secretary Wilkie Immediately," *Military Times*, December 16, 2020.

8 Mandy Smithberger, "Brass Parachutes: The Problem of the Pentagon Revolving Door," Project on Government Oversight (POGO), November 5, 2018, pogo.org.

9 "Pursuit of Excellence," InterFuze, interfuze.com/who-we-are.

23 The Princeton Tory

1 Brad Reed, "'Most Loser Shit I Have Ever Seen': Pete Hegseth's Unhinged Speech to Generals Sparks Instant Ridicule," *Common Dreams*, September 30, 2025, commondreams.org.

2 Alexander Bolton, "Ernst Will Vote for Hegseth, Handing Trump Big Win," *The Hill*, January 14, 2025.

3 Dave Phillips, "Veterans See Costs and Risks in Hegseth's Military Rewind to 1990," *New York Times*, October 2, 2025.

4 Greg Jaffe, "The Army Was the Only Life She Knew. Trump's Trans Ban Cast Her Out," *New York Times*, June 16, 2025.
5 John Ismay, "Air Force Denies Early Retirement for Transgender Men and Women," *New York Times*, August 8, 2025.
6 Martha McHardy, "Ashli Babbitt Getting Military Funeral Honors Sparks Anger," *Newsweek*, August 29, 2025.
7 Pete Hegseth, *The War on Warriors: Behind the Betrayal of the Men Who Keep Us Free* (Broadside Books, 2024).
8 Jasper Craven, "Pete Hegseth's Crusade to Turn the Military into a Christian Weapon," *Politico*, December 6, 2024, politico.com.
9 "Letters to the Editor," *Daily Princetonian*, September 23, 2001.
10 "Iraq Veteran Takes on McCain in New Ad," *New York Times*, July 23, 2008.
11 Jane Mayer, "Pete Hegseth's Secret History," *New Yorker*, December 1, 2024.
12 Jennifer Steinhauer, "What's Right and Wrong About Trump's Defense Secretary Pick," *New York Times*, November 18, 2024.
13 Michelle Ye Hee Lee, Lisa Rein, and David Weigel, "How a Koch-Backed Veterans Group Gained Influence in Trump's Washington," *Washington Post*, April 7, 2018.
14 Concerned Veterans for America, "DISASTER: Veteran Care Failures, Obamacare Link," PR Newswire, December 17, 2013, prnewswire.com.
15 Jasper Craven, "Trump's Cronies Threw the VA into Chaos. Millions of Veterans' Lives Are on the Line Again," *The Intercept*, October 28, 2024, theintercept.com.
16 Suzanne Gordon and Steve Early, "Public Service the Hard Way," *Washington Monthly*, December 17, 2019, washingtonmonthly.com.
17 Sarah Tan, "Quick Facts About Pete Hegseth: Divorces and Affairs, Net Worth, and Salary as Secretary of Defense," *International Business Times UK*, November 13, 2024.
18 Dan Caldwell and Darin Selnick, "Our Troops Deserve Better than Moldy Barracks," *New York Times*, July 28, 2025.
19 Hiroko Tabuchi, "Defense Department Delays Cleanup of 'Forever Chemicals' Nationwide," *New York Times*, September 23, 2025.

24 An Air Force Chaplain from Georgia

1 Ben Leonard, "Democrats Press VA Secretary Nominee on Abortion, Project 2025," *Politico*, January 21, 2025, politico.com.
2 Roni Caryn Rabin and Nicholas Nehamas, "Chaos at the V.A.: Inside the DOGE Cuts Disrupting the Veterans Agency," *New York Times*, March 9, 2025.
3 Suzanne Gordon and Steve Early, "VA Research Funding Slashed," *American Prospect*, February 25, 2025, prospect.org.
4 Jessica Washington, "Veterans Are 'Guinea Pigs' in Trump's First National Abortion Ban Experiment," *The Intercept*, August 13, 2025, theintercept.com.
5 Brian Todd, "VA Hospital Staff See Plunging Morale as Shortages Leave Doctors Prepping Rooms and Nurses Chasing Supplies," CNN, July 1, 2025, cnn.com.
6 Jasper Craven, "VA's Nonexpert Health Expert," *American Prospect*, September 26, 2025, prospect.org.
7 Brandon Roberts, Vernal Coleman, and Eric Umansky, "DOGE Developed Error-Prone AI Tool to 'Munch' Veterans Affairs Contracts," ProPublica, June 6, 2025, propublica.org.
8 Suzanne Gordon and Steve Early, "VA Secretary Says No Department Wide RIFs,

but It's No Time to Cheer," *Washington Monthly*, August 8, 2025, washingtonmonthly.com.

9 Alex Chadwick, "'Love My Rifle': A Woman Soldier's Guide to Iraq," NPR, September 12, 2005, npr.org.

10 Aaron Glantz, "VA Doctors Warn Cuts, Privatization Threaten Veterans' Healthcare," *Guardian*, September 24, 2025.

11 "Women Are the Fastest Growing Group in the Veteran Population," Women Veterans Health Care, US Department of Veterans Affairs, September 23, 2025, womenshealth.va.gov/materials-and-resources/facts-and-statistics.asp.

12 Brienna N. Meffert et al., "US Veterans Who Do and Do Not Utilize Veterans Affairs Health Care Services: Demographic, Military, Medical, and Psychosocial Characteristics," *Primary Care Companion for CNS Disorders* 21, no. 1 (2019).

13 Women Veterans Health Care, US Department of Veteran Affairs, accessed October 15, 2025, womenshealth.va.gov.

14 ACES Act, H.R. 530, 119th Cong. (2025–2026).

15 "Uveal Melanoma," Melanoma Research Alliance (MRA), curemelanoma.org/about-melanoma/types/uveal-melanoma.

16 Elaine Schmidt, "Early Detection of Rare Eye Cancer Is Important," UCLA Health, June 5, 2018, uclahealth.org.

17 "Fight Back Against Trump's Cuts to Veteran Healthcare," *Common Defense*, accessed October 15, 2025, commondefense.us/actions. Email message to Common Defense Supporters in possession of authors.

18 Joanna Sweatt, "Opinion: I Fought for My Country, So Why Isn't My Country Fighting for Me?," NBC News, June 28, 2022. (Archived at: nbcnews.com/think/opinion/abortion-military-service-roe-women-might-not-serve-rcna35755.)

19 "Veterans' Community Care: VA Needs Improved Oversight of Behavioral Health Medical Records and Provider Training," US Government Accountability Office, May 5, 2025, gao.gov.

20 Ellen Barry, Nicholas Nehamas, and Roni Caryn Rabin, "Trump and DOGE Propel V.A. Mental Health System into Turmoil," *New York Times*, March 24, 2025.

21 "Military Sexual Trauma (MST)," US Department of Veterans Affairs, va.gov.

25 Can "Service Candidates" Save the Republic?

1 Linda Qui, "Explaining Claims About Tim Walz's Military Service," *New York Times*, August 21, 2024.

2 Suzanne Gordon and Steve Early, "Democrats Hope Walz and the Party's Military Veterans Have the Right Stuff," *Washington Monthly*, October 1, 2024, washingtonmonthly.com.

3 Jennifer Steinhauer, "In the Battle for the Capitol, Veterans Fought on Opposite Sides," *New York Times*, February 8, 2021.

4 Eloise Goldsmith, "With the Crypto Industry War Chest Looming, Senate Democrats Help GOP Pass GENIUS Act," *Common Dreams*, June 19, 2025, commondreams.org.

5 Adam Wren, "Slotkin Is Testing a 'War Plan' to Beat Trump. She Wants Dems to Ditch Wokeness and Muscle Up," *Politico*, April 24, 2025, politico.com.

6 Honoring the Life of Charles "Charlie" James Kirk, H. R. 719, 119th Cong. (2025–2026).

7 Michelle Goldberg, "How to Make Senate Republicans Pay for Their Awful Bill," *New York Times*, July 8, 2025.

26 Federal Workers Find Their Voice

1 Suzanne Gordon and Steve Early, "A 'Middle Finger' to Vets," *American Prospect*, February 19, 2025, prospect.org.
2 Luis Feliz Leon, "It's Time for a United Front to Take on Billionaire Rule," *In These Times*, February 11, 2025.
3 Mark Smith, "Federal Workers Organize Bottom-Up to Tell Musk Hands Off!," *The Call*, February 19, 2025, socialistcall.com.
4 Colin Smalley, "Federal Workers Are Mobilizing Against Musk's Purge," *Jacobin*, February 16, 2025.
5 Federal Unionists Network, federalunionists.net.
6 "Save Our Services Day of Action," Action Network, accessed October 15, 2025, actionnetwork.org.
7 Molly Burke, "'It's Maddening': Federal Workers in S.F. Protest Trump, Musk Cutbacks," *San Francisco Chronicle*, February 19, 2025.
8 Rebecca Davis O'Brien, "Unions Form Pro Bono Legal Network for Federal Workers Targeted by Trump," *New York Times*, April 16, 2025.
9 "AFGE Membership Highest in History as Government Workers Join in Droves to Stand Up for Public Service," American Federation of Government Employees, February 10, 2025, afge.org.
10 "AFGE E-Dues = Taking Our Power Back," American Federation of Government Employees, September 2, 2019, afge.org.
11 Joseph A. McCartin, "Will Federal Workers Rediscover Their Militancy?," *Dissent*, Spring 2025.
12 US Merit Systems Protection Board, mspb.gov.
13 Chris Dols and Alissa Tafti, "Federal Workers Are Organizing for Democracy—from the Inside Out," *Nonprofit Quarterly*, June 25, 2025, nonprofitquarterly.org.

27 Progressive Vets Versus Trump and Vance

1 Neta C. Crawford, "The U.S. Budgetary Costs of the Post-9/11 Wars," Watson Institute, Brown University, September 1, 2021, costsofwar.watson.brown.edu.
2 Naveed Shah, "Democrats, Remember: Veterans and Military Families Are Not a Monolithic Voting Bloc," *The Hill*, April 14, 2024.
3 Clementine Doyle, "JD and Usha Vance Live a Lavish Life," The List, December 17, 2024, thelist.com.
4 "Tim Walz Is Kamala Harris's Choice for Vice President," *New York Times*, August 6, 2024.
5 "Walz in the National Guard: A Steady Rise Ending with a Hard Decision," *New York Times*, August 10, 2024.
6 "How Tim Walz's Time in the House Paved the Way for His Ascent," *New York Times*, August 8, 2024.

Index

"Passim" (literally "scattered") indicates intermittent discussion of a topic over a cluster of pages.

About the Authors

Steve Early has been active in the Communications Workers of America for forty-six years. He was an international union representative and is now a rank-and-file member of the News Guild/CWA. From 1980 to 2007, he assisted organizing, bargaining, and strikes by workers at Verizon, AT&T, and other firms in the Northeast.

He has worked with Labor Notes, Teamsters for a Democratic Union, the Association for Union Democracy, Jobs with Justice, and Labor for Bernie. After a 2012 move to California, he joined the East Bay Democratic Socialists of America and the Richmond Progressive Alliance. He is the former chair of the City of Richmond Personnel Board, an appeals body for municipal employee grievances.

Early is the author or coauthor of five previous books: *Our Veterans: Winners, Losers, Friends, and Enemies on the New Terrain of Veterans Affairs* (Duke University Press); *Refinery Town: Big Oil, Big Money, and the Remaking of An American City* (Beacon Press); *The Civil Wars in U.S. Labor* (Haymarket); and two from Monthly Review Press, *Save Our Unions* and *Embedded with Organized Labor*.

Early's reporting and commentary have appeared in *The Nation*, *Jacobin*, *New Politics*, *American Prospect*, the *Progressive*, *Washington Monthly*, *Dissent*, *Democratic Left*, and many daily newspapers throughout the country. See ourvetsbook.com for links to this and other reporting. Early can be reached at Lsupport@aol.com.

Suzanne Gordon is an award-winning journalist and author who also belongs to the News Guild/CWA. She has written for the *New York Times*, *Los Angeles Times*, *Washington Post*, *Atlantic*, *Nation*, *Washington Monthly*, *American Prospect*, *Boston Globe*, *Globe and Mail*, *JAMA*, *Annals of Internal Medicine*, *British Medical Journal*, and others.

She is the cofounder of the Veterans Healthcare Policy Institute and serves as a senior policy analyst. Gordon was the coeditor of the Culture and Politics of Health Care Work series at Cornell University Press and is the author, editor, or coauthor of twenty books. They include three previous ones on veterans' issues: *Wounds of War: How the VA Delivers Health, Healing, and Hope to the Nation's Veterans*; *The Battle for Veterans' Healthcare: Dispatches from the Frontlines of Policy Making and Patient Care*; and *Our Veterans*. Her other healthcare-related titles include *Life Support: Three Nurses on the Front Lines* and *Beyond the Checklist: What Else Healthcare Can Learn from Aviation Teamwork and Safety*. She received a Special Recognition Award from the Disabled American Veterans for her writing about veteran issues. For more information on her speaking, writing, and workshop facilitation, see suzannegordon.com.

ABOUT PM PRESS

PM Press is an independent, radical publisher of critically necessary books for our tumultuous times. Our aim is to deliver bold political ideas and vital stories to all walks of life and arm the dreamers to demand the impossible. Founded in 2007 by a small group of people with decades of publishing, media, and organizing experience, we have sold millions of copies of our books, most often one at a time, face to face. We're old enough to know what we're doing and young enough to know what's at stake. Join us to create a better world.

PM Press
PO Box 23912
Oakland, CA 94623
www.pmpress.org

PM Press in Europe
europe@pmpress.org
www.pmpress.org.uk

FRIENDS OF PM PRESS

These are indisputably momentous times—the financial system is melting down globally and the Empire is stumbling. Now more than ever there is a vital need for radical ideas.

In the many years since its founding—and on a mere shoestring—PM Press has risen to the formidable challenge of publishing and distributing knowledge and entertainment for the struggles ahead. With hundreds of releases to date, we have published an impressive and stimulating array of literature, art, music, politics, and culture. Using every available medium, we've succeeded in connecting those hungry for ideas and information to those putting them into practice.

Friends of PM allows you to directly help impact, amplify, and revitalize the discourse and actions of radical writers, filmmakers, and artists. It provides us with a stable foundation from which we can build upon our early successes and provides a much-needed subsidy for the materials that can't necessarily pay their own way. You can help make that happen—and receive every new title automatically delivered to your door once a month—by joining as a Friend of PM Press. And, we'll throw in a free T-shirt when you sign up.

Here are your options:

- **$30 a month** Get all books and pamphlets plus a 50% discount on all webstore purchases

- **$40 a month** Get all PM Press releases (including CDs and DVDs) plus a 50% discount on all webstore purchases

- **$100 a month** Superstar—Everything plus PM merchandise, free downloads, and a 50% discount on all webstore purchases

For those who can't afford $30 or more a month, we have **Sustainer Rates** at $15, $10, and $5. Sustainers get a free PM Press T-shirt and a 50% discount on all purchases from our website.

Your Visa or Mastercard will be billed once a month, until you tell us to stop. Or until our efforts succeed in bringing the revolution around. Or the financial meltdown of Capital makes plastic redundant. Whichever comes first.

Insurgent Labor: The Vermont AFL-CIO 2017–2023

David Van Deusen with a Foreword by Kim Kelly and an Introduction by Steve Early

ISBN: 979-8-88744-036-1
$19.95 288 pages

Insurgent Labor tracks the trials and tribulations of bringing a formerly stagnant labor council into national relevance with an unapologetically left-wing agenda.

David Van Deusen charts the rise of the UNITED! slate to create a progressive and militant labor organization. He chronicles the many victories throughout his tenure including expanding union democracy into the rank and file, moving power away from single individuals and into democratic structures, supporting farm workers, supporting Black self-determination, and providing solidarity with the Revolution in Rojava.

The boldest step undertaken by the Vermont AFL-CIO—and marker of years of steady progress in labor organizing and raising of political consciousness in Vermont—was authorizing a call for a general strike throughout Vermont as a possible response to the November 2020 coup threat by then US President Donald Trump.

This book should be of interest to anyone, whether they have merely thought of joining a union or are an old union hand. Most importantly, Insurgent Labor offers a blueprint for militant labor's advances in an era of capitalist polycrisis and offers hope for a brighter future based around equality, justice, and true democracy.

"Employing historically effective left strategies Van Duesen shows how a Central Labor Body organized to fight for both the economic and political interests of workers can unite with other social movements to blunt right-wing attacks on workers at the workplace and globally. Essential reading for those who believe in democracy."
—Fernando E. Gapasin, principal researcher for AFL-CIO 1996 "Union Cities" project and coauthor with Bill Fletcher, Jr. of *Solidarity Divided*

"Labor Councils focused on member involvement and action are needed now more than ever. Vermont is a model for cross union solidarity and David Van Deusen's account should inspire others."
—Larry Cohen, former national president of Communications Workers of America and AFL-CIO Executive Council member; current chair of Our Revolution

Fighting Times: Organizing on the Front Lines of the Class War

Jon Melrod

ISBN: 978-1-62963-965-9
$24.95 320 pages

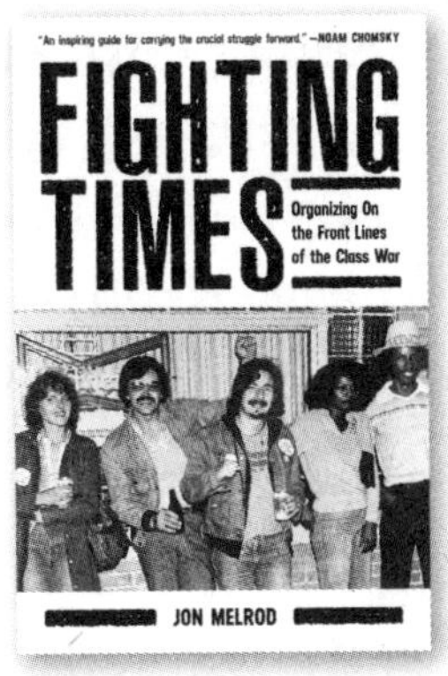

Deeply personal, astutely political, *Fighting Times: Organizing on the Front Lines of the Class War* recounts the thirteen-year journey of Jon Melrod to harness working-class militancy and jump start a revolution on the shop floor of American Motors. Melrod faces termination, dodges the FBI, outwits collaborators in the UAW, and becomes a central figure in a lawsuit against the rank-and-file newsletter *Fighting Times*, as he strives to build a class-conscious workers' movement from the bottom up.

A radical to the core, Melrod was a key part of campus insurrection at the University of Wisconsin, Madison. He left campus for the factory in 1972, hired along with hundreds of youthful job seekers onto the mind-numbing assembly line. *Fighting Times* paints a portrait of these rebellious and alienated young hires, many of whom were Black Vietnam vets.

Containing dozens of archival photographs, *Fighting Times* captures the journey of a militant antiracist revolutionary who rose to the highest elected ranks of his UAW local without compromising his politics or his dedication to building a class-conscious workers' movement. The book will arm and inspire a new generation of labor organizers with the skills and attitude to challenge the odds and fight the egregious abuses of the exploitative capitalist system.

"An eloquent voice from the frontlines of the hard, bitter, exhilarating struggles for freedom and justice that have made the world a better place, and an inspiring guide for carrying the crucial struggle forward."
—Noam Chomsky

"To organize communities and workers, you have to listen to them. Jon Melrod's many stories show he did just that—and had a blast, too, as they turned their creativity and solidarity against the boss. Yes, there's a lot to be learned from Melrod's tales, but they're also a joy to read."
—Ken Paff, cofounder of Teamsters for a Democratic Union

"In Fighting Times, *Jon Melrod shares his personal experiences in historical context about his human rights battles against social injustices. Jon was an early supporter of the Black Panther Party and the struggle for Black liberation. As you will read, he became a target of the FBI after landing on the Bureau's radar when he called the Chicago office to coordinate sales of* The Black Panther *community newspaper in Madison, WI. A must-read for all freedom-loving peoples."*
—Emory Douglas, social justice artist and minister of culture for the Black Panther Party, 1967–1981

Keep Going: A Guide to Organizing When It's Hard

Ellen David Friedman, illustrated by Fernando Martí

ISBN: 979-8-88744-099-6
$25.00 288 pages

This book is a guide to help workplace organizers get started, keep going, and get unstuck when things aren't going as expected.

Organizing is full of challenges and dilemmas. How do you decide who to talk to, if your coworkers all seem scared or apathetic? What if you invite people to a meeting and no one comes? What should you do when your organizing committee is splitting apart? What if your own union leaders break your heart? This book will help you evaluate any situation and find a way forward.

Drawing on a half century of experiences in training and advising thousands of workplace activists, Ellen David Friedman teaches four essential principles and four basic ingredients of organizing. She shows how to apply these principles and ingredients to familiar situations and invites you to rethink common missteps. You'll start to see how you can get yourself unstuck, no matter what situation you're in.

Eight featured true stories of workplace organizers bring the ideas to life, gorgeously illustrated by Fernando Martí.

"*Against the seemingly limitless power of corporations and billionaires, and the cruelty of a government turning against its own people, there are workers everywhere standing up and fighting back. I've known Ellen David Friedman for many years. She knows what it takes to organize and give people real hope. This book contains that experience and helps anyone who is building power in the workplace—step by step, facing endless challenges—to keep going.*"
—Senator Bernie Sanders

"*While many organizing books focus narrowly on techniques,* Keep Going *hits on key fundamentals putting questions of union democracy and power front and center. It combines practical advice with fundamentals insights on organizing.*"
—Joe Burns, labor attorney/negotiator and author of *Class Struggle Unionism*

"*The book* Keep Going *captures the need for humility in organizing, especially when things get hard. Through storytelling, Ellen shares organizing lessons that are in response to common organizing questions and challenges and that provoke thought about the processes of organizing often taken for granted or forgotten.*"
—Diamonté Brown, president of the Baltimore Teachers Union